Kate Albert   May
                               '87

LETTERS FOR

Letters For My Children

Life is hectic for **Deirdre Rhys-Thomas** and, like many women, she struggles to balance the demands of her job with those of her husband, two children and a beagle. Her turn to do Meals on Wheels comes around once a month, she is an active member of the parent-teacher association and of a committee to collect funds for the Royal National Lifeboat Institution in her land-locked Welsh town. She says, 'It is only when I'm cycling that I have time to think.'

In the early 1950s, **Janice Owens** worked as a technician in a genetic laboratory which bred flies, fish and newts. She has campaigned against the spread of nuclear technology since that time and, recently, has started speaking out more forcibly about the health dangers of radioactivity. Janice Owens is the Green Party's prospective parliamentary candidate for Vauxhall, Lambeth.

PANDORA PRESS FOCUS

LETTERS FOR MY CHILDREN

ONE MOTHER'S QUEST FOR ANSWERS ABOUT THE NUCLEAR THREAT

Deirdre Rhys-Thomas

Explanatory notes by Janice Owens

PANDORA

London and New York

First published in 1987 by
Pandora Press (Routledge & Kegan Paul Ltd)
11 New Fetter Lane, London EC4P 4EE

Published in the USA by
Pandora Press (Routledge & Kegan Paul Inc.)
in association with Methuen Inc.
29 West 35th Street, New York, NY 10001

Set in Sabon, 10 on 11pt
by Columns of Reading
and printed in Great Britain
by The Guernsey Press Co Ltd
Guernsey, Channel Islands

Library of Congress Cataloging in Publication Data

Rhys-Thomas, Deirdre.
Letters for my children.
1. Nuclear warfare. 2. Antinuclear movement –
England. 3. Rhys-Thomas, Deirdre. I. Owens,
Janice. II. Title.
U263.R47 1987 355'.0217 86-25498

British Library CIP Data also available

ISBN 0-86358-181-1 (c)
      0-86358-055-6 (p)

For my sons, Theo and Toby

Contents

Preface

How can we expect our young to develop a sense of family and future if they are so uncertain about what the future holds for them, if they cannot imagine themselves, let alone their own children, growing up? This was the question that Dr Coppolillo, a leading American child psychologist, put to me in his letter four years ago.

I began writing these letters after my 12-year-old son, Theo, asked if I thought that there would be a nuclear war. Since then I have written to hundreds of people all over the world in an attempt to find an answer to Theo's question and to ask their views about the nuclear industry which threatens all our lives. At times I have felt as though I was hacking my way through the densest jungle. When I started writing these letters I had no thoughts of publication but, as time went on, I began to think that other mothers who shared my fears, who were also baffled by bureaucracy and weary of official statements, might gain some insight into the nuclear issue by reading the responses I had received. The people who were good enough to take the time and trouble to write to me were, I believe, expressing their honest views; I am publishing these letters in the belief and hope that they would want other, equally concerned parents to read them.

I would like to thank all the people who have given me help and encouragement, especially my husband, Peter, my friend Geraldine who is like a sister to me, Dr Don Arnott, Olive Chick, Hugh and Mags Richards, Mandy Herman, Iona MacGregor, my editor Jane Hawksley, and Janice Owens for all her hard work on the research.

Prologue

Shrewsbury
9 December 1982

Dearest Deirdre,
Just a line. Please do be careful if you decide to go to Greenham
Common.
    I know you shouldn't believe all you read in the papers but
I do hope there won't be any trouble.
    Do look after yourself. Phone me when you get home.
    All my love,
    Mummy

Saturday evening 11 December 1982

Hope to get to bed early. Lay breakfast for boys and Peter. Threaten
Puzzle (our new Beagle puppy) that if she barks as I creep out of the
house at daybreak, I'll take her to Greenham Common.[1] . . .

    Dilemma over what to wear. Common sense tells me to wrap up
warmly, definitely trousers, as forecast shows possible snow and
icy-cold winds, but I know only too well, the dear old media
equating trousers with lesbianism! How often do we read of
waistcoat-wrapped paunchy, shiny-seated, suited males? I care not
whether someone is a hippy, middle-class, lower-middle-class,
working-class, upper-class, coloured, white, spotty, tall, thin, short,
fat, as long as he or she doesn't threaten me. So much lip-service is
given to freedom of choice, where only prejudice abounds.

    I get out delicate, lace-trimmed thermal underwear, socks, and
my husband offers me his sailing jacket and trousers. So without
yacht, but 100% waterproof, in dashing red, I will set sail for
Greenham Common.

Sunday 12 December 1982 Greenham Common

Fixed on the wire fence is a life-size cardboard figure clothed in
Welsh dress, with 'My Mum' written on her. She smiles down at me.

Note 1: The women's peace camp has been at Greenham Common Air
Force Base since 5 September 1981, as a protest against the deployment
of 96 Cruise missiles and their launchers and in opposition to all nuclear
weapons. See Lynne Jones, *Keeping the Peace*, The Women's Press,
London, 1983.

At Gate 4, an exit gate used by American servicemen to cross over to their barracks, on the wire fence there is a most beautifully prepared card. Four fading, sepia photos – precious to their owner – all young men of 17, 18 years, one showing a soft wispy moustache, his first. In copperplate writing, their names, all Welshmen. The dead of the First World War. And written 'To be remembered today, to seek their peace'.

From our section of the perimeter fence we can see the deformed earth mound: a blanket for the cruise missiles. All day the floodlights stay on . . . waiting for the next Act in the Nuclear Drama. RAF Land Rovers drive up and down. Most unusual, say locals, usually only American Dodge trucks patrol the perimeter. Police helicopters circle overhead all day.

Near our Gate 4, the American barracks – a misnomer, no question of money spared in the building of what looks like a luxury block of flats set in well-lawned grounds, mature English trees offering shade and protection – have been cordoned off for the day. Police guard the lodge entrance. During the day American servicemen in civilian clothes come out onto the lawn. Some watch through binoculars from upstairs windows. I am aware of the immense gulf between us, obviously not physical but mental: though we supposedly speak the same language I feel I might be better able to communicate with E.T. Phone Home?

Newbury & Crookham Golf Club have to cancel its Christmas Competition. Locals tell me that American personnel rarely mix in the town, or pubs, too many upsets. Not as a consequence of the women's peace camp.

As dusk draws near, candles are lit, carols float through the air. Many Quakers line the fence, they are so sure: to hold their hands is to feel hope. Felt Doves of Peace, handmade, are fixed flying along our fence towards the word PEACE woven from the dead summer twigs of Greenham Common.

Whenever an American Dodge truck, or American bus, appears a spontaneous whooping noise comes forth, gradually involving all the women round the Base. I can only liken it to keening, or the plaintive call of Red Indian women. A sound that comes through from our ancestors.

Police keep a very low profile. Those near us are most pleasant and I feel concerned (after all when they take off their uniforms they too have to answer their children's fear of nuclear war).

A written plea tied to the fence: 'God Save the Queen . . . and the Rest of us.'

When dark comes, like vampire bats, the American servicemen

come out: for the first time in military dress: in their bus, quickly driven through Gate 4 across the airfield.

The candles placed in the ground all along the perimeter fence light up the faded teddy bears (well-worn but loved) looking down at us, the babies' first shoes, cherished photos. It looks as if we have been celebrating a pagan festival, a desperate summoning up of the spirits of our ancestors to help us now in the most dangerous time of mankind.

With great care, I tie my memento to the wire fence, the photos of my smiling children, of my husband, and two chosen poems written by women during the First World War –

'Fight-on' the Armament-kings
besought,
Nobody asked what the
women thought.

When the day was
done,
My little son
Wondered at his bath-time
Why I kissed him so,
Naked upon my knee
How could he know
The sudden terror that
Assaulted me?

That short poem sums up for me the obscenity and terror of the threat of war that hangs over all our children today, the stifled, unspoken fear that we parents carry in our hearts but dare not unburden on to them.

When it first hit me it was even worse than that, because it was my own 12-year-old son who brought the subject up. I had gone upstairs as usual to say goodnight to him. We'd always had a little giggle at night-time and said the ridiculous things my father used to say to me – 'Night, night, sleep tight, see the bugs don't bite . . . .' The same kind of traditional silly jokes that every family has.

That particular night it was different. Perhaps it was something he had seen on the news: something which had caught and held his attention in a way which touched his deepest fears. Theo spoke in that deceptively quiet way that children do when they're frozen with terror and can't get their feelings out. 'Do you think there's going to be a nuclear war, Mum?'

For an odd, still moment I couldn't think or speak. I sat down

3

on the bed again, took his hands, tried not to let him see how upset I was, tried to reassure and comfort him so that he could go to sleep. He'd always brought his problems to me, utterly confident that I would be able to solve them for him. Now he'd brought this gigantic fear, and I didn't want to let him down.

And yet afterwards I stood outside his door, immobilised by a strange mixture of anger and panic. I had had to lie to Theo to comfort him, and in doing so I felt that I had betrayed his trust in me, the implicit trust he has in Peter and I as his parents, his protectors. This trust had enabled him finally to drift off to sleep soothed by my empty promises into a false sense of security. How many other mothers, I thought, all over the country, all over the world, are being placed in this position?

Peter and I had never discussed the nuclear question with our children. We treated it as we treated all the things that children are inquisitive about: we waited for them to bring something up themselves, and then answered their questions as honestly as we could, according to their age at the time. Indeed, I can't say that it had been a question particularly to the forefront of my mind. I'd been too busy with the boys and our family life, and building up my career again. Every year in a child's life is different; there are new interests to explore, fresh things to take up your time. Now I was telling myself I should have paid more attention to what was happening in the world outside. I felt guilty that I had been so unprepared for Theo's question, and that I just didn't know the responsible approach to take.

Yet most of all I was angry. I felt, suddenly, that I had been the victim of a massive set-up in which my maternal role as a source of stability and comfort had been abused. I, and all the other parents like me, endlessly reassuring, smoothing the brows, being left to cope with our children's questions and relied upon not to ask too many questions ourselves. It seemed to Peter and I, as we sat in the living room later that night, discussing our child's worry, that we had come to a bridge in our lives as parents. Later we came to know of the research done by psychologists on children's responses to the nuclear threat; but at the time we only knew instinctively that to react less than honestly to their questions was worse than no solution. We had to say truthfully 'I don't know' but not 'I don't care' or 'I feel helpless'.

When I tried to think what I did know it was very little. I had seen some copies of *Protect and Survive*, the government leaflet on the action families should take in the event of nuclear attack, in my

4

local library. Even then the neat drawings of father constructing a nuclear shelter out of an old door and black dustbin liners seemed pathetically inadequate. I knew nothing about radiation, either from nuclear power or nuclear bombs: I had only a hazy idea of the effects and no way of judging the dangers.

I made up my mind that night that the solution could only be to seek answers to my questions and to actively involve my children in the process, Theo to begin with, then Toby later on. I decided that the way to do this was to address my simple, blunt questions directly to the people who *had* the answers: the planners, the scientists, the politicians. That way Theo would get his answers directly from them, unmediated by me, and he could make his own judgments about them. It would also involve those faceless bureaucrats in the responsibility they were otherwise leaving up to me as a parent. And it would show my children that I cared.

That was how I began to write these letters. And that is how I came to be standing that night among the failing candles in the cold and mud and companionship of Greenham Common.

When I got home, I wrote again to my mother.

late 12 December

Dearest Mummy,

I'm back from Greenham Common. I know how worried you were for me so I decided to write down everything about my day at Greenham Common. I would like to share it with you.

There were no arrests. Honestly, the way the press go on about lesbians, just because a number of women meet together – I don't think they go on the same way about the international rugby matches, the football matches, etc. etc. There were mothers, grandmothers, even met one great-grandmother, working, middle-class, no class, a complete mixture of British women.

The one thing we all had in common was our determination not to become Mrs Bloggs!

I'm so tired, see you next week for lunch in Shrewsbury.

Best love to you,

Your daughter,

Deirdre

P.S. Mrs Bloggs appears in a book – *When the Wind Blows*, by Raymond Briggs. Even when the bomb drops she can't believe it's happening and pretends it isn't.

The letters

13 December 1982

To: Mr Imbert,
Chief Constable,
Headquarters,
Thames Valley Police,
Kidlington,
Oxon.

Dear Mr Imbert,
I would be extremely grateful if you would convey my thanks to
those of your policemen who patrolled and protected Gate 4
and environs at USAF Base Greenham Common on Sunday, 12
December.

Their kindly, courteous behaviour was exemplary.

It also pleases me that the Riot Police who had been ferried
into the USAF Base at first light were not called out. In addition
that there was not one single incident during the day with over
30,000 people present.

May I wish you and your Police Officers a Happy
Christmas.
Yours sincerely,
Deirdre Rhys-Thomas

22 December 1982

Dear Deirdre Rhys-Thomas,
Thank you for your letter dated 13 December 1982.

It was very kind of you indeed to write informing me of the
kindly and courteous behaviour of the police officers on duty at
Greenham Common on Sunday, 12 December 1982.

As you are aware, this was a very delicate situation and I
am pleased that all the police officers dealt with it so well. I will
ensure that your kind remarks are brought to the attention of
the officers concerned.

There is one point I would wish to make, and that is, there are no 'riot' police in this Force nor in any other Force in the country. The police officers who were actually based inside the airfield were ordinary police officers and were not riot police. I am sorry to labour this point, but I am anxious that all members of the public realise that those police officers who perform duty at demonstrations, football matches, etc. are the same police officers who normally perform ordinary police tasks in our towns and villages.

Once again, many thanks for writing – I am delighted you thought the demonstration such a success.

I wish you a happy Christmas.

Yours sincerely,

Peter Imbert

Chief Constable

Thames Valley Police

11 January 1983

Dear Mummy,

I'm sorry but I don't honestly feel like coming over to see you at the moment. It's a laugh really, remember how concerned you were for me when I went to Greenham Common?

Well, the phone went yesterday, and it was an Inspector Thomas (woman) from Police Headquarters, Carmarthen. She said she had been told that I had said complimentary things about the Police at Greenham Common. I couldn't think how she knew but she said a Det. Chief Supt. Pointer of Wiltshire Constabulary had told her.

Actually I had written to the Chief Constable of Thames Valley Police Force asking him to pass on my thanks to the policemen near the fence near Gate 4 (on 12 December) who were friendly and helpful. The Chief Constable replied to me, and I told the Inspector of these letters.

Although I agreed to meet the Inspector on 20 January, I had to phone her back this morning to change the date to 14 January, and suggested we meet in a local Hotel. I was taken aback when the Inspector agreed to meeting there but said an official Statement could only be made in a Police Station.

Never having made an official Statement, let alone knowing

7

what the form looks like, or ever having been in a Police Station I think I'll have a word with our solicitor.

Don't worry, Mummy, after all we are forever being told we live in a free society, and after all, all I have done is write complimentary letters to the police.
Much love,
Deirdre

9 February 1983

Dear Mummy,
Yes, I met the Inspector yesterday in Llandrindod Wells, at a hotel, and after we had chatted she asked me for a Statement.

I repeated that I didn't see the need for a statement as the Police had the letters of the Chief Constable and mine on file. But the Inspector said if I didn't make a Statement she felt she would be asked to contact me again.

So I agreed to make a negative Statement, which the Inspector suggested: I phoned our solicitor before making it. I kept a note of it in my Diary –

Statement taken at 2.47

I attended the demonstration at Greenham Common on the 12th December 1982.

I decline to make a written Statement on the grounds that I have said everything in my letter to the Chief Constable of Thames Valley.

My feelings about this are very confused. I feel resentful, that my privacy has been invaded and the words a free society sound a little hollow as it doesn't seem to me that I had much freedom of choice in this.

See you on Wednesday.
Much love,
Deirdre

Just after I had come back from Greenham Common I read an interview with a Mr and Mrs McGuire. They complained that the entranceway to their home had been damaged by the women demonstrators. I thought: I object to being put into that generalization as an irresponsible, trespassing vandal, so I sent them a cheque towards the cost of putting things right.

13 December 1982

To: Mr and Mrs R. McGuire,
Greenham Common,
Nr Newbury,
Berks.

Dear Mr and Mrs McGuire,
Having read of your plight in today's *Guardian*,[2] I would like to apologize for the inconvenience caused to you. As a token of my concern, I would like you to accept the enclosed cheque.

I am so pleased you don't like the Bomb but I cannot understand why you don't believe this sort of thing will make it go away. May I suggest you look at the actions and achievements of Gandhi. Peaceful, positive public action has usually been the only way to make politicians realise that their first responsibility is to the people, and such action has stopped politicians from being immured in the House of Commons.

Again, please accept my sincere apology on behalf of those who have caused you discomfort.
Yours sincerely,
Deirdre Rhys-Thomas

Note 2: 'Long-suffering local residents Roger and Carol McGuire had their front drive used as a car park. They had their house invaded by hippies in the past and an airgun pellet through a window.
Mr McGuire said: "A lot of them are sincere but they attract undesirables who cause trouble and it is us who have to bear the brunt. It costs us money as ratepayers and the land is turned to mud by thousands of tramping feet. We don't like the bomb but we don't believe this sort of thing will make it go away."' (*Guardian*, 13 December 1983, p.1)

9

They didn't write back, but I saw on my bank statement that my cheque had been cleared.

My next attempt to counter the media image of 'Greenham harridans' fell on equally deaf ears.

13 December 1982

To: Mr Church,
Members' Secretary
Newbury & Crookham Golf Club,
Greenham Common,
Nr Newbury, Berks.

Dear Mr Church,
As one of 'the mob' (as used by your Stewards) present at USAF Base Greenham Common on Sunday, 12 December, I would be grateful if you would offer my sincere apology to your Members. I am so sorry they had to cancel their Christmas Golf Competition.

Having several golf-playing relations, indeed one who is a Champion Golfer, I do so appreciate the importance of golf in your Members' lives. Unfortunately the pursuit of sport is proving of little consolation to my 10 and 13 years old sons. Both being terribly well read they have inevitably become aware of the threat of nuclear war. As many adults seem unable to face up to the full implications of nuclear war if the nuclear deterrent policy fails, bearing in mind that informed opinion now recognises that the deployment of new weapons is changing nuclear policies from nuclear deterrence based on mutual assured destruction to nuclear-war fighting.

Perhaps Members of your Golf Club could find the words I may use to my sons to alleviate their fear?

Regarding your cancelled Competition, I will put it to several concerned anti-nuclear friends who would, I hope, like to donate a cup to one of your forthcoming Competitions.

May I wish you and your Members a Happy Christmas.
Yours sincerely,
Deirdre Rhys-Thomas

10

To: Mr Church,
Members' Secretary
Newbury & Crookham Golf Club,
Greenham Common,
Nr Newbury,
Berks.

10 February 1983

Dear Mr Church,
I am sure it is because of your Club's Christmas celebrations
that I have not yet received a reply from you. I look forward to
hearing from you shortly.

I do hope the members of Newbury & Crookham Golf
Club have accepted my offer of an Anti Nuclear Cup to be
presented at one of your Competitions in 1983.
Yours sincerely,
Deirdre Rhys-Thomas

22nd February, 1983

Dear Mrs. Rhys-Thomas,
Thank you for your letters of the 13th December, 1982, and
10th February, 1983.

I do not dispute the benevolent regime under which we live
gives you and I the privilege of demonstrating our beliefs.

Like yourself I would not dispute that my Steward has the
personal right to express his opinion whether you or I believe it.

I also believe that members of the public should be allowed
to get about their lawful business without hindrance and if this
involves them wishing to play golf in their leisure time then so
be it. I have personally been prevented from attending my place
of work on several occasions because of action outside the Base
but have to accept this, however reluctantly, as my cross to bear
in a 'truly democratic' community.

I must tell you that although your offer of a cup to play for
is I know well intentioned, because we have a full programme I
must say I am unable to accept this.
Yours sincerely,
R.F. Church

Children's fears of the Bomb

Denver, Colorado: More and more children fear an all-out nuclear war and many say they do not expect to reach adulthood, an American psychiatrist says.

Some see the Bomb as a symbol of the evils they fear, but they have learned to keep these fears secret, according to Dr Coppolillo, head of child psychiatry at the University of Colorado's health sciences centre.

He told a schools panel on nuclear issues that parents did not want to discuss their own fears of nuclear war because 'these emotions are simply too disturbing to live with day to day.

'Our children, who take many of their cues from the adults in the environment, have also come to feel that this is not a topic of discussion.'

The Bomb was often viewed in the same light as the devil among children of earlier generations, he said. But, while earlier generations were offered the hope of escaping the devil through religion, there was no such ready escape from the Bomb.

Guardian, 2 November 1982

2 November 1982

To: Dr Coppolillo,
Head of Child Psychiatry,
Health Services Center, University of Colorado,
Denver, Colorado, U.S.A.

Dear Dr Coppolillo,
Please help me. Today I have read in my newspaper an article on your findings on American children – their fears of the Bomb.

Deep in my heart, I have always hidden my fear of the nuclear threat. I know as a child that I was conscious of the Bomb.

Many adults I talk to now are irritated, laugh dismissively, adopt the ostrich attitude. Oh, yes, we nuclear children have taken our unexpressed fears about the Bomb into adulthood.

But Dr Coppolillo, if American children are frightened, how frightened British children must be? My children?

Our newspapers daily report on the latest nuclear theatre weapons to be installed in Britain or Europe – they hear the Forces talk of protracted nuclear war – they see on Television Reagan talking of the nuclear arms race – they hear Thatcher siding with Reagan 'her Nuke best friend' – and the Pentagon's 'For God's sake keep it in Britain or Europe' attitude – all these increase our fear.

America, it is said, is providing the nuclear umbrella but we seem to be holding it. And the person holding it is usually the one who gets struck by lightning. In a nuclear thunderstorm the lightning bolts are likely to be frequent and fatal. I don't like the prospect of my family sheltering under the nuclear umbrella.

Mrs Thatcher (Prime Minister) has recognised the erosion of family life in Britain. Surely political measures designed to enhance the prospects of family life must include the removal of this psychologically crippling fear of a dark and radioactive future?

Yours sincerely,
Deirdre Rhys Thomas

University of Colorado Health Sciences Center
December 3, 1982

Dear Mrs Thomas:

Thank you for your poignant letter of November second. It arrived only yesterday, but I hasten to answer because I was moved and touched by your expressions and find that they inspire me to try to do more.

You begin your letter by saying, 'Please help me', and I certainly feel that your plea is justified and I will hear it repeated in my mind in my daily work. Let me ask, however, if it would not be better if we began to ask at this time that we all help each other. By this, I mean that we can no longer live in a world in which the interests and welfare of single nations or single institutions can be allowed to be paramount even in the minds of those nations or institutions. The first item of priority for the world must be that of the physical and psychological safety and welfare of all of our children. If *one* (even just one)

13

British or German or French child dies or is physically or psychologically impaired in order to serve the interests of America or Russia or of a giant industry or institution, then every child in the world will continue to be vulnerable. As you have so accurately pointed out our children carry this vulnerability into their adult lives.

As you have stated in your letter, our leaders say they are aware of the erosion of family life within our countries. It seems to me, however, that thus far all we have done is to give lip service to solving the problem. How can we expect our young to develop a sense of family and future if they are so uncertain about what the future holds that they cannot imagine themselves as grown up, let alone imagine their children growing up.

I think we must all unite in proclaiming whenever we have the chance that the time has come for us to stop talking about we and they. Children are to be protected *all over the world*. The time has come for the leaders in the world to see that for the first time in the world's history they are deciding between survival and *oblivion* for the *whole world*, and that the results will be total. We will either all survive or all become part of a void filled only by radioactive particles.

I hope that our counterparts in Britain and in the rest of the world (Physicians for Social Responsibility, Educators for Social Responsibility, etc.) will join all the concerned parents of the world in raising their voices to save our children.

Thank you again Mrs Thomas for taking the time and trouble to write me.

With cordial best wishes, I am,
Sincerely yours
Henry P. Coppolillo, M.D.
Professor and Director
Division of Child Psychiatry
University of Colorado
Health Sciences Center

To: The President of the United States of America,
Oval Office,
The White House,
Washington,
Washington, D.C.
U.S.A.

Mr President,
Does it matter to you, Mr President, that millions of children –
British, French, Rumanian, American, Russian – are living in
fear of nuclear war? Indeed the children of the World?

Perhaps because it's 'millions' it is too difficult for you to
relate to. Let me help you, Mr President. My son is frightened
of nuclear war. I cannot find the words to use to him at his
bedside when he wakes from a nuclear nightmare. Could you,
Mr President, if you were at his bedside find the words to stop
his fear? It's hardly surprising as most adults can't cope with the
prospect of nuclear war, adopting the ostrich attitude.

Research from America is showing that American children
are so frightened of the Nuclear Bomb that it is, and has,
seriously changed their basic hopes. How much more frightened
children in Britain and Europe must be?

Please don't give me the old chestnut – 'this nuclear
situation is the most complicated'. I know it is. I am fully
conversant with the nuclear scenario – ICBMs, SLBMs, theatre
nuclear weapons, overkill, balance of arms, interpretation of
balance.

The fact is: now in 1983 we have every possible nuclear
variant.

Little constructive has come out of the Treaties or
Conventions, or arms control talks. Informed opinion (of
leading strategists and scientists) recognizes that the deployment
of new nuclear weapons is changing nuclear policies from
nuclear deterrence based on mutual assured destruction to
nuclear-war fighting.

On television last week, Mr President you said 'moderate
words are convincing only when they are matched by moderate
behaviour'. Exactly so. I hope that the very reliable rumour
coming out at the moment that the USA is going to rush in to
Britain the Transporter Erector Launchers (TELs) for the Cruise

15

Missiles is not true? If it is, is this your example of moderate behaviour?

Is it surprising, Mr President, that so many people throughout the world are not convinced that the USA or Russia genuinely want to achieve realistic arms control but would rather play power politics?
Deirdre Rhys-Thomas

Embassy of the
United States of America
London W1A 1AE

March 11, 1983

Dear Mrs Rhys-Thomas,

Thank you for your letter concerning nuclear weapons which you sent to the President, and to which I have been asked to respond.

Because you have written about this important matter I am sure you will find the enclosed booklets – *In Search of Peace* and *Peace through Deterrence and Arms Reduction* – of interest.

Yours sincerely,
[illegible signature]
Acting Counselor for Public Affairs

To: Dr Anthony Clare,
Institute of Psychiatry,
De Crespigny Park, London S.E.5

30 November 1982

Dear Dr Clare,

Though I listened to your radio series *In the Psychiatrist's Chair* with considerable interest it is not as a psychiatrist but as a parent I wish to ask you – how do you lie to your children?

This dreadful decision has had to be made by me. My son voiced his profound fear of nuclear war. As most adults seem unable to cope with this fear, seeming to adopt the ostrich attitude, I felt it was essential to protect his peace of mind and

16

so I lied to him by saying that there is absolutely no possibility of a nuclear war.

I feel so angry that for the first time in our relationship I have had to lie, and been forced into doing this by politicians and the armaments lobby who believe the arms race is the only way forward.

I do recognise that deep in my heart I have always hidden my fear of the nuclear threat. I know as a child that I was conscious of the Bomb. Oh yes, we nuclear children have taken our unexpressed fears about the Bomb into adulthood.

Apparently research from America is showing that American children are so frightened of the Bomb that it is, and has seriously changed their basic hopes. How much more frightened British children must be, Dr Clare?

America, it is said, is providing the nuclear umbrella but we in Britain seem to be holding it. And the person holding it is usually the one who gets struck by lightning. In a nuclear thunderstorm the lightning bolts are likely to be frequent and fatal. I don't like the prospect of my family sheltering under the nuclear umbrella.

Politicians, amongst them Mrs Thatcher, have recognised the erosion of family life in Britain. Surely measures designed to enhance the prospects of family life must include the removal of this psychologically, crippling fear of a dark and radioactive future which my son and so many other British children fear?
Yours sincerely,
Deirdre Rhys-Thomas

Institute of Psychiatry
University of London
De Crespigny Park
Denmark Hill
London

5th January, 1983

Dear Mrs Rhys-Thomas,
    I am sorry to have taken so long to reply to your fascinating letter of the 30th November, 1982. I think the question that you put to me is a very difficult one indeed. I have six children and at various times each has asked me just such a

17

question, and depending on their age I have had to do what you did. I think that children up to a certain age cannot cope with the grim reality of nuclear destruction. I myself don't know of any research into the effects of this particular preoccupation, and I am asking some of my colleagues whether they know any.[3] In view of the final paragraph of your letter, perhaps you should write a similar letter to Mrs Thatcher, particularly in the light of the growing concern being expressed by British women regarding nuclear weapons.

Many thanks for writing to me.

Yours sincerely,

Anthony W. Clare, M.D.,

Senior Lecturer

Note 3: In March 1983 a symposium on the subject of children and war was organised by the Peace Union of Finland at Siunto Baths, and the proceedings published. In the introduction the editors point out that although in the First World War 5 per cent of the human victims were civilians, in the Second World War the proportion had risen to 50 per cent, in Vietnam between 80-90 per cent and in Lebanon 97 per cent. See Kahnert, Marianne, David Pitt and Ilkka Taipale, eds, *Children and War*, GIPRI, IPB, Finland 1983.

24 February, 1983

To: The Rt Hon. Prime Minister, Mrs Margaret Thatcher
10 Downing Street,
London S.W.1.

Dear Mrs Thatcher

Cruise missiles will not be functional until 1986. Their reliability has been questioned in the USA at the highest level. Why are you and your Minister of Defence, Mr Heseltine so eager to support their deployment?

You are always speaking of your support for multi-lateral disarmament. I would be obliged if you would explain to me why your Government's Ambassador to the United Nations has continually voted against the proposals for moves towards a nuclear freeze, including steps towards nuclear disarmament?

I am forever hearing you talk of your happy family life above the grocer's shop. A happy family life lays the foundations for responsible adulthood. Today, this is being denied many intelligent, well-read children. They are frightened of nuclear war (crystallised for them in the book *When the Wind Blows*). Many parents are totally unaware of their children's fear of nuclear war. Many children sense their parents have opted out of their nuclear responsibilities and so do not confide in them. They are withdrawing their trust in adults.

Could you, Mrs Thatcher, find the words to use to my son at his bedside when he wakes from a nuclear nightmare?

You, and your 'family group' Ministers, have recognised the erosion of family life in Britain. Surely measures designed to enhance the prospects of family life must include the removal of this psychologically crippling fear of a dark and radioactive future which my son and so many other British children fear?

Yours sincerely,
Deirdre Rhys-Thomas

From: S P Lock, Defence Secretariat 17
Ministry of Defence
Main Building, Whitehall, London
Our reference D/D517/1/26

10th May 1983

Thank you for your letter of 24 February 1983 to the Prime Minister. I have been asked to reply.

First, let me say that I entirely appreciate your concern over nuclear weapons, but reassure you and your son that the Government does not for one moment hold that nuclear war is inevitable, or even likely. There has been considerable discussion in the media about the prospects of a nuclear war, but despite relations between East and West, being far from ideal there is no reason to believe that such a war is imminent. The chief aim of the Government's defence and foreign policies is to preserve and strengthen peace, and to ensure that nuclear weapons are never again used.

This is why we in the United Kingdom, together with our NATO Allies, have adopted the strategy of deterrence. Our main objective is not to win a war but to prevent one starting in the first place. Our aim is to make it quite clear to any potential aggressor that the risks he would incur would be out of all proportion to any gains he might expect to make. I cannot emphasise too strongly that this strategy is intended to maintain peace between East and West in Europe, as it has done for over thirty years, despite circumstances that were often difficult. To abandon our security system now, in favour of some alternative one which would be quite unproven would be immensely dangerous. The hard truth is that without a nuclear capability the Alliance would be unable to deter attack or to resist blackmail based on the threat of attack.

There is a common misconception that a unilaterally disarmed Britain would be safer. Some unilateralists argue that the Russians pose no danger, other unilateralists contradict this and argue almost the opposite; that because the Russians are so powerful and because the possibility of nuclear war is so appalling, we should opt out altogether. However the real world in which we have to live is one in which nuclear weapons inescapably exist, and the idea that if we were unilaterally to renounce our nuclear forces we should be spared from attack in a nuclear war is wishful thinking. If we abandon our nuclear weapons but at the same time remain in NATO we shall be no less vulnerable to a nuclear attack by the Soviet Union in the event of war than we are now. Our geographical position and strategic importance make us a prime target. If, on the other hand, we renounce our nuclear weapons and at the same time leave NATO, we shall not only be abandoning an Alliance which has safeguarded our security for thirty years, but quite probably prompting it to collapse altogether. European security would be drastically weakened in consequence, and the risk of Soviet aggression correspondingly increased.

The point is that 'Nuclear-Free' does not mean 'Nuclear-Safe'. The best way of deterring an adversary from threatening to use nuclear weapons against us is to retain our own nuclear weapons until all nuclear powers agree to disarm. Possession of nuclear weapons has actually made it less likely that Britain would be a nuclear target, not more so. Soviet planners could never be certain, as long as Britain possessed a strategic nuclear deterrent, that a nuclear attack on this country would not carry the unacceptable risk for them of a British nuclear response.

Cruise missiles will form an important part of NATO's strategy of deterrence. The Soviet Union has in recent years considerably enhanced the capabilities of its intermediate range nuclear force (INF) by deploying, more than 350 mobile and extremely accurate SS20 missiles, each with three warheads, together with the Backfire bomber which has an inherent intercontinental capability and also poses a serious threat to targets in Western Europe from bases deep within the Soviet Union. These improvements are taking place at a time when NATO's INF are ageing and becoming increasingly vulnerable. It was against this background that we and our Allies decided on a modernisation of our INF capability, including the deployment of cruise missiles, in order that the Soviet Union should not believe that it might be able to exploit NATO's possible weakness at the intermediate nuclear level. I should add that the decision to modernise our INF capability was accompanied by an offer to the Soviet Union to negotiate balanced limitations of the weapons on both sides. To start with the Russians refused to talk. It was only when faced with NATO's determination to proceed with the modernisation decision, that the Russians came to the negotiating table. In the real world, where business has to be done with the Russians, the West will not secure arms control by giving them what they want before negotiation starts.

I did not, as it happens, see the report to which you refer, but there have been a number of accounts casting doubt on the efficiency of the cruise missile. Perhaps I could comment in general terms on the situation as we see it. The Americans are engaged in a comprehensive development on a whole range of cruise missile variants. The only type which concerns this country directly is the ground launched cruise missile, which is due to begin to be deployed at Greenham Common by the end of the year unless there are satisfactory results in the Geneva negotiations. We keep in touch with the Americans about this, and all the information we have suggests that this particular programme is proceeding according to schedule. It is of course inevitable that there will be some failures during tests; indeed the whole object of the tests is to expose and iron out the faults before the missiles enter service. I do assure you however that there is no question of the missiles being deployed before all the necessary development and safety tests have been completed.

Perhaps I could make two further points. First, the missiles will not be fired from this country, except in the event that they are required for an actual war. Secondly, as one of the many safety checks included in the weapon, the nuclear warhead is armed only when the computer guidance system recognises and acquires the target immediately before hitting it. There is no question of a premature nuclear explosion if the rocket for some reason fails in flight.

The reason why the British Government has been unable to support the idea of a 'freeze' on nuclear weapons (as has for example been advocated by some US senators and certain countries at the United Nations) is not because it is in any way opposed to nuclear arms control and disarmament but because such a move would confirm a Soviet superiority in practically all aspects of nuclear forces and reduce their incentive to negotiate meaningfully towards reduction. In recent years the Soviet Union has invested massively in new nuclear weapons both at the strategic level (such as the SS18 ICBM) and below (such as the SS20 missile). The West by contrast, has introduced very few new nuclear systems. To freeze now would confirm this Soviet superiority and contractualise an imbalance in forces. A freeze would be difficult and time consuming to negotiate, and difficult to verify. It would also divert effort away from the urgent and important task of seeking to negotiate *reductions* in the levels of nuclear forces of both sides (as is happening in talks in Geneva) rather than merely seeking to hold forces at existing levels. For these reasons the Government believes that the best course is to work for balanced reductions in the forces of both sides, and supports the US positions in the Geneva negotiations as the way forward.

At the Intermediate Nuclear Forces (INF) talks in Geneva the Americans have put forward the radical proposal of the 'Zero Option'. Agreement to this would mean that NATO would scrap its plans to deploy cruise and Pershing II missiles in return for the dismantling of similar Soviet missiles (the SS20 and older SS4 and SS5). We sincerely hope that the Russians will respond positively to this initiative which would totally eliminate the nuclear missiles of most concern to both sides. We have always been prepared, however, to consider other solutions, at least as an interim step. If the Soviet Union is not prepared to negotiate the 'Zero Option', then the West will look for other solutions. President Reagan has made it clear that the 'Zero Option' is not a take it or leave it offer, and that the American negotiating team has instructions to explore any proposal consistent with the principle of balance. With NATO's full support, the US announced in March that they were prepared to negotiate an interim agreement, under which NATO would reduce its planned deployment if the Soviet Union would reduce their corresponding missile warheads to an equal level. This demonstrates our flexibility and determination to reach an agreement if at all possible. It is now up to the Soviet Union to prove that they are serious in their negotiating intent by responding positively and constructively to this proposal.

We welcome the resumption of talks on strategic weapons (START) and the commitment of the Americans to work for massive reductions in the levels of these forces. So far they have proposed a dramatic cut of over 50% in the number of strategic nuclear missiles and a cut of a third in the number of nuclear warheads as a first step in reducing the massive arsenals of the two Super-powers. These talks take time – they involve complex and difficult issues and national security – but they offer a major chance to work for real progress in disarmament and must be given a chance to succeed.

In summary, then, all the Government's efforts are devoted towards preserving peace. They believe that while NATO continues to maintain its defences, war in Europe is not likely. At the same time, they will take every opportunity to seek balanced and verifiable arms control agreements through diplomatic activity and negotiations, and to work for a safer future, in which the security of our country and of other States can be upheld at a lower level of risk. I hope that this explanation will help to allay the concern which you feel.

20 May 1983

To: The Rt Hon. Prime Minister, Mrs Margaret Thatcher,
10 Downing Street,
London S.W.1.

Dear Mrs Thatcher,
I have received a letter dated 10th May, from the Ministry of Defence, in reply to my personal letter to you.

I cannot help but feel that my Victorian grandfather, a landowner and a Tory Agent to the Duchess of Atholl, would have frowned upon your not having replied personally to my letter to you.

Your personal lack of response can hardly be seen to exemplify the Victorian values you claim to uphold.
Yours sincerely,
Deirdre Rhys-Thomas

Peter and I moved to Wales soon after we were married. We wanted to get back to the Celtic areas of Britain. We felt we had an affinity there: Peter is Welsh, and although I was brought up in England I am half Welsh and half Scots.

When we met in London Peter was combining teaching with the making of documentary films, and I was in PR. After the wedding we moved to Knighton in Radnorshire; Peter took a post in a comprehensive school, teaching science.

Knighton is in the heart of the Welsh border country, the Marches. It's quite a hilly area, with lots of woodland. Knighton is a small market town with a population of just under three thousand. We have a few small factories but mainly it functions as a centre for the local agricultural community. On market days the farmers bring their sheep in and the pubs stay open all day. There's a little single-track railway which we've been able to hang on to because we are a marginal seat, and it's an important local issue. Until we were detached from the South Wales valleys this was a labour constituency, but in 1980 it swung to the Conservatives. There are other elements; some old-style Liberals and a Green Group. A Knighton Peace Group started up, but it faded away. Politically, we are quite a mixture.

Nowadays Knighton is a quiet little place; but it used to be like a Texas border town. Offa's Dyke runs right through the middle, though you now have to go outside the town to pick up the visible remains. King Offa of Mercia built it in the eighth century right down the Welsh Marches to keep out the Welsh. Some people say it's just a demarcation boundary. Someone told me that 'Knighton' means 'the town of the riding men – knights'. They used to base themselves here and patrol up and down the Dyke.

On Sunday afternoons we often walk out there with Theo and Toby – mainly to exercise our beagle, Puzzle. There's a large ditch and an earth bank that's twenty feet high in places. I used to be on the Rights of Way Committee. We fought very hard to get it opened for everyone. Now it is run by the Offa's Dyke Association and there's a public footpath all the way along the top from Chester to Chepstow. People come from all over Britain to walk the Dyke, and even from as far away as Holland and Japan.

24

I'm quite involved in the local life of the town. With my friend Geraldine Barnes I run a company which promotes real Welsh farmhouse holidays for guests from abroad. The farmhouse holidays led to our becoming involved in the Royal Welsh Show. This is our premier agricultural show held once a year at Builth Wells. The Queen is our patron. The show lasts four days and usually a member of the Royal Family attends.

I've presented rosettes in the Main Ring, and the company gets asked to sponsor some of the entries. We agreed to sponsor our native Welsh sheep, the badger-face. It has a black stripe on its face and underbelly and tail. It had been almost bred out, and it didn't have a Flock Book. Some of the farmers were bemoaning this; but in order to start showing it, a Class had to be sponsored. Our company agreed to do this and we sponsored the breed for four years.

We have also sponsored the Concours d'Elégance turn-out, mainly in Welsh cobs and ponies. We chose carefully, picking only those entries we felt would be helpful to the Welsh way of life, and which represented genuine Welsh culture rather than being an artificial continuation.

At the Royal Welsh Show I once started talking to someone on the Lifeboat stand. He had a record of a male voice choir singing sea songs and shanties. I couldn't wheedle it out of him as it was the only copy. But he promised to send me another. Two months later the LP arrived from the RNLI in Cardiff. With it was a cryptic note saying that they had decided to start a Lifeboat branch in Knighton and that I was to be on the Committee.

In fact I feel strongly about raising money for the lifeboat service. When we go sailing we see the work done by the volunteer crew there. In Cardigan Bay the sea can be quite dangerous. And I remember vividly how, when I was a child at Swanage, we'd all rush off to the lifeboat station when the red maroons went off. Even in the middle of Sunday lunch everyone would leave the table to watch the lifeboatmen go out. It wasn't morbid curiosity, but as if there was some spiritual help for them in our watching.

We hold barndances and the like to raise money for the lifeboats. Of course Knighton is completely landlocked and seventy miles from the sea. I feel rather strange trying to persuade people to give money when I'm out on the street on Flag Day. I always tell people that they'll need a lifeboat when the great flood comes because there won't be room for all of us on the hills!

When I started to write the letters they grew very much out of my immediate local concerns — my family, my work, my community and my town.

14 September 1982

To: Mr M. Dray,
Emergency Planning Officer,
Powys County Council,
Llandrindod Wells,
Powys.

Dear Sir,
I have been told there is a nuclear shelter under the Radnor District Council office at Llandrindod Wells.

Having no nuclear shelter, I would like my family to take advantage of the Council shelter and seek refuge in it, if or when there is a nuclear war/contretemps.
Yours faithfully,
Deirdre Rhys-Thomas

Powys County Council
Cyngor Sir

17th Sept 1982

Dear Mrs Thomas,
Nuclear Shelters
I am in receipt of your letter regarding nuclear shelters and I am afraid that somebody has been giving you false information, not intentionally I hope, as there are no purpose built nuclear shelters in Powys.

The ground floor/basement area of the Radnor District Council offices at Llandrindod Wells was used as Civil Defence control in the last war and this would also be used as the County control centre in the event of a nuclear war, in which case additional protection against radioactive fallout would have to be provided by sandbagging, etc.

The Government are at present looking at measures to provide shelters in urban and city areas or evacuate to rural areas, such as Powys which would be unlikely to suffer from the heat/blast effects of nuclear weapons and whose major problem would be fallout protection.

Simple measures to improve the standard of protection against fallout are set out in the publication *Protect & Survive* which can be obtained from H.M. Stationery Office branches and larger bookshops. This publication is being up-dated and a revised edition will be published next year. I would also draw your attention to another H.M.S.O. publication – *Domestic Nuclear Shelters*, price 50p which gives details for home-built shelters.

Yours sincerely,
County Emergency Planning Officer

I rang up Mike Dray, and he kindly invited me to meet with him. He's a charming man. He had a lovely map on the wall with coloured pins in it. He showed me how the wind from Brawdy (a nearby US base) would come over in neat little corridors marked with arrows. It looked reassuring but winds are unpredictable. It looked to me as if it had been decided administratively which way the wind would blow after a nuclear war.

Mr Dray gave me another copy of *Protect and Survive*.

My friend Geraldine, with whom I run Country House Farms of Wales, is an expert on traditional Welsh cooking, and we try to get the farms to use the authentic old recipes in their catering for foreign guests. We keep an eye on food and catering literature, and I saw an article which led to the following:

14 September 1982

To: The Chairman,
The Guernsey Tomato Board,
St Sampson's,
Guernsey.

Dear Sir,
I do not know whether to continue buying tomatoes, vegetables and fruits grown in the Channel Islands and at present on sale in shops throughout Britain.

Can you assure me that there is no radioactive contamination of these fruits and vegetables?

I understand that radioactive materials discharged from the French nuclear processing plant at Cap de la Hague are being reconcentrated in seaweed around the Channel Islands.[4]
Yours faithfully,
Deirdre Rhys-Thomas

Note 4: Some explanation of where plutonium and americium – called 'transuranic radioisotopes' because they are heavier than uranium – come from, and how they get into the sea might help. When the world began many of the chemicals it was made of were unstable, and they went through a series of transformations, with bits flying apart, and rays of energy swirling in abundance. Most of them eventually settled down to the safe and familiar rocks, sand and water in which living plants and animals were able to evolve. A few stayed 'radioactive', like radium which gives off rays that leave their trace on photographic film even in pitch darkness. Some uranium atoms split apart naturally, and if they are separated from their more stable counterparts and concentrated into a 'critical mass', they can be made to split simultaneously as in the first atom bomb dropped on Hiroshima. When uranium is packed into a hollow rod of steel, or another metal alloy, and many rods are built into the core of a nuclear reactor, the splitting apart of the atoms, called 'fission', can be controlled and the immense energy emitted can be used to boil water to generate electricity. Just as the splitting apart of uranium atoms in weapons creates a cloud of radioactive dust – fallout – so the production of energy from uranium fuel rods creates a similar, but more complicated mixture inside the rods. Some of the uranium traps bits and becomes heavier, being transformed into plutonium, americium, neptunium, etc. – the 'transuranics'.

The plutonium is wanted for the production of nuclear weapons, or for use in a different type of nuclear reactor, called the Fast Breeder Reactor, where it can be used as fuel. At Cap de la Hague in France, the fuel rods are stripped, and the contaminated uranium goes through a series of chemical processes to dissolve out the plutonium and some unused uranium. This is called reprocessing, and it creates a great deal of radioactive gas and liquid. The gas is sent up the chimney, and filtered to trap some of the radioactive particles. The liquid is filtered and when it has very little plutonium, etc., left in it, it is sent down a long pipeline into the sea. Plutonium is an 'alpha-emitter' (see diagram) and the total alpha discharge allowed at Cap de la Hague is 90 curies in any one year.

Types of radiation

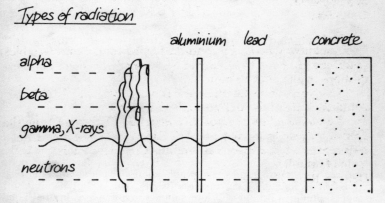

As the diagram shows, alpha particles cannot get through skin, but if they are absorbed into plants eaten by people specks of plutonium can go on giving off alpha particles for a very long time – 240 thousand years – and cause damage inside the body.

The Ministry of Agriculture, Fisheries and Food are responsible for monitoring the amount of radioactive contamination that is getting into the sea and sea-plants and fish. In 1983 they took eleven samples of two different kinds of seaweed near Guernsey, and reported that 'concentrations of artificial radionuclides ... were of negligible radiological significance'. They do not refer to use of seaweed as fertiliser, which is mentioned in the report Deirdre refers to.

The significance of low levels of radiation in causing damage to public health is under debate at present, and many experts disagree with previous assumptions, maintaining the view that the risk may be many times greater than was recognised in the past.

The Guernsey Tomato Marketing Board
17th September, 1982

Dear Madam,
I am only too happy to assure you that you need have no fear of radioactive contamination of tomatoes and other fruit and vegetables from the Channel Islands on sale in the United Kingdom.

Whilst you are correct in that the French nuclear plant at Cap de le Hague has been subject of much controversy in regard to radioactive discharge, there is to the best of my knowledge no evidence of any harmful effects being identified, or measurements taken which are not well within acceptable limits.[5]

I see no reason to fear contamination of Island crops any more than I see likelihood of U.K. crops, milk, water, animals, becoming unacceptably affected by U.K. nuclear plant emissions.

Trusting that you will continue to buy our tomatoes and other produce for a very long time, I remain
Yours sincerely,
M. J. Tanguy
Chairman

Note 5: Acceptable limits of radioactive discharges into the air and sea have been the subject of continual revision. What was thought to be 'acceptable' in 1952 is much higher than present-day levels. The body responsible for setting the 'acceptable limits' is the International Commission on Radiological Protection (ICRP). The 'acceptable limit' for the general public in Britain is 20 times higher than the level in the United States.
Scientists agree that any increase in the level of radiation to which people are exposed carries an increased risk of cancer, genetic damage and other illnesses occurring among the population exposed. There is no *safe* dose of radiation, but because the kind of illness that occurs is the same as occurs naturally, and the time a cancer can take to develop is very long, up to 40 years or more, collecting scientific information about the process is long drawn out. The ICRP acknowledged in 1959 that any damage to public health would only be seen by carrying out large-scale studies on millions of people. So far, very few such studies have been done, but those that have been reported show a direct link between a rise in radiation exposure and an increase in childhood diseases, or an earlier onset of adult diseases. It will be many years before the genetic effects can be observed, since they remain hidden for several generations. See Bertell, Rosalie, *No Immediate Danger*, The Women's Press, London, 1985.

When I received the reply from Mr Tanguy I looked up the exact reference in the article I had originally seen, and traced it back to a scientific report which said:

> Finally, the question arises as to whether the current levels of contamination could constitute a public health hazard to the population of the Channel Islands. It is recognised that these alpha-emitting nuclides are of radiological significance only as internal sources of radiation (i.e. they must be inhaled or ingested in some form). It is not the purpose of this paper to discuss the various pathways for human exposure or their relative importance (see, e.g. Hunt, 1979). However, a point which may have been overlooked, and which we feel is of particular significance, is the fact that seaweed (chiefly Fucus vesiculosus) is used extensively as an agricultural and garden fertiliser and soil conditioner in the Channel Islands. Therefore, several radioisotopes from seawater to terrestrial food chains. The significance of these pathways is possibly increased by the relatively large dependence of the Islands' population on locally produced foodstuffs, e.g. vegetables, milk and beef, in addition to marine foodstuffs. Although it is unlikely that any significant radiological hazard yet exists from the presence of plutonium or americium in food in the Channel Islands, present monitoring appears to be restricted to two seafood items (Hunt, 1979). More extended monitoring of foodstuffs might soon be advisable. ('Plutonium and Americium in seaweed from the Channel Islands', J.E. Cross and J.P. Day, Department of Chemistry, University of Manchester, *Environmental Pollution*, 2, 1981, p. 256).

6 October, 1982

To: M.J. Tanguy, Esq.,
Chairman,
The Guernsey Tomato Marketing Board, Guernsey.

Dear Mr Tanguy,
I thank you for your letter of 17 September.

My fear concerning produce grown in the Channel Islands has arisen because of a report in *Environmental Pollution*.

As I mentioned in my earlier letter, discharge from the French nuclear processing plant is being reconstructed in

31

seaweed around the Channel Islands. Apparently large quantities of this seaweed are harvested and used as fertilizer on farmlands and on smallholdings. Measurements of bladder wrack off the Cornish coast showed no radioactivity above that expected from fallout: the Channel Islands samples showed increased radioactivity amounting to about 3% of the total background alpha radiation activity.

Although the present concentrations are still low, potential problems will arise. Do I understand from your letter that the agricultural foodchains are now being monitored?

Can you show conclusively that in spite of using this seaweed there is no chance of radioactivity being passed through the food chain?

I am always doubtful as to how to interpret 'acceptable limits', so as a family I feel we must set our own 'acceptable limits' i.e. zero above natural background radiation.

Yours sincerely,
Deirdre Rhys-Thomas

The Guernsey Tomato Marketing Board

13th October, 1982

Dear Madam,
I thank you for your letter dated 6th October 1982.

Bladder vraic, or any other sea weed for that matter is not used in the cultivation of tomatoes or any other crop grown under glass in Guernsey. Indeed it requires an outdoor environment in order to break it down into a fertilizer and we do not export any vegetable or fruit crops grown out of doors. Furthermore, it is a number of years now since I have seen seaweed being gathered from the local shores and I would seriously question the present day economics of doing so.

So far as food from the sea is concerned, no one could have a greater concern about this than we Islanders, and in this respect our local department of agriculture and fisheries are constantly monitoring the situation and I, my family and my friends have every reason to be confident in the assurances which our authorities are giving to us.

Yours sincerely,
M. J. Tanguy
Chairman.

30 November 1982

To: Dr Philip Day,
Chemistry Department,
University of Manchester,
Manchester.

Dear Dr Philip Day,
I enclose a press cutting: having read this, I wrote to Mr
Tanguy, Chairman of The Guernsey Tomato Marketing Board
(copy of my letter enclosed).

    I quote from his letter to me: 'Bladder wrack, or any other
sea weed for that matter is not used in the cultivation of
tomatoes or any other crop grown under glass in Guernsey.
Indeed it requires an outdoor environment in order to break it
down into a fertilizer and we do not export any vegetable or
fruit crops grown out of doors. Furthermore, it is a number of
years now since I have seen seaweed being gathered from the
local shores and I would seriously question the present day
economics of doing so.'

    I wonder if you could clarify this for me.
Yours sincerely,
Deirdre Rhys-Thomas

Department of Chemistry
University of Manchester
Manchester
4 February 1983

Dear Mrs. Rhys-Thomas,
Thank you for your letter, and later telephone call. I again
apologize for not having replied.

    I note that Mr. Tanguy states that 'seaweed is not used in
the cultivation of tomatoes or any crops grown under glass in
Guernsey'. This is quite probably correct in so far as the larger
(exporting) growers are concerned, and therefore the tomatoes
available over here are unlikely to be contaminated by that route.
However, seaweed (bladder wrack) is used quite extensively in
outdoor cultivation, which is in fact what I referred to in my
original paper (copy enclosed, see p.256). The Guernsey soil is
on the whole very light and sandy, lacking in humus, and
seaweed is ideal to remedy this. I know the Islands well, having

33

lived there for 12 years. It is possible that radioactive contamination may pass from the seaweed to food crops grown in soil treated in this way. Thus, it is the local population who are at risk, if indeed anyone is at risk. Which is actually what I said originally, but the emphasis changed slightly when my paper was reported in the *Guardian*.

Like yourself, I feel that radioactive contamination begins at zero above background radiation.[6] However, in practical terms, I see no reason to stop eating Guernsey tomatoes at present, but I feel that all Channel Islands food crops should be kept under observation (this is now happening to a greater extent than before).

However, I certainly would advise against eating shellfish from the Cumbria/Lancashire coast, because of radioactive contamination from the Windscale outlet, and I think that laver bread (sold, I believe, in South Wales) is also best avoided, as the seaweed (porphyra) from which it is made concentrates radioactive ruthenium from seawater. But these are actually isolated and very specific cases, and at the moment I think the artificial radioactivity levels in our normal foods are low enough to be genuinely 'insignificant'.

Once again, I'm sorry not to have replied to you before. Please write again if I can help with any other radioactivity matters.

Yours sincerely,

Philip Day

Note 6: We live in a naturally radioactive environment, where cosmic rays from the sun and outer space, radiation from some rocks and earth used in building materials, phosphorus in some of our food and drink, all add up to 'background radiation'. Because the radiation from rocks varies from place to place, background radiation also varies. It is largely this that was responsible in the past for a certain number of children in each generation carrying damaged genes, such that they were born with a disease like cystic fibrosis, or some forms of hormone deficiency. Many babies with gene damage (or mutation) did not survive to have their own families, but the numbers remained fairly constant, although they were always variable from place to place. For instance, in Kerala, a state in North India, there is a range of hills separating people of the same culture. On one side the background radiation is very high, and the number of children with Down's Syndrome, or with other incapacities is higher than among the people on the other side of the hills, where background radiation is lower.

Since 1945 background radiation has been raised by 13 per cent due to:

- the Hiroshima and Nagasaki bombs;
- the nuclear weapons exploded in above ground tests, whose fallout circled the globe in $2\frac{1}{2}$ years, and traces of which are still settling to the ground;
- the nuclear factories for making weapons, which produce contaminated waste some of which is buried and some has been dumped at sea;
- nuclear power stations which discharge gas and liquid to the local environment. These discharges become 'background radiation' when the station has been operating for 1 year;
- accidents at nuclear facilities, such as the Windscale fire in 1957, Three Mile Island in 1979, Chernobyl in 1986, and hundreds of smaller accidents that occur weekly throughout the world;
- the nuclear submarines which are rather a problem when they become too radioactive for crews to work in them;
- the high level wastes created by reprocessing and the gas and liquid discharged from reprocessing factories such as Sellafield and Cap de la Hague; etc., etc.

The increased use of X-rays and radioisotopes in diagnosing and treating illnesses accounts for much of the extra radiation to which most people are exposed. This is the cause of an additional 1,400 deaths from cancer each year in Britain. A single X-ray to an unborn child is so dangerous that only in cases of extreme need will a pregnant woman nowadays have a pelvic X-ray.

7 October 1982

To: Ms Prue Leith,
The Guardian,
119 Farringdon Road, London

Dear Prue Leith,
For several months I have been delighted to read your *Guardian* column on cooking; also the *Sunday Times* feature – 'A Day in Your Life'. Being aware of your expertise I would be so grateful for your help.

Arising from Doris Lessing's article in the *Guardian*[7] which seems to me to exhort one to prepare positively to survive the aftermath of nuclear war, I feel it will be pretty ironic to have my nuclear larder bare . . .

My family will be in a fallout area, so the officials tell us, a family of 4 existing in a home-made shelter built according to the plans in the H.M.S.O. publication – *Domestic Nuclear Shelters*.

Assuming the above, with the following – no freely-available drinking water – no mains electricity – no mains gas –

please advise me on a suitably adapted food supply to provide a balanced diet for a period of at least 2 weeks (apparently 2 weeks is a 'rule of thumb period during which civilian populations would be expected to stay in fallout shelters' from the WEU Report).

What sort of diet would you recommend on emerging from our shelter? Will Fine Fare, Tesco, Sainsburys be delivering as usual?

Yours gratefully,
Deirdre Rhys-Thomas

Note 7: 'These Shores of Sweet Unreason', *Guardian*, 25 September 1982, p.11.

> The Guardian
> 119 Farringdon Road
> London
> 29 October 1982

Dear Mrs Rhys-Thomas
Thank you for your thought-provoking letter about feeding the family following a nuclear war.

For the sort of diet you would need on emerging from your fall-out shelter I rather think you need advice from the nuclear medics.

As to the two weeks you say is the rule-of-thumb period one is expected to stay inside a shelter following a nuclear blast, I assume that purpose-built shelters come with all mod cons, so that your supply of food should be that giving you a normal balanced diet to feed your family on as you would in normal, non-nuclear circumstances.

Yours sincerely,
Prue Leith,
Cookery Editor.

P.S. Personally I am planning on a diet of 2 cyanide pills!

A popular commentator on gardening matters is Clay Jones, who appears on BBC TV's *Gardener's World*, and BBC radio's *Gardener's Question Time*. He came as a guest speaker to one of our lifeboat fundraising events, a Gardening Evening. People brought their dehydrated cacti and he advised them. I thought that even if he didn't know the answers to my questions he could put me on to the experts who would, and I was right.

10 December 1982

To: Mr Clay Jones,
Chepstow.

Dear Clay Jones,
As the Government has drawn up contingency plans in anticipation of a nuclear war, it seems only logical to me for householders to do the same. No doubt in the aftermath there will be very little the Government can do for the individual with the fabric of society crumbling round us. Would you therefore be so kind as to tell me:

Which vegetables and fruit are least likely to absorb radioactive elements?[8]

Are these seeds available yet to gardeners, and if so could you give me the name of the supplier?
Thank you,
Yours sincerely,
Deirdre Rhys-Thomas

Note 8: Although the fallout Deirdre was thinking about was from nuclear war, the accident at the nuclear reactor at Chernobyl has shown us that fallout from power station accidents can lead to contamination of food. The trouble with radioactive elements like caesium and strontium getting into vegetables or meat is that the body mistakes them for the harmless chemicals like potassium or calcium that are necessary for building up muscles and bones. Even 800 miles away, we have experienced concentrations of caesium brought down by rain and built into the bodies of lambs. The caesium now settling into the soil in those areas will not lose its radioactivity for 300 years, although it will decrease over time, and some will avoid being drawn into the food chain.

After the Superpowers had a bumper time testing nuclear weapons in the 1950s, the Physical Institute in Kiel tested a wide range of foodstuffs for the content of radioactive strontium. Although there has been a great emphasis on the caesium released in the Chernobyl cloud, there was also strontium present. This is the more damaging substance for the health of babies and children as it gets built into the bones and stays in the body a long time, unlike caesium which has usually been excreted within $1\frac{1}{2}$-2 years. This was what they found:

37

Oranges	10	veal	1	bream	.1
bananas	5	potatoes	20	pork	1.6
pears	5	lamb	4.7	asparagus	45
cauliflower	20	ling	.6	spinach	32
bread	30	maize	44	runner beans	2.6
butter	1	milk	12	Swedish turnips	13
eggs	5	plums	5	tomatoes	80
goose	4.8	venison	9	white beans	1
cabbage	12	rice (polished)	9	white cabbage	7
cucumbers	3	rice (unpolished)	150	cornmeal	31
oatflakes	8	rhubarb	2.5	savoy cabbage	24
hare	10	beef	3.6	sausage	4
herring	.1	rye meal	20	cinnamon	85
stag	65	brussels sprouts	7.5	sugar	1
cheese	10	raisins	5	onions	30

The table shows levels of Strontium-90 found in foodstuffs after the above-ground atom bomb tests in the 1950s. See *Contemporary Issues*, Vol. II, no. 42, Sept./Oct. 1961.

D.B. Clay Jones B.Sc. F.R.H.S.
Horticultural Journalist,
Broadcaster and Consultant
28.12.82

Dear Mrs Rhys-Thomas,
Thank you very much for your letter.
    Frankly I have no answer to the questions you pose, and theorising would be futile. May I suggest you write to:—
1. Lawrence D. Hills
   The Henry Doubleday Research Assoc.
   20 Convent Lane
   Backing
   Braintree
   Essex.
2. The National Vegetable Research Station
   Wellesbourne
   Warwickshire.
Yours sincerely,
Clay Jones

National Vegetable Research Station
Wellesbourne
Warwick
11 January 1983

Dear Ms Thomas
I asked Dr Fraser, Head of our Biochemistry Section, to do his best to respond to your questions. I enclose a copy of the notes he prepared and a Table taken from the Letcombe Annual Report which enforces the latter part of his (3).

We have never been asked by Government to work on aspects of the nuclear scenario. As Dr Fraser points out the Letcombe Laboratory did, however, do quite a lot in the 60s and 70s. They did not cover the storage of seed to grow food crops for survivors. Whilst the long-term availability of seed could be met by imports the short-term needs might be best met from home stores. My own thoughts on the best single crop for such a seed store are that turnips would be a strong candidate as you can eat the tops as greens, hence getting a quick return, and also have the 'variety' of the roots in due course. Our climate is such that there are times of the year when you could be very hungry waiting for the turnips to grow.

I hope this helps.
Yours sincerely,
John Bleasdale
Director
Copy to Mr Clay Jones

Henry Doubleday Research Association
Braintree, Essex.
13th January, 1983

Dear Mrs Thomas,
Many thanks for your letter of 4th January and your enclosure of your copy letter to Clay Jones. I do not know this man but your letter has got the usual treatment that a nuclear enquiry gets – silence.

We are not working in this field so I enclose a leaflet that will tell you about us and you will see we are concerned with gardening and farming without chemicals. There is no agricultural A.R.P. in this country and I would suggest that you write to the papers and your M.P. asking for the best design of shelter to accommodate a herd of 50 bulls and a cow, with

39

fodder, for a fortnight, and the best covering for pasture fields to keep off the fallout. Should it be done with aluminium foil or polythene?

As far as I know all fruit and vegetables are going to be contaminated with radioactive fallout and though in America various smart operators have been trying to sell protective pills no one is going to know whether they work or not until too late. The main objective of the shelter policy is to make our citizens self-burying. There is very strong evidence that fallout will not stay in the neat circles usually depicted round Manchester, Moscow and New York but will spread to the other countries of the world. Counting America, Russia and the other countries there are merely 500,000,000 people involved. About another 3,000,000,000 live in Third World countries like India and Indonesia, where I have seen a great many people who have not even got a door to hide under. Nuclear war is not possible.

I would suggest that as you are seriously concerned, as I and all thinking people are, that you should try writing to M.P.s and the Ministry perhaps using some of my points. They might answer but I do not think they will, they will just evade. If you are in a position to do something about it and have the perseverance, best of luck.

Yours sincerely,
Lawrence D. Hills
Director

We went up to Aberdovey for a weekend sailing. In the local pub, the Penhelig Arms, we heard a couple of old fishermen and a farmer we know who has river banks on the Dyfi saying that their catches were going steadily down over the years. They wondered if there were things being pumped into the sea that were not doing these fish any good. I came home with another topic for research.

Windscale, located on the Cumbrian coast on the western side of Britain, is the dirtiest nuclear reprocessing plant in the world. The plant reprocesses spent fuel from nuclear power plants to extract the uranium and plutonium and in doing so produces radioactive waste. It started discharging waste in the early 1950s and since then it has discharged more than all the other nuclear plants in the world put together. Windscale reprocesses spent fuel for other countries, and in doing so makes huge profits. The USA doesn't reprocess spent fuel at all. There is at least ¼ ton of plutonium in the Irish sea.

The government-owned company, British Nuclear Fuels Ltd, which operates Windscale decided to re-name it in 1981. It is now called Sellafield but its history is the same.

30 November 1982

To: Mr Peter Taylor
PERG
(The Political Ecology Research Group)
Oxford

Dear Peter Taylor
Hugh Richards of the Central Wales Ecology Group has given me your name.

Recognizing that the Windscale nuclear reprocessing plant discharges more radioactive elements, plutonium and americium, than any other installation in the World, it must surely follow that the Irish Sea is now the most radioactive in the World?[9]

Doesn't this also indicate that the seafood is the most radioactive in the world?

It has yet to be established what is the 'acceptable' toxicity

41

level of radioactivity absorbed into food chains. Are not the scientists' levels of acceptability arbitrary in the sense that you may not die of radiation sickness after five years but there is no way to show that there are no long-term toxic, lethal effects?

As someone who loves cooking, it seems so sad to think that soon may come the day when Salmon, Cockles, Dublin Bay Prawns, Sewin and Laverbread from the Irish Sea may no longer be eaten in our Welsh or Irish traditional dishes, or when alongside our knife and fork we have a geiger counter!
Yours sincerely,
Deirdre Rhys-Thomas

Note 9: Sellafield was permitted (until 1 January 1985) to discharge: 2,000 curies of alpha emitters including plutonium in any 3 months, up to an annual maximum of 6,000 curies; 75,000 curies of beta emitters including caesium in any three months, up to an annual maximum of 300,000.

The limits have been reduced to 30 curies of alpha in any 2 days, 200 in any three months, and an annual maximum of 600 curies of alpha, plus 7,000 curies of beta in any 2 days, 50,000 in any three months, annual permissible total of 200,000. See Valentine, John, *Atomic Crossroads: Before and After Sizewell*, Merlin Press, London 1985.

On 19 August 1986 reprocessing at Sellafield had to be stopped because the 2-day limit could not be kept.

Peter Taylor
Technology Policy & Environmental Assessment
11 January 1983

Dear Ms Thomas,

Thank you for your letter of 30th November.

You draw attention to the high levels of radioactivity in the Irish Sea and ask 'is it not now the most radioactive sea in the world?', and does this also affect the seafood? You also state that it has yet to be established what an 'acceptable' level of radioactivity in food might be, and that are not scientists' levels of acceptability arbitrary?

There are a number of separate issues raised here, and I shall do my best to answer briefly.

Firstly, it is most certainly the case that the Irish Sea, and particularly the fisheries, are the most contaminated waters and source of human food that you are likely to come across anywhere in the world (it is possible that an odd corner of the atomic bomb testing atolls might have higher levels, but there is no comparable large-scale dispersal of radioactivity to the food chain).

Moreover, having reviewed other countries' regulations, I am quite certain Windscale would not get a licence to operate anywhere in the industrial world.

It is not quite true to say that 'scientists' set the 'acceptable' limits. Rather they advise the regulatory authorities (Dept of the Environment) on both the likely health impact *and* whether they think that impact 'acceptable'. In making that judgement they compare the impact with other polluting industries and also assess the cost of controlling the pollution against some index of cost of the health damage. All this, of course, takes place behind closed doors, with the exception of the odd 'consult document' sent to academics and environmental lobbyists for their comment.

I can tell you that within the current regulatory system, the DOE has received intense criticism for its policy and way of setting the limits. Briefly, the approach they take neglects two factors: (i) large sections of the community may view nuclear power as a net disbenefit, so why should they accept any health damage at all, (ii) the risks and benefits (e.g. jobs in Cumbria) do not always fall to the same communities, especially where the pollution crosses international boundaries (Windscale pollution reaches Ireland and even Denmark, which are, of course, non-nuclear states).

There are many further questions:

– the regulations are based on present knowledge of radioactivity and its effects on the body, and whereas the cancer effect is relatively securely predicted, genetic effects and non-cancer diseases are not.

– current policy assumes the future pathways of the toxic material are predictable, whereas in the case of plutonium, there is a great deal of controversy within scientific circles.

– I enclose some scientific material which may help you, including some reports that I produced with PERG[10] for the Greenpeace organisation specifically dealing with the Irish Sea.

Yours sincerely,
Peter Taylor

Note 10: The Political Ecology Research Group (PERG) was set up by a group of scientists and others who were concerned about the impact of industry – and especially the nuclear industry – on the environment. They have taken part in public inquiries, advised government Select Committees, and carried out research for local authorities and others, including Greenpeace. They have published independent work on many potential trouble spots in the nuclear industry, such as contamination of the Irish Sea by reprocessing operations at Sellafield, and the potential dangers of transporting radioactive high-level waste by sea.

18 January 1983

To: Ms. Delia Smith,
'Cookery' programme,
BBC 2, London

Dear Delia Smith,
Your television programmes on cooking are always useful. When inspiration has been exhausted a tip of yours comes to mind!

Perhaps you read a recent article by Doris Lessing, in which she seems to me to exhort one to prepare for the aftermath of nuclear war. I feel it will be pretty ironic to have my nuclear larder bare! I don't think this is a subject you have dealt with on any of your programmes? 'The Nuclear Cook Book'?

My family, so the officials tell us, will be in a fallout area. A family of 4 persons, plus one beagle, existing in a home-made shelter built according to the plans in the H.M.S.O. publication – 'Domestic Nuclear Shelters'. No £10,000 purpose built-nuclear shelter, with all mod.cons. but under the stairs, the toy cupboard, or cloakroom, so . . .

Assuming the above, with the following – no freely-available drinking water, no mains electricity, no mains gas, please advise me on a suitably adapted food supply to provide a balanced diet for a period of at least 2 weeks. (Apparently 2 weeks is a 'rule of thumb' period during which civilian populations would be expected to stay in fallout shelters', from the WEU Report).

What sort of diet would you recommend on emerging from our shelter as presumably Fine Fare, Tesco, Sainsburys will not be delivering as usual?
Yours gratefully,
Deirdre Rhys-Thomas

British Broadcasting Corporation
1st March 1983

Dear Mrs Rhys-Thomas,
Thank you for your letters. I'm sorry you have not yet had a reply to your first, but the fact is I receive well over a hundred letters a week.

I try to answer them all as usefully and quickly as I can. But working as a freelance (and running a home) I'm sure you can see that it's pretty nearly impossible to keep up with them all.

Your question – serious though it is – would involve hours of thought and research even to begin to answer sensibly. Indeed, I would have thought some government official could be productively employed full-time in working out such a diet. Forgive me, therefore, for not being in a position to help.

Yours sincerely,
Delia Smith.

5 March 1983

Mr Glynn Christian
The Cookery Expert,
'Breakfast-Time'
BBC Television Centre,
London

Dear Glynn Christian,
I was most interested in your Laverbread* dish you cooked on St David's Day, 1st March.

Do you have a BBC Welsh Recipes leaflet? Can you tell me where I can buy Laverbread? And as I give my family a nutritionally, well-balanced diet I wonder if the inclusion of Laverbread would be beneficial?

Thank you for your reply,
Yours sincerely,
Deirdre Rhys-Thomas

*Laverbread is seaweed. It is one of the national dishes of Wales. You can mix it with oatmeal and fry it in bacon fat and eat with sausages, bacon, as a cooked breakfast.
Also, laverbread can be thickened with sour cream and flavoured with lemon juice, served on oatmeal biscuits as canapes.

British Broadcasting Corporation
Lime Grove Studios London
March 23rd, 1983

Dear Mrs Rhys-Thomas
Thank you for your letter.
I'm afraid that I cannot answer your questions about laver bread.
To get all the facts and figures I suggest you get in touch with the Welsh Tourist Office who will be able to tell you all you want to know.
Good luck
Sincerely
Conal Walsh
Assistant to Glynn Christian
BBC Breakfast Time

30 March 1983

To: Mr Glynn Christian,
BBC Breakfast Time,
BBC TV,
London

Dear Glynn Christian,
BBC Breakfast Time
Thank you for your letter of 23 March.
I couldn't remember why I had such a feeling of unease watching you prepare laverbread on BBC Breakfast Time on 1 March. Now I know. I do hope Selina Scott and Frank Bough didn't eat any of it.
It took me sometime to put my hands on a letter I had from Dr Philip Day, a leading British scientist. He strongly advises against eating laverbread. Laverbread is highly dangerous as it has been contaminated by radioactivity.
Bearing in mind that your colourful presentation will I am sure tempt quite a few viewers to try laverbread do you not think the BBC Breakfast Time programme should publish a health warning say during your cooking spot?
Yours sincerely,
Deirdre Rhys-Thomas

For the personal attention of: General Bernard Rogers

12 March 1983

To: General Bernard Rogers,
Supreme Commander of Allied Forces in Europe,
NATO Headquarters,
Brussels,
Belgium.

Dear General Rogers,
I have read a profile of you in *The Times*.

I will not forget your remark about war: 'It's a lousy way
to do business, and there must be a better way . . . .'

As the Supreme Commander of the Allied Forces in Europe
(NATO) do you think it is morally right to have made Britain
and Europe a buffer between America and Russia? Would you
not agree that this makes Americans feel more secure than they
would otherwise feel? In the sense that Britain is being used as
nothing more than an advanced warning outpost under the
pretext of being part of a grand strategy of defence called
NATO.

This is exemplified by the American Sonar Surveillance
System at Brawdy, Wales, of key importance to America's first
strike ability. It will be the people of Wales who will be killed to
protect America.
Yours sincerely,
Deirdre Rhys-Thomas

U.S. Information Service
Embassy of the
United States of America
London W1A 1AE
March 21, 1983

Dear Ms. Rhys-Thomas,
General Rogers' office has asked me to reply to your recent
letter.

I cannot agree that Britain and Europe are simply a buffer between the United States and the Soviet Union. Instead, Britain and the western democracies and the United States are all joined together in the common purpose of defending our individual and national freedoms. Our NATO alliance is voluntary and has, I think, proven to be most effective during the past generation.

Yours sincerely,
Counselor for Public Affairs

I saw Paul Warnke on television. He was the Chief Negotiator for the USA during the SALT II talks in 1977, and the former head of the US Arms Control and Disarmament Agency.

14 March 1983

To: Mr Paul Warnke,
Washington,
Washington D.C. 20006.

Dear Mr Warnke,[11]
I am sure you are a very busy man, and receive many letters every day. But please answer my letter.

Did I hear you say on television that cruise missiles need not be based in Britain, instead there could be sea-launch cruise missiles?

Did you say that the verification of nuclear missiles/ weapons would be simple and reliable with photo recognizance satellites?

Thank you for your reply; it is most important to me.

Yours sincerely,
Deirdre Rhys Thomas

Note 11: Paul Warnke, a lawyer, was appointed head of the United States Arms Control and Disarmament Agency by President Jimmy Carter in 1977. He was chief negotiator on the US side during the Strategic Arms Limitations Talks (SALT II). Cruise, Pershing, and SS20s are all missiles that are supposed to have a strategic use in fighting a nuclear war. His position on arms control is based on his belief that the United States and the Soviet Union have had for some time the strategic capability to annihilate each other. Further additions to the weapons arsenal are, in

Warnke's view, not only unnecessary from the military standpoint but are also potentially injurious to the negotiations of future arms control agreements. He is regarded as a 'dove'.

Clifford & Warnke
Attorneys and Counsellors at Law
Washington, D.C. 20006
March 28, 1983

Dear Ms Deirdre:

This is in reply to your letter of March 14, 1983. With regard to the issue of American cruise missiles and Pershing II missiles to be stationed in Europe, what I have said frequently is that they are unneeded for any military purpose. All of the targets that would be covered by these 572 missiles (including the 96 scheduled for deployment in Britain) are already covered by almost 10,000 strategic warheads. The fallacy in the argument that European-based missiles which can strike Soviet targets are necessary to complete deterrence is based on the fallacy that the point of launch of the retaliatory forces is of some significance in determining the willingness of the Soviet Union to initiate a nuclear war.

In fact, what deters a Soviet nuclear strike – against either the United States or its NATO allies – is the certainty that Soviet society would be destroyed in a retaliatory strike. Soviet awareness that the United States would respond is not logically affected by the fact that the response might come from a launch point in Britain or West Germany rather than from the continental United States or an American ballistic submarine.

The contention is sometimes made that the Soviet SS-20 threat requires that NATO have its own missiles. As you know, however, the cruise missiles and Pershing IIs would not be turned over to the Western European members of NATO but would remain under U.S. control.

The issue, therefore, is strictly a political one and should be decided on political grounds, the most important of which is the willingness or unwillingness of the West European countries to accept the deployment.

As far as verification is concerned, the provisions that have been negotiated in SALT I and SALT II are thoroughly verifiable by photo-reconnaissance satellites and other national technical means. The deployment of ground-launched and/or sea-launched missiles would, however, be promptly matched by the Soviets, and create new verification problems. This is an additional reason why such deployments should take place only after thorough consideration.

Thank you for writing and I hope these comments may be of some interest to you.

Very truly yours,
Paul C. Warnke

20 May 1984

To: The Secretary of State for Defence, The Rt Hon. Michael Heseltine, M.P.
Ministry of Defence,
Whitehall,
London

Dear Mr Heseltine,
I remember you saying that the deployment of Cruise missiles would bring the Russians back to the conference table.

Today I read in my copy of the *Observer* that the Russians have deployed new missiles, in answer to Cruise, now targeted for the first time on Britain.

Marshal Ustinov states that the Soviet Union will only go back to the conference table if the West stops the deployment and removes those Cruise and Pershing missiles already in place.

Democracy means to me that you require me to trust your judgement and in so doing I trust you to safeguard my children's futures. In no way can I see that a newly-deployed missile now targeted on my children has increased their safety!

I require your personal explanation, not that of one of your Whitehall mandarins.
Yours sincerely,
Deirdre Rhys-Thomas (Mrs)

From: Miss M L Mahon, Defence Secretariat 17
Ministry of Defence
Whitehall London
Our reference D/DS17/1/26
29 May 1984

Dear Mrs Rhys-Thomas,

Thank you for your letter of 20 May 1984 to the Secretary of State. I have been asked to reply.

I am enclosing a copy of a leaflet which sets out the reasons for the deployment of cruise missiles in Europe, and addresses some of the more common misunderstandings about NATO's plans. You will see that the aim of the deployment is to modernise the Alliance's existing capability; but NATO has always made clear that its plans could be adjusted, if a reduction could be achieved through arms control negotiations in the threat which faces us. Initially the Soviet Union simply refused to talk at all. It was only when they became convinced that the Alliance was indeed determined to proceed with deployment that they were prepared to come to the negotiating table. But it then became apparent that their intention was simply to prevent NATO deploying any modernised weapons, while they retained the major part of their formidable SS20 deployments. Moreover they continued with their own deployments of SS20's while the negotiations were in progress. To cancel our own plans now, simply because the Soviet Union have walked out on the talks and made a variety of threatening noises as a result of their failure to dictate a settlement on their terms, would simply reward the Soviets for bullying and aggressive behaviour while doing nothing to ensure our own safety. We want an agreement that offers real security to both sides; and we hope that when the Soviet Union have considered their position fully they will recognise that their interest in such a settlement is as great as ours.

I am sure that you will understand that the Secretary of State is not able to reply personally to the very large number of letters he receives on this and other issues. However, I hope that this reply has been helpful.

To: The Secretary of State for Defence, The Rt Hon. Michael
Heseltine M.P.
The Ministry of Defence,
Whitehall,
London

Your letter – 29 May '84. D/DS17/1/26
30 June 1984

Dear Mr Heseltine/Miss Mahon,
Look, all I am interested in is the safety of my children and no
amount of convoluted hypothesis by you changes the fact that
now, TODAY, as I write this, new Russian missiles are pointing
at my children in answer to Cruise and my children are less safe.

My children are the most important thing in my life. I don't
have to subscribe to the stiff-upper-lip school so I know
emotionally, logically, intuitively what is good for my children.
The escalating nuclear arms race is not. It does not make my
children safe.

You write of 'the Russians' bullying and aggressive
behaviour', please give me examples. To preclude your pigeon-
holing me I am neither anti-American nor anti-Russian. Indeed I
have American relations – big, orange-growing capitalists in the
million-dollars bracket in California.
Yours sincerely,
Deirdre Rhys-Thomas

28 March 1983

To: Mr Norris McWhirter,
Editor,
Guinness Book of Records
Enfield,
Middlesex.

Dear Norris McWhirter,
I would like you to advise me on how I go about entering a
Record in the Guinness Book of Records.
    The Record I wish to enter is newly significant. It is not a
personal record but a British Record which is evidence of
International competitiveness reflecting the 20th Century in
which we all live.
    I thank you for your attention.
Yours sincerely,
Deirdre Rhys-Thomas

Guinness Books
Guinness Superlatives Limited
Enfield, Middlesex

5 April 1983

Dear Deirdre Rhys-Thomas
Thank you for your letter of 28 March.
    By all means feel free to let us have details of the record
idea you have in mind and to assist you I enclose some notes of
a general nature as regards authentication.
    With best wishes,
Yours sincerely
Colin Smith
Correspondence Editor
Guinness Book of Records

14 April 1983

To: Mr Colin Smith,
Correspondence Editor,
Guinness Book of Records,
Guinness Superlatives Ltd.,
Enfield,
Middlesex

Dear Colin Smith,
I thank you for your letter of 5 April and enclosure.
I wish to enter the following record for the Guinness Book of Records:

THE MOST RADIOACTIVE SEA IN THE WORLD – THE IRISH SEA

Verification available.
Yours sincerely,
Deirdre Rhys-Thomas

Guinness Books
Guinness Superlatives Limited
Enfield, Middlesex

25 April 1983

Dear Deirdre Rhys-Thomas
Thank you for your letter of 14 April.
While we are always interested in collecting information of this type, the terms of any kind of record submission are likely in this instance to be rather too narrowly drawn for the purpose of raising an inaugural category in a book as general as ours. Nevertheless, by all means feel free to let us have such information as you may possess although it is likely that rather more specialised publications are going to be able to do justice to the subject.
With best wishes,
Yours sincerely,
Colin Smith
Correspondence Editor
Guinness Book of Records

To: Mr Colin Smith,
Correspondence Editor,
Guinness Book of Records,
Guinness Superlatives Ltd.,
Enfield, Middlesex

Dear Colin Smith,
Thank you for your letter of 23 April.

Try as I may I can't understand why you write 'that more specialised publications are going to be able to do justice to the subject'. I thought the whole point of the Guinness Book of Records was to list Records, from who can swallow most oysters in the shortest time, to records of world importance.

I would have thought quite a lot of readers would be interested to know that the Most Radioactive Sea in the World is the Irish Sea.

I enclose copy of the research report *The Impact of Nuclear Waste Disposals to the Marine Environment*. I am sure that Peter Taylor of the Political Ecology Research Group will give you all the information you require, and I would suggest you contact a leading marine geochemist Dr V.T. Bowen of Woods Hole Oceanographic Institute. His address is available from Mr Taylor.

I would be grateful if you would return my copy as soon as possible.
Yours sincerely,
Deirdre Rhys-Thomas

Guinness Books
Guinness Superlatives Limited
Enfield, Middlesex

3 June 1983

Dear Deirdre Rhys-Thomas
Thank you for your further letter and enclosures of 11 May. We are glad to have the reference concerning Peter Taylor of the PERG and if the Editor is able to pursue the idea then this will

obviously be helpful to us. In the interim I have returned the
PERG Report as requested.

    With best wishes,

Yours sincerely,

Colin Smith

Correspondence Editor

Guinness Book of Records

Theo had read a copy of *Protect and Survive*. He went round the home one evening surveying the best place for our makeshift nuclear shelter. He decided on the downstairs cloakroom.

We set out to explore the logic of the government's advice.

30 March 1983

To: Mr E. R. Griffiths,
Managing Director,
Sainsburys (Grocers) Ltd.,
London S.E.1.

Dear Mr Griffiths,
For years I have been a satisfied Sainsburys customer.

I am an efficient housekeeper but I do have a problem. Would you be so kind as to suggest a nuclear shopping list for a nuclear family, i.e. 2 adults + 2 children, for 2 weeks in a nuclear shelter, following advice in Government *Protect and Survive* booklet.

Thank you so much.
Yours sincerely,
Deirdre Rhys-Thomas

J Sainsbury plc
London SE1
27th April 1983

Dear Mrs Rhys-Thomas
Thank you for your letter addressed to the Managing Director which has been passed to this Department.

Referring to *Protect and Survive* we note the comments on page 13 giving a broad outline of suggested items. The detail will, of course, depend on family preferences. The quantities, too, will be more easily judged by reference to your own usual shopping requirements, as well as the storage space available, and are rather difficult for us to predict. If, however, you are planning to keep this stock separately from the rest of your

57

supplies it will, of course, be necessary to rotate it on a regular basis.

I do not really think I can be more specific on these points but please do not hesitate to write to us again if you have any further enquiries.

Yours sincerely
Miss J A Lewis
Manager
Customer Relations Department

28 April 1983

To: Miss J.A. Lewis,
Manager,
Customer Relations Department,
Sainsbury's,
London SE1

Dear Miss Lewis,

Thank you for your letter of 27 April, in reply to my letter to your Managing Director, Mr Griffiths.

I have tried to make a nuclear shopping list by referring to my usual shopping requirements but quite honestly my mind goes blank. I don't know why this happens, it's probably because I realize that I am preparing for the unthinkable.[12]

But my common sense tells me that if the Government, the Local Authorities, the Civil Defence have at this moment already made contingency plans for nuclear war, then it is foolhardy not to follow their examples and make my own domestic contingency plans. I know I don't function well when I panic, and I just know I will panic when I hear the BBC and ITN give out the news 'there is going to be a nuclear war'.

So again may I ask Sainsbury's for help. Could you perhaps feed the necessary information for a nuclear shopping list for the average nuclear family – 2 adults + 2 children – with average appetites, for 2 weeks into your computer? I think this is the only way to overcome the emotional blank-out which comes over one when trying to prepare for nuclear war.

After all if I miscalculate and have to leave our Inner Refuge for a tin of soup it could be a matter of life and death.

Thank you so much.

Yours sincerely,
Deirdre Rhys-Thomas

Note 12: The way in which the thought of nuclear war causes people to suffer 'emotional blank-out' is discussed in several books, among them Kovel, Joel, *Against the State of Nuclear Terror*, Pan Books, London, 1983 and Rowe, Dorothy, *Living with the Bomb*, Routledge & Kegan Paul, London, 1985.

Most of us are aware of the threat of nuclear war or accident, just as we are aware of acid rain and other threats to the survival of the planet, but we cannot live on a day-to-day basis feeling the enormity of earth's destruction. We push the feelings out of the way, and behave as if we were indifferent to what we know is being done.

J Sainsbury plc
London
18th May 1983

Dear Mrs Rhys-Thomas,
Thank you for your further letter and telephone call.

As I said before, a lot does depend on the appetite and personal preferences of the individual family. If we were to feed into a computer an 'average' family shopping list we could well end up with a shortfall such as you mention or indeed an excess, for individual families.

May I suggest that you take a detailed note of your usual shopping list for a two-week period adapting the perishables to fit in with the storage facilities you are likely to have available?

This would seem to be the best method of judging your requirements most accurately which, as I understand it, is your prime concern.
Yours sincerely,
Miss J.A. Lewis
Manager
Customer Relations Department

8 April 1983

To: Mr Terence Conran,
Habitat,
Wallingford,
Berks.

Dear Terence Conran,
Would you be so kind as to recommend a suitable colour scheme and furnishings for a purpose-built nuclear shelter.

I understand some colours are more soothing than others, and I think I will need all the soothing possible; possibly cyanide pills.

The Building Society hasn't yet OK'd a mortage but I hope they will see it as a jolly good investment.
Yours sincerely,
Deirdre Rhys-Thomas

Habitat/Mothercare
London WC2
4th May 1983

Dear Ms Rhys-Thomas
Thank you for your letter. I think the colour scheme for your nuclear shelter should be white with details painted bright yellow – for optimism!
Yours sincerely
Terence Conran

This was the time when I began writing more and more letters which might be labelled 'tongue-in-cheek'. It may seem strange to bring frivolity into such a serious subject. It started because I needed a touch of humour – however black – to lighten the load. The more replies I received the blacker and more hopeless the whole nuclear scenario appeared. It was not just the nuclear arms race but everything connected with it – the dangers connected with disposing of nuclear waste, the Australian uranium, the radioactivity of the Irish Sea so close to us and the whole juggernaut of war propaganda that seemed to be heading inexorably in one direction.

I had become inflexibly anti-nuclear; I hoped I was being logical and not emotional. But then, when your child is being threatened how can you stop yourself from being emotional? If you stop being emotional as a mother you might as well give up on the job.

I had to be certain that I was right. I wanted to explore every possible approach so that no one could ever say to me, 'You've got a closed mind about this.'

The more humorous letters were a way of breaking down the nuclear taboo and forcing people to think. Even to elicit a light-hearted comment can be quite revealing about the way a person thinks. I had an open mind to everybody's viewpoint; but the replies showed that often the writers hadn't thought the nuclear issue through. They just had the ostrich approach: close your eyes and it'll go away.

I was writing to everyone I could think of trying, if possible, to wake them up and make them think. I was surprised at the number of prominent people who hadn't received any other letters like mine.

Then as more and more replies came back to me it became more and more difficult to explain things to Theo. The humorous approach was a way of bringing the issue on to another level so that I would still be able to talk about it with him.

1 April 1983

To: Ms Judi Dench
The National Theatre,
London S.E.1.

Dear Judi Dench,
When the curtain comes down in this nuclear play, Final
Act/Nuclear War (?) how will your years of training as an
actress help you cope with the Final Act?
        If as in the words of the Bard 'All the world's a stage . . .'
what do you think of the script of this nuclear play we are all
in?
Yours sincerely,
Deirdre Rhys-Thomas

Dear Deidre Rhys-Thomas,
Being an actress will have no bearing whatsoever on how I
confront a Nuclear holocaust. Being a mother — it concerns me
greatly.
        Yours sincerely,
        Judi Dench

2 April 1983

To: Mr K.W. Overton,
Managing Director,
Ladbrokes,
Harrow,
Middlesex.

Dear Mr Overton,
Please be so kind as to quote me the odds on a nuclear war in
the next 10 years?
        I thank you.
Yours sincerely,
Deirdre Rhys-Thomas

Ladbrokes
Ladbroke Racing Limited
The retail betting division of the Ladbroke Group
18th April, 1983

Dear Ms. Rhys-Thomas,
Thank you very much for your letter of the 2nd April, which
was only received this morning.
    I regret to advise you, however, that we do not bet on
disasters.
Yours sincerely,
K.W. Overton
Managing Director

15 November 1982

To: Dr Hugh Jolly,
c/o The Jimmy Young Show, BBC Radio, London W1.

Dear Dr Jolly,
I recently saw you on *Medical Express* television programme
advising on babycare, I think, to compliment the birth of the
Royal Baby.
    As I sat listening to your words of wisdom, it struck me as
the supreme irony that that very day, after 12 years of loving
care, my son had voiced his profound fear of nuclear war. For
the first time in our relationship, Dr Jolly, I had to lie to him
and say that there was absolutely no possibility of nuclear war.
    Is it any wonder when my son reads the *Sunday Times*, the
Observer, the *Telegraph*, and hears on television reports of the
latest nuclear theatre weapons to be installed in Britain or
Europe – hears the Forces talk of protracted nuclear war – sees
on television Reagan talking of the increase in the nuclear arms
race – is aware of Thatcher siding with Reagan her 'Nuclear
best friend' – is aware of the Pentagon's 'For God's sake keep it
in Britain or Europe' attitude – that he is so aware of this fear.
    Research from America is showing the American children
are so frightened of the Bomb that it is, and has, seriously
changed their basic hopes. How much more frightened British
children must be, Dr Jolly?
    America it is said, is providing the nuclear umbrella but we
in Britain seem to be holding it. And the person holding it is

63

usually the one who gets struck by lightning. In a nuclear
thunderstorm the lightning bolts are likely to be frequent and
fatal. I don't like the prospect of my family sheltering under the
nuclear umbrella.

Mrs Thatcher has recognized the erosion of family life in
Britain. Surely political measures designed to enhance the
prospects of family life must surely include the removal of this
psychologically, crippling fear of a dark and radioactive future
which my son and so many other British children face?

Yours sincerely,
Deirdre Rhys-Thomas

23 February 1983

To: Dr Hugh Jolly,
Department of Paediatrics,
Charing Cross Hospital,
London

Dear Dr Jolly,
Last November I wrote to you, c/o The Jimmy Young Show. I
wrote a heartfelt letter to you as I have always been impressed
with your realistic understanding of children.

I am terribly disappointed not to have heard from you,
though I understand you have been Overseas.

I would be most grateful, Dr Jolly, if you could be so kind
as to reply to my letter (copy enclosed). The questions raised in
my letter are becoming ever more difficult for mothers to deal
with. Our intelligent, questioning, well-informed children are
becoming ever more doubtful that adults do have their best
interests at heart. In point of fact, withdrawing their trust.

Coupled with their attitude to unemployment, one is
hearing many children now say, oh well, who cares, what's the
point we'll all be dead in a couple of years. Surely, this attitude
can't be healthy?

Yours sincerely,
Deirdre Rhys-Thomas

Charing Cross Hospital Medical School
(University of London)
Department of Paediatrics
Dr. Hugh Jolly
8th April 1983

Dear Mrs Rhys Thomas
Thank you for your letter of 23rd February. I think your son is
realistic in being frightened of nuclear war – I certainly am.

You are kind enough to refer to my understanding of
children. This aspect leads me to believe that to lie to a child
only makes it more complicated.
Yours sincerely
Hugh Jolly

7 January 1983

To: H.R.H. The Prince of Wales,
Kensington Palace,
London S.W.1.

Your Royal Highness,
I hope that this Christmas was the most fulfilled and happy for
you and your family in the presence of your newborn son.

Sadly, as a parent of growing sons this Christmas was the
most sorrowful of all. With the escalating nuclear discussion on
television, on radio, in our papers, it is impossible for well-
informed children to escape their fear of nuclear war. Indeed
research from America has shown that the basic hopes of
American children have changed because of their fear of the
nuclear Bomb. One wonders how frightened Welsh, Scottish,
English, Dutch, German, Polish, Rumanian, Russian children
must be? Indeed the children of the World?

Informed opinion recognizes that the deployment of new
weapons is changing nuclear policies from nuclear deterrence
based on mutual assured destruction to nuclear-war fighting.

Great men, the Earl Mountbatten of Burma, Albert
Einstein, Bertrand Russell have all realised that if the nuclear
arms race goes on unchecked there will be only one outcome.

I appreciate, Sir, that many try to make political gain out of
the nuclear threat but I only wish you to know, Sir, that to
many loving parents now is a time of much searching in our
quest for survival.

One can only hope in the words of General Eisenhower,
President of the United States that 'Some day, the demand for
disarmament by hundreds of millions will become so universal
and so insistent that no man, no nation, can withstand it'.

Buckingham Palace
17th January, 1983

Dear Mrs Thomas
Thank you for your letter of 7th January to The Prince of
Wales. Your views on this difficult subject have, of course, been
noted and His Royal Highness is very grateful to you for
writing.
Yours sincerely
Francis Cornish.
The Assistant Private Secretary to H.R.H. The Prince of Wales

20 April 1983

To: The Worshipful Mayor of Knighton,
Town Hall,
Knighton,
Powys.

Your Worship,
Are you able to tell me which sound (either 3 loud bangs or
whistles in quick succession) will be used in Knighton for The
Fall Out Warning?

You may recall I asked you about this about 8 weeks ago
having read the Government's booklet *Protect and Survive*. I
understand that the Government plan to put it through the
letterbox of every household in Britain if nuclear war is
imminent. But it would probably be psychologically unsound to
have a dummy run of The Fall Out Warning at that late stage
for fear of spreading alarm and despair prematurely.

Don't you think it would be a good idea to have a dummy
run of The Fall Out Warning to be used in Knighton?

And as an after-thought, could you tell me what The All
Clear will be?
Yours sincerely,
Deirdre Rhys-Thomas

Cyngor Sir
Powys County Council
15th June 1983

Dear Mrs Rhys-Thomas,
Fall Out Warning
Your letter, dated 20th of April, addressed to the Mayor of Knighton has now been forwarded to me for reply.

First of all I must emphasise that the warning system and matters relating thereto is the responsibility of the Police and they maintain and administer the scheme as well as carrying out the routine tests.

A summary of the information you request is set out in *Protect & Survive* and I have enclosed copies of the relevant pages. You live close enough to Knighton Police Station to hear the maroons (3 bangs) and this could well be re-enforced by whistles soon after to indicate the approach of fall-out.

The All Clear is a long steady note on the siren.

With regard to a 'dummy-run' this is entirely a matter for Home Office and the Police but my own view is that any practical exercises involving the general public are not on at this time. War is not imminent and such public involvement at this time would, in my opinion, cause unnecessary distress especially to those who still remember the air raids and blitz of the last war.

Yours sincerely,
M. Dray
County Emergency Planning Officer

I read of the publication of the Report made to the British Medical Association by its Board of Science in my morning paper.

14 April 1983

To: Dr John Dawson,
Head of the Professional, Scientific and International Division,
The British Medical Association,
London

Dear Dr Dawson,
BMA Report – The Medical Effects of Nuclear War
There are more sheep than people in Mid Wales. The sheep all graze on open hills and mountains. How will they be affected by radioactive fallout?

Geographically Mid Wales looks far from nuclear conflict but with Trawsfynydd and Wylfa Nuclear Power Stations, the largest U.S. Surveillance Station at Brawdy, Aberporth on our nuclear doorstep, and a frequency of westerly winds radiation fallout will be inevitable.[13]

The National Farmer's Union, The Farmer's Union of Wales, and the Civil Defence, say that no 'barbecued' sheep or sheep offal should be eaten but all other sheep may be eaten. From the BMA Report I understand that farm animals are sensitive to radiation; your advice would be most helpful.
Yours sincerely,
Deirdre Rhys-Thomas

Note 13: There are 18 nuclear power stations in the UK: Bradwell, Sizewell A, Dungeness A, Dungeness B, Hinkley Point A, Hinkley Point B, Heysham A, Heysham B, Hartlepool, Berkeley, Trawsfynydd, Wylfa, Hunterston A, Hunterston B, Torness, Calder Hall, Chapelcross.

There are a number of other nuclear facilities, the most well-known being the factories at Sellafield, Harwell, Winfrith, Dounreay, Chapelcross, Springfields, Risley, Capenhurst, Cardiff, Amersham, Aldermaston and Burghfield.

Radioactive materials are constantly on the move between them, by lorry, train, ship and aircraft. The people of Billingham, Elstow and Killinghalme are putting up resistance to the attempts to survey sites near them for the burial of radioactive waste.

British Medical Association
London
21 April 1983

Dear Ms Rhys-Thomas

Thank you for your letter of 14 April addressed to Dr Dawson concerning the Board of Science's Report on the Medical Effects of Nuclear War.

The Board of Science Inquiry was set up to look at the medical effects of nuclear war and the value of civil defence. Obviously, following on from the immediate medical effects of a nuclear attack it is necessary to look at the long-term medical effects on survivors of an 'average' attack for a period of about two years. For this reason in chapter 4 of the Report we examined the problems likely to be experienced with shelter, water, food and power supplies. In the chapter we came to the conclusion that the LD50 for sheep is approxmately 3.5Gy and that for cattle 4.4Gy.[14] I enclose an order form for the Report which has now been published and suggest that you read chapter 4 for any further information you require about the effects of radiation on agriculture.

Yours sincerely,
Maryse Barwood
Secretary
Board of Science and Education

Note 14: LD50 is the abbreviation for Lethal Dose to 50 out of every 100. It means that whatever animal you are looking at, there is a dose of radiation that will kill half of the total. So if 200 sheep get a dose of 3.5Gray (a measure of radioactivity), 100 of them will die immediately, or within a few days. The rest will get a lot of cancer and other illnesses, but they can expect to live a few more years. Cattle being bigger animals will need a higher dose to kill half of them. For humans the LD50 is estimated at 4 Grays, half-way between sheep and cattle.

Chapter 4 of the BMA Report of the Board of Science and Education Inquiry into the Medical Effects of Nuclear War makes it clear that the greatest problem would be to maintain a supply of water that was free of contamination from fallout, as people can change their eating habits, but water is necessary for life.

6 April 1983

To: Mr P.V. Doyle,
Chairman,
Irish Tourist Board,
Dublin
Ireland

Dear Mr Doyle,
Do you think that now the Irish sea is the most radioactive sea
in the World, this will be a tourist attraction for Ireland?[15]
     Molly Malone's words 'cockles and mussels alive, alive o',
could take on an entirely new meaning.
Yours sincerely,
Deirdre Rhys-Thomas

Note 15: From the end of the Second World War until recent years, the
US, Japan and Britain have dumped nuclear waste at sea. The first
practical steps to stop this happening were taken by the National Union
of Seamen, who with other transport unions, refused to handle the drums
of radioactive waste in 1983.
Scientists used to believe that the sea was big enough to dilute the waste
as it leaked out of the drums, and there would be no trouble, but over the
years some of the drums have been washed ashore on the coast of the US,
submarines have rammed into heaps of leaking barrels and become
dangerously contaminated, and instead of spreading evenly throughout
the whole ocean, the waste has a tendency to drift towards land, and to
be eaten by fish. In 1985 the international body responsible for regulating
sea dumping of nuclear waste has recommended that the practice should
stop until it can be proved conclusively that it causes no harm.
Most of the radioactivity in the Irish Sea, however, is caused by the
discharges of liquid waste containing plutonium, americium, caesium and
other materials from the reprocessing plant at Sellafield.

Bord Fäilte – Irish Tourist Board
26 April 1983

Dear Mrs Rhys-Thomas
Thank you for your letter of 6 April about radioactivity in the
Irish Sea.
     One of the main concerns of our Tourist Board is to
preserve the international reputation of Ireland as an unspoilt,
beautiful country. Clearly that reputation could be damaged by
the evidence that has emerged in recent years of the high level of
radiation that has been allowed to seep into the Irish Sea from

nuclear waste disposal activities at Windscale.

An important paper entitled 'Marine Disposal of Nuclear Waste' was delivered by Dr Noel Murray, a well known expert on the subject at Trinity College Dublin very recently. It might interest you to get a copy of that paper which I understand outlines current thinking on this highly involved question. Mr Ian McAuley of Trinity College Dublin would, I understand, be able to obtain a copy for you.

Ireland's position on nuclear matters is handled by our Nuclear Energy Board, 20 Lower Hatch Street, Dublin 2, tel. 764375 and they should be able to answer any detailed queries you might have on the subject at a wider level. The person to contact there is Mr John Cunningham.

As the Chairman of our Tourist Board and someone with a life-long love of Ireland I would certainly prefer to see the original meaning of 'Molly Malone's' words preserved . . .
Yours sincerely,
P.V. Doyle
Chairman

12 April 1983

To: Mr Barry Norman
'Film Night',
BBC TV,
London

Dear Barry Norman,
The other night I couldn't get to sleep so instead of counting sheep I tried to remember my favourite films – probably triggered off by the Oscar Ceremony.

But as so often happens when sleep escapes me, my imagination took a morbid turn and I began to wonder what films I would take into the nuclear shelter: not *Dr Strangelove* and not *On the Beach*.

Perhaps the C.O.I. has already compiled the film library for the Government nuclear shelter under Whitehall?

What films would you take in to the nuclear shelter?
Yours sincerely,
Deirdre Rhys-Thomas

British Broadcasting Corporation
London
28th April 1983

Dear Deirdre Rhys-Thomas,
    Thanks for your letter.
    An interesting idea – but the films I took with me would
depend largely on my mood during the four minutes I had in
which to choose them.
    Best wishes,
    Yours sincerely,
    Barry Norman

22 April 1983

To: Mr Alan Cummings,
Chairman,
Building Societies Association,
London

Dear Mr Cummings,
As Chairman of the Building Societies Association do you
regard a domestic nuclear shelter as a good investment? Would
a mortgage be granted for a nuclear shelter?
    I understand the Government has a city nuclear shelter
built deep under Whitehall, and a country nuclear shelter built
under the Chilterns. (And it is rumoured – in the Valleys – that
the Royal Family has a nuclear shelter in Wales, hollowed out
of a Welsh mountain). So following their example, it is
obviously time for serious thought to be given to building a
family nuclear shelter.
    As tax payers' monies have been used in the building of all
Government, Local Authorities, and military nuclear shelters I
hope the ordinary man and woman has not yet again been left
out and that you will tell me that there are tax concessions, or
grants given for domestic nuclear shelters?
Yours sincerely,
Deirdre Rhys-Thomas

The Building Societies Association
London
28 April 1983

Dear Miss Rhys-Thomas
Mr Cummings has asked me to reply to your letter of 22 April
1983 about domestic nuclear shelters.

A building society in granting a loan has to have regard to
the value of the security which it is given and in no
circumstances can it lend in excess of that value. That is the
overriding consideration and each society formulates its own
lending policy within that framework. It may be therefore that a
case could be made out to a society for a loan to be granted
for this purpose.

As to taxation, interest relief for a loan would be available
if the Inland Revenue could be persuaded that a shelter
constituted an improvement. We do not in fact know their
policy on this.
Yours sincerely,
K R P Shears
Deputy Secretary

29 April 1983

To:Mr Cyril English
Chief General Manager,
Nationwide Building Society,
London

Dear Mr English,
I would be obliged if you would tell me if the Nationwide
Building Society considers a domestic nuclear shelter a sound
investment, and in the event of my applying for an additional
mortgage for a domestic nuclear shelter would a loan be
granted?

At the same time would you be so kind as to advise me on
Government grants for domestic nuclear shelters: I know of
grants for Home Improvements, loft insulation, etc. but I do not
know if the Government considers a nuclear shelter a home
improvement?

Thank you so much.
Yours sincerely,
Deirdre Rhys-Thomas

73

Nationwide Building Society
London
9 May 1983

Dear Miss Rhys-Thomas
Your letter to Mr English of 29 April has been passed to me to reply.

It is not the Nationwide Building Society's policy to grant loans for the provision of nuclear shelters and I do not know of any government grants which are available for the provision of same. I am of course not aware of the full details of your existing mortgage and it may well be that there is sufficient equity already in your property to allow the local branch manager to consider a further advance and I would suggest that you call and discuss the matter fully with him.

Yours sincerely
A J Wonnacott FRICS
Chief Surveyor

When I had read through the BMA report on the Medical Effects
of Nuclear War, I decided to write to Sir John Stallworthy, who
was the Chairman of the Working Party which produced the
Report.

18 April 1983

To: Sir John Stallworthy,
Emeritus Professor of Obstetrics and Gynaecology,
Oxford University,
Oxford.

Dear Sir John Stallworthy,
I have recently read of research which has been carried out in
America and has shown that because of their fear of the Bomb
and fear of nuclear war the basic hopes of American children
have been changed.
    As the Mother of a 13-year-old son, who is well able to
take in all the talk of limited nuclear war and the escalation of
the nuclear arms race, would you be so kind as to tell me what
research is being carried out in Britain on British children
concerning their fears of the Bomb and nuclear war?
Yours sincerely,
Deirdre Rhys-Thomas

Headington,

Oxford
6th May 1983

Dear Mrs Rhys-Thomas,
Thank you for your letter of April 18th, which I have been
unable to answer until today. As you will see from the BMA
book on *The Medical Effects of Nuclear War*, which was
published this week, reference has been made to the
psychological effects which major disasters can produce in
surviving population, but not with particular reference to
anticipatory fears, nor the manifestations likely to be produced

in children either before or after such catastrophes. Such research as you suggest at this stage is not to the best of my knowledge being undertaken, and perhaps this is wise. I realise this would be a matter of opinion.

The major efforts of those who are devoting a great deal of time and thought to the whole problem facing mankind seem to be divided between those who on the one hand are seeking to use modern technology to make powerful weapons even more powerful and/or more accurate, and on the other hand those who are striving to create a social atmosphere in which it is to be hoped it may be realised that war fought with modern weapons, whether nuclear, bacteriological, chemical, or all combined, is an outrage in an allegedly civilised society.

The answer to your specific question, therefore, to the best of my knowledge is that there is no research in Britain in relation to the effect on children which the threat of nuclear war might produce. I am sure you have realised that whatever this effect might be, it is likely to be largely influenced by the attitude within the children's own home. It may well be that you would obtain help, if you are anxious to pursue this further, by seeking advice from one of the senior psychiatrists in your area. The alternative, and this might be more helpful, would be to write to Dr John Dawson, Scientific Officer, Board of Science and Education, B.M.A. House, Tavistock Square, London, WC1H 9JP.

Yours sincerely,
Sir John Stallworthy

8 April 1983

To: Mr Raymond Briggs,
Hamish Hamilton Ltd.,
London

Dear Raymond Briggs,
I can't help feeling we will all end up like Jim and Hilda Bloggs.[16]

When Paul Warnke, former Head of the US Disarmament Agency writes to me 'With regard to the issue of American cruise missiles and Pershing II missiles to be stationed in Europe, what I have said frequently is they are un-needed for any military purpose. All of the targets that would be covered by these 572 missiles (including the 96 scheduled for deployment in Britain) are already covered by almost 10,000 strategic warheads', and then I hear Mrs Thatcher yet again say that cruise is necessary to balance the SS20's and is highly reliable, I just know that we (the Bloggs of Britain) have never been told the truth, the whole truth, and nothing but the truth about nuclear arms.

My sons, Theo and Toby, had become so fond of Gentleman Jim.

Even though one is up against the 'nuclear brick wall' it will not prevent me from doing what I can because if I have to lead my children into that nuclear shelter I will do so knowing that I did everything I could to stop the first, and last, nuclear war.

Yours sincerely,
Deirdre Rhys-Thomas

Note 16: Raymond Briggs wrote a cartoon book, *When the Wind Blows*, whose characters, Jim and Hilda Bloggs, a middle-aged couple living in a semi-detached house, try to follow the instructions in the Government pamphlet *Protect and Survive*. They compare the steps they are taking with the Air Raid Precautions of the Second World War, but in the end they die of radiation sickness. See Briggs, Raymond, *When the Wind Blows*, Hamish Hamilton, and Penguin, London, 1983.

Raymond Briggs,
Hassocks
Sussex
5 May 1983

Dear Deirdre Rhys-Thomas,
I was very pleased to hear your boys had liked 'Gentleman Jim'. It is particularly painful for people such as yourself who have young children. My own lady friend is in the same position and finds it too upsetting to even discuss it, although she is a convinced CND-er.

Thank you for your letter and the amazing statement by Paul Warnke, which I had never heard before. It should be more widely publicised.

Yours sincerely,
Raymond Briggs

Aylesbury stocks up a hot line in nuclear rations

THE BUSY but otherwise peaceful market town of Aylesbury, Buckinghamshire, rarely features in news of natural or man-made disasters. If hurricanes hardly happen in Herefordshire, bombings barely bother Bucks.

Yet, at 8 am, one recent morning, a lorry drew up at the telephone exchange in the town centre. Under the watchful eyes of senior British Telecom managers from Oxford, men unloaded eight pallets stacked with 288 large boxes, stamped EMRAT, meaning Emergency Rations.

There was enough food – neatly labelled Menus A, B, C and D – to last between 16 and 20 people for 144 days. What calamity was expected? Flooding of the nearby River Thame? An indefinite sit-in by switchboard operators?

British Telecom was not best pleased to be asked. It had hoped that the delivery had been unobserved. In due course, a press officer read out a statement: 'As the major provider of communications services for the UK, British Telecom has the responsibility for their maintenance in all circumstances.'

The press officer added helpfully that such supplies would be useful when, for example, dealing with a rail crash. Aylesbury, on a suburban line, is not noted for the frequency of its rail crashes. But the press officer would not elucidate.

An exchange employee, however, volunteered the information that the food was for an underground bunker beneath the exchange (BT has since launched an inquiry to find the source of the leak). Aylesbury exchange was preparing for the worst disaster of all – nuclear war.

Like a number of other exchanges, Aylesbury's has a dual purpose. In the bunker is a manual switchboard, part of the EMSS – the Emergency Manual Switching System – which will attempt to maintain a skeleton trunk network after nuclear war has begun.

Peaceful Aylesbury has, in fact, a strategic significance – it is close to the prime minister's house at Chequers, to the new US European Command headquarters at Daws Hill, and to the RAF strike command headquarters at Naphill. Direct lines have been laid between the Aylesbury bunker and Chequers and Naphill.

Back at BT, the press officer was tight-lipped. 'We do not discuss security matters', he said. Nor would he divulge the contents of Menus A, B, C and D. A food company which supplies

EMRATs was no more revealing. 'That,' it said, 'is covered by the Official Secrets Act.'

(*Sunday Times*, 8th May 1983, p.9.)

9 May 1983

To: Telephone Manager
Main Telephone Exchange,
Aylesbury,
Bucks.

Dear Sir,
I read in the *Sunday Times* (8 May) that the main telephone exchange at Aylesbury has just put together a nuclear larder: apparently enough food for 144 days to feed the 16-20 people who will be in the underground bunker beneath the exchange after/during a nuclear war.

This is so coincidental. I too, prompted by such examples as yours, have been giving serious thought to my domestic nuclear larder. It would be so helpful if you would be so kind as to share your Menus with me – I understand you have 4 – Menus A. B. C. D.

I appreciate that their cost will have been subsidised by taxpayers but nevertheless perhaps you could give me an idea of how much they would cost the ordinary housewife to buy?

Thank you so much,
Yours sincerely,
Deirdre Rhys-Thomas

British Telecom Oxford
20th May 1983

Dear Ms Rhys-Thomas
Thank you for your letter of 9 May 1983 concerning an article in the *Sunday Times* (8 May) which featured Aylesbury Telephone Exchange.

The newspaper faithfully reported British Telecom's statement namely 'As the major provider of communications services for the UK, British Telecom has the responsibility for their maintenance in all circumstances.' To do this BT has contingency plans designed to cater for a wide range of

79

emergency conditions. Stores, including food, which may be required in such emergencies are held in a number of convenient locations throughout the country, including Aylesbury.

BTs expertise is in telecommunications however, and we are not qualified to advise on what food would be suitable in the event of a nuclear attack on this country. This is the responsibility of the Home Office and may I suggest that you direct your enquiries on this matter to them.

Yours sincerely,

R.C. Orr

Customer Relations Manager

I remember Theo coming home during the Falklands War and telling us the father of a boy at his school had been killed. He was in an SAS helicopter which crashed into the South Atlantic.

Shortly afterwards someone told me that David Tinker had been killed. David Tinker was a Naval lieutenant serving aboard HMS *Glamorgan* when it was sunk by Exocet missiles during the war with Argentina. He was very critical of the conduct of that encounter, and in order to commemorate his death his parents arranged the publication of his poems and letters in *A Message from the Falklands* (Junction Books, London, 1982). It was Mummy who told me about this book; one of the boys at Shrewsbury School had given her a copy. David's book says all there is to say about war. Reading it, I was so upset, so outraged and so frightened at how easily we can slide into military conflict. I asked the Vicar of Clungunford to forward my letter to David's parents.

I often cycle over to Clungunford Church, sometimes taking a picnic with me, and sit under David's tree. I find myself crying at the sheer waste of his life, of the lives of all those who died in the Falklands War. David Tinker was only 25.

I can't forget him. He and his wife were doing up a cottage near Knighton. I didn't meet him but, for all I know, perhaps I passed him in the street when they came into Knighton to go shopping.

11 April 1983

Mr and Mrs H. Tinker,
Clungunford,
Shropshire.

Dear Mr and Mrs Tinker,
Today I read the last of David's letters from the Falklands, sitting on the Church wall at Clungunford. I live 9 miles from Clungunford. I cried for him and for an Argentinian who died in the Falklands.

My brother lives and works in Argentina and on his return to Britain during the war told me of his concern for an Argentinian friend of his with 3 sons, all conscripts of 18, 19 years, sent to the Falklands. One was killed.

Over the last 18 months I have been trying to personally do something to stop the nuclear arms race. Though I have visited the European Parliament, the House of Commons, I am dismayed at the casualness and misinformation of so many politicians concerning things nuclear. The Falklands War crystallised my fear of leaving such decisions to politicians.

Please accept my sympathy,
Yours sincerely,
Deirdre Rhys-Thomas

10 May 1983

Dear Deirdre Rhys-Thomas
Thank you very much for writing to us about David and his book. He would like it that you read that last letter sitting on the church wall at Clungunford. Did you notice the recently planted cherry tree on the right of the path? Hugh and I put it in last November, it is probably blossoming now. It is soon to have an inscription let into a stone at the foot, the words will be those of Rupert Brooke which are quoted at the end of the book.[17] I wonder whether you were able to get into the Church? There is a lovely stained glass window on the left of the nave, nearest the Chancel. It is of shepherds with their sheep and David was very fond of it. Also his name has been added to the brass war memorial tablet at the back of the church.

The father of the Argentinian boy who was killed should soon be able to read Dave's letters. The book is soon to be published there. Our greatest hope is that it will be an influence for peace, and there is great sorrow in our hearts for the relatives of those young Argentinians who died, just the same as for our own people.

How I hope your efforts to stop the nuclear arms race will prosper! I often feel that there are very few politicians that can really be trusted, it is up to the ordinary folk to protest at the horror and stupidity of it all.

Nothing in this world can make up for what happened to our marvellous David, but we do thank you for your sympathy and send you our very best wishes.
Yours sincerely,
Elisabeth Tinker

Note 17: The inscription on David Tinker's grave reads:

> He wears
> The ungathered blossom of quiet; stiller he
> Than a deep well at noon, or lovers met,
> Than sleep, or the heart after wrath. He is
> The silence following great words of peace.

from Rupert Brooke's poem 'Fragments written during the voyage to Gallipoli, April 1915.'

I had mixed reactions to the letters that came back to me. Nuclear fission and radioactivity are complicated subjects, and grasping them is an ongoing learning process. When I felt I was beginning to sort them out that encouraged me to feel more confident: I was able to isolate important information and understand it. Things were moving in a positive way.

Then the next day I would be utterly depressed by some communication from the Ministry of Defence or Harwell or the CEGB. I wrote to all these bodies on slightly different subjects; but the tone of the replies was always the same: nothing you could call a lie but fobbing-off and all couched in those recognisable 'Yes, Minister'-type sentences. It's a programme I laugh at on television. But this was real and affected all our lives. I didn't find it funny at all.

Theo was fascinated by the replies and wanted to read the whole lot. He saw the letters I wrote the evening before I posted them. The replies I would show him when he came home from school after tea. He made spontaneous remarks such as, 'Well, that's just what you'd expect.' He was about fourteen by then.

If there were three or four replies on the same day he would grade them into 'believable', 'typical', 'thank goodness that one makes me laugh', 'that was really great'.

He was astonishingly perceptive. From another point of view it was disheartening to find that he could be so cynical. Peter and I think it our democratic duty to vote at elections, although we feel sceptical about politicians. But Theo was totally cynical about all these bureaucratic letters, and even about the forthcoming arms talks.

During dinner we would talk about what Toby had done that day at school. We would also mull over the letters together and discuss them at length. I had to think carefully about Toby's response to all this. He is $3\frac{1}{2}$ years younger than Theo and I had thought Theo was young at twelve to start being concerned about nuclear war. Now I know from Dr Coppolillo and Dr Clare that children can start to worry about it from about eleven onwards.

I had a talk with Theo when Toby wasn't present. He's very kind towards his brother; that's the sort of person he is.

'Theo, when you were younger you asked about nuclear war

because you were frightened of it, didn't you? When we discuss the letters over dinner we'll just analyse them and say why we believe what's in them, or why we don't. We'll let Toby join in if he wants to. But we won't mention nuclear war or why it frightens you. We don't want Toby to become aware of that side of it until he actually thinks and speaks up about it for himself. Then when he mentions being afraid he won't be hiding anything or being frightened on his own. We'll all be talking about it together.'

We had considered the possibility of Theo beginning to write his own letters. But he knew for himself that the majority of adults talk down to children, and he might not get a proper reply. Peter and I have always talked to our children as equals. We've talked about anything that Theo has wanted to talk about, though obviously holding our parental roles. Some adults might be quite surprised at a teenager having so much information.

Theo didn't feel that he would get a proper answer if he wrote the letters and became quite cross. 'I think my opinion does matter,' he said. 'They just think because I'm young, it doesn't matter. But it ought to.' So we agreed that I would write for him, asking about anything he wanted to know. He was particularly concerned about Sellafield. When he was thirteen he had already worked out that in his view the scientists could not be so dogmatic about safety levels of radiation. From my writing the letters he received his own personal replies to his questions, without interpretation. Because of this I have no qualms about people saying that in this way I was trying to indoctrinate my children.

By this time we were building up quite a store of information at home. At first we kept it all in our beagle's old puppy box, which was the largest cardboard box we had. Now it's kept under Theo's bed in various other boxes, so that it is easy to look at. We got information from everywhere – from America, Russia, the United Nations, the European Parliament, Windscale, the Central Electricity Generating Board, Holland, research papers from universities and so on.

As I began to become more knowledgeable, by reading all this information which was coming through the post every day, I noticed how the replies to me changed. Often I would write a first letter in a direct, straightforward way, asking my question and explaining that I wanted to know because I was a mother of two sons, a housewife concerned about her family. I would usually get back a letter which gave me a pat on the head and a bland reassurance. Then I would write back, this time quoting from an academic or scientific report. Their next letter was suddenly quite different in tone: you could almost hear them saying, 'Who the hell *is* this woman?'

Some of the replies to me, of course, say virtually nothing – but their very silence is deeply indicative. Others use many words to say nothing at all. I found it interesting to see who would take the trouble to give me a serious reply and who would offer only an abrupt or a 'polite' dismissal.

8 April 1983

To: Mr Hugo Young,
Political Editor
The Sunday Times
London

Dear Hugo Young,
It worries me how remote I feel from politicians, how I doubt their integrity. This feeling was crystallised for me during the Falklands War when my brother came back to Britain from Argentina (he works and lives in Argentina, but has since returned there), and we spoke of the war.

My political doubts have grown over the last 18 months during my personal search to try and make sense of the nuclear arms race.

Of some help to me in trying to work out what makes politicians 'tick' has been the Report – *Human Fallibility in the Control of Nuclear Weapons*. I enclose a section which I found of interest and I would be most grateful for your comments. I can't help feeling that I can recognize more than one of the symptoms of 'Group-Think' in today's leading politicians.[18]

As a professional politician-watcher have you any words of help for a voter for whom there appears to be no party?
Yours sincerely,
Deirdre Rhys-Thomas

Note 18: *Group-think* The psychologist Janis notes six symptoms of how people in small groups tend to think:

1 An illusion of invulnerability that becomes shared by most members of the group.

86

2 Collective attempts to ignore or rationalise away items of information challenging shaky but cherished assumptions.
3 An unquestioned belief in the group's inherent morality.
4 Stereotyping the enemy as either too evil for negotiations or too stupid to be a threat.
5 A shared illusion of unanimity in a majority viewpoint.
6 Self-appointed 'mind-guards' to protect the group from adverse information.

Since most decisions in our society are made by very small groups it is important for us to keep them in touch with the wider world. One of the greatest difficulties faced by such groups, especially when there is a crisis and they must make decisions quickly, is for information to reach them from those who have to take actions according to their instructions, since they find it hard to hear or understand anything that conflicts with their view of events, however unrealistic that may be.

For a discussion of the thinking behind nuclear decisions see: McLean, Scilla, *How Nuclear Weapon Decisions Are Made*, Macmillan, London, 1986.

The Sunday Times
London
18 May 1983

Dear Ms Rhys-Thomas,
I cannot apologise enough for my delay in responding to your letter of April 8. It arrived when I was on holiday and somehow unforgivably got overlooked thereafter. Now I hear you have had to telephone me and write another copy of the letter – which makes me quite certain that I will be unable to live up to the expectations you must have of my being able to answer your questions.

In a sense, I hope my various columns in this newspaper address themselves to the kind of doubts you feel about politicians as a class. It is very hard to make general observations of the kind you seem to be seeking. Perhaps you will have seen a BBC television programme, *The Heart of the Matter*, last Sunday which I mention not for my own contribution, but because a number of politicians were asked to contemplate their own moral standing over matters such as truth and honesty. I quite profoundly believe that all six of the propositions you mention from the psychologist Janis are the kind of things which newspapers exist to challenge. We must not believe that group-think can be so invulnerable to outside influences. In respect of nuclear weapons, although no doubt secrecy and security protect the tiny group of decision-makers in the different countries in the ways you suggest, public ventilation of the arguments and the horrors make their own contribution to deterrence. Even defence, in other words, is not an area of decision making which exists in quarantine.

As I have sometimes tried to write in various ways, I don't think many politicians are knaves, although some are fools. By and large they think they are doing what is best by some standards beyond party and self-interest. This does not lead to any conclusions about which party you should vote for. But I always think that a genuine 'floater' like yourself would be well advised to look hard at the individual candidates in their own constituency and possibly vote for them on the basis of personal merit.

Yours sincerely,
Hugo Young
Political Editor

29 April 1983

To: H.R.H. Prince Philip, Duke of Edinburgh,
Buckingham Palace,
London SW1

Your Royal Highness,
I sincerely hope, Sir, that now you have publicly entered into the nuclear arms debate you will be reading the Report – *Defence without the Bomb* – by the Alternative Defence Commission whose Chairman Frank Blackaby was a former Director of the Stockholm International Peace Research Institute.

The Report, published this week, is based on a practical analysis of the risks involved in Britain's present reliance on nuclear weapons compared with those involved in giving them up.

I cannot help but fear, Sir, that unless we halt the nuclear arms build-up the words of the late Earl Mountbatten of Burma, a Member of the Scientific Council of the Stockholm International Peace Research Institute, may prove to be prophetic:

'And when it is all over what will the world be like? Our fine great buildings, our homes will exist no more. The thousands of years it took to develop our civilization will have been in vain. Our works of art will be lost. Radio, television, newspapers will disappear. There will be no hospitals. No help can be expected for the few mutilated survivors in any town to be sent from a neighbouring town — there will be no neighbouring towns left, no neighbours, there will be no help, there will be no hope.'

Deirdre Rhys-Thomas

From: Major The Hon. Andrew Wigram
Buckingham Palace
11th May, 1983

Dear Miss Rhys-Thomas
    The Duke of Edinburgh has asked me to thank you for your letter about his comments on nuclear weapons.
    You may like to have the enclosed copy of the speech he made on 26th April to the Symposium on the Social and Cultural Challenge of Modern Technology organised by the Fellowship of Engineering.
    Yours sincerely
    Andrew Wigram

23 May 1983

To: Major The Hon. Andrew Wigram,
Buckingham Palace,
London SW1

Dear Major Wigram,
I would be obliged if you would thank The Duke of Edinburgh for the copy of his Speech which I have read with much interest.
    Indeed nuclear power stations do not produce acid rain but they produce nuclear waste. This nuclear waste is responsible for making the Irish Sea the most radioactive sea in the World.
    Like acid rain, nuclear waste recognises no national boundaries. Plutonium and other chief transuranic americium are now distributed widely in the Irish Sea; around the coast of Ireland: in Scottish coastal waters, off Norway and Denmark.
    I do hope that The Duke of Edinburgh, as a conservationist, will be disturbed to know that British scientists

have stated that laverbread from the Irish Sea should not be eaten. This is highly significant because when such a change occurs the pollutants are passed on through the food chain.
Yours sincerely,
Deirdre Rhys-Thomas

10 May 1983

Sir Walter Marshall,
Chairman,
Central Electricity Generating Board
London

Dear Sir Walter Marshall,
I recently watched a television programme which examined your very close association with the PWR[19] manufacturers in the States, who are in a desperate financial state having been unable to sell their PWRs in the USA since the Three Mile Island accident and must now depend on British, European, etc. sales.[20]

A follow-up BBC2 programme explaining the melt-down at Three Mile Island and the unawareness of those in charge as to what was happening was very illuminating.

As an electricity consumer I would like you to explain to me why you say that nuclear-generated electricity is cheaper than coal-generated electricity, when one considers the risk of transportation of nuclear waste and radioactive products by rail (this method of transport banned in the States) and the security risks also additional police (CEGB?) needed at nuclear power stations etc.[21]

Perhaps your attitude and my attitude regarding Britain are completely opposite when I read your business philosophy. 'The service provided by the CEGB does not stem from a benign philosophy and we are not the conscience of UK Ltd.'[22]

When you are making decisions which have life or death considerations environmental, health, pollution, you would best be advised to be the conscience of UK Ltd. It is your moral, not business, duty to Britain.
Yours sincerely,
Deirdre Rhys-Thomas

Note 19: The Pressurised Water Reactor (PWR) was developed by Westinghouse in the USA, and has been sold to countries all over the world. It uses fuel that is more radioactive than the uranium used in most British reactors, and when the fuel rods come out of the reactor core they have to be stored under water for several years until they have become cool enough to be transported. The Public Inquiry at Sizewell, which lasted over two years, was to give advice to the Government about the decision whether to build a PWR at Sizewell, next to the reactor already there.

Sir Walter Marshall, who came to the CEGB from the Atomic Energy Authority, is very keen on nuclear power, and has lobbied for years for permission to build a PWR. He recently said that if we turn away from nuclear power the output of electricity would fall by 40 per cent, but this seems a bit exaggerated considering that even during the miners' strike when the nuclear power stations were producing the maximum they were capable of, they only got up to 20 per cent for part of a year.

Note 20: Three Mile Island is a nuclear power station in the USA, 12 miles from Harrisburg, Pennsylvania. On 28 March 1979 the core of the reactor came very close to a 'meltdown', similar to the accident that blew the roof off Chernobyl. The containment building at TMI is extra strong, because the designers were asked to make it thick enough to stay intact if a jumbo jet crashed into it.

Work on cleaning up the ruined reactor is still going on, and the cost is estimated in billions of dollars. At the moment, 17,000 lawsuits have been entered by people who claim to have suffered health or property damage from the accident, and at least six claims have been met.

This accident spelt the end of nuclear power expansion in the USA. Even before TMI no new orders for nuclear power stations had been placed in the preceding two years, but from then on a number of power stations being constructed were cancelled, and others were converted to burn oil or coal. See Lepzerr, Robert, *Voices from Three Mile Island*, The Crossing Press, New York, 1980, for the experiences of the people of TMI in their own words.

Note 21: There is a lot of disagreement about the real cost of electricity from nuclear power as compared with coal. Even the CEGB figures for 1983/4 Generation Costs seem to show that coal is cheaper:

COSTS PER kWh.

Older stations		*Recent stations*	
Magnox (nuclear)	Coal	Hinckley B (AGR nuclear)	Coal
2.60	2.38	2.64	2.46

The nuclear industry does not include the full cost of 'decommissioning' the nuclear power stations when they are at an end of their productive life. The experience at Three Mile Island with trying to dispose of the buildings and equipment which become radioactive causes some people to wonder whether this dismantling of old nuclear power stations will be quite so simple as has been suggested. The costs of keeping the radioactive wastes separated from the environment for the next quarter of a million years has also not been taken into account, nor the costs of maintaining a healthy population in conditions of slowly rising background radiation. See Patterson, Walt, *Nuclear Power*, Penguin, London, 1983, for a good description of different types of nuclear reactors.

Note 22: The British electricity industry was nationalised in April 1948, and in June 1957 the Central Electricity Generating Board (CEGB) was set up to be in charge of the production and distribution of electricity for England and Wales. The first Chairman, Sir Christopher Hinton, was transferred to the CEGB from the United Kingdom Atomic Energy Authority. He had spent many years in the atomic energy industry; in 1946 he was put in charge of the atomic energy production organisation which was established to build nuclear reactors and factories for the production of nuclear explosive (fissive) material. It is not surprising that the CEGB has shown such a tremendous commitment to producing electricity from nuclear power stations when you think of the enthusiasm the new Chairman must have brought to the job. At that time the scientists working on nuclear energy must have experienced many of the characteristics noted by Janis (see note 18) when faced with decisions in a field of technology where the forces they were dealing with were truly awesome. It is altogether too easy to understand how they would regard even the terrible accident when the nuclear reactor at Windscale caught fire as a challenge rather than a warning.

As early as February 1947 the Medical Research Council were sounding a warning note about the harmful genetic effects of radiation, pointing out that no threshold dose existed, and small repeated doses add together; there was no build-up of resistance as there is, for example, to illnesses such as measles. Such information must have seemed unwelcome to the nuclear boys, many of whom still dispute the effects of low levels of radiation in damaging health, although there is a great deal of evidence about it.

See *The Development of Atomic Energy 1939-1984: Chronology of Events* available from the UKAEA Information Services Branch, 11 Charles II Street, London SW1Y 4QP, price £5,00, publ. 1984.

Central Electricity Generating Board
London
19 May 1983

Dear Ms Rhys-Thomas

Thank you for your letter of 10 May to the Chairman about nuclear safety and the Board's business objectives. Sir Walter is absent from the office on business for a few days and has asked me to reply.

Your letter raises numerous issues in passing but the first point I would make is that the Board does attach a very high priority to ensuring the safety of both the public and its own staff. This is reflected in the very large effort and expenditure devoted to safe plant design and operation and also the excellent safety record of the Board's nuclear and fossil-fired power stations.

In respect of our business philosophy, our objectives stem from those established by Parliament which, under the 1957 Electricity Act, charged the Board with the duty of developing and maintaining an efficient, co-ordinated and economical system of electricity supply in bulk. This objective is fundamental to the strength of the national economy and the effective pursuit of it is our major contribution to 'UK Limited'. The extract from the CEGB Paper referred to in the *Guardian* article of 11 May has been taken out of context and the business philosophy outlined there is not a statement of our philosophy but only one alternative put forward to assist the Board in defining its position. We do of course regard ourselves as responsible members of the community and the Board's safety and environmental standards are not sacrificed in the interests of cheap production. Beyond this, however, we do not regard it as our role to identify and evaluate independently other possibly conflicting national economic or social priorities which may themselves conflict with the interests of the electricity consumer. This is the responsibility of the elected Government to whose guidance, direction and statutory powers the Board is subject on matters of national policy.

In respect of your more detailed points, we consider nuclear generated electricity is cheaper than coal because, over the lifetime of the plant, the higher capital cost of nuclear stations is more than out-weighed by their cheaper operating costs. We believe that this can be achieved in a safe and environmentally acceptable manner and indeed, before a nuclear power station can be constructed the Board must also satisfy both the Nuclear Installation Inspectorate in order to obtain a site licence and the Secretary of State for Energy in order to obtain statutory consent.[23]

As you will know from press reports of the Sizewell Inquiry, both these processes are exceedingly thorough and painstaking.

Currently 80% of electricity is generated by CEGB from coal and coal will remain the Board's major source of fuel until at least the end of the century. The UK's oil and gas resources are however regrettably only finite and coal will increasingly be needed as a substitute. In these circumstances you may wish to consider the extent to which the UK should remain so dependent on a single source of fuel for its electricity supplies both from the point of view of its cost and availability. In our view, the development of nuclear power is both economic and strategically necessary to ensure continued security of supplies in the longer term.

Yours sincerely,
John Anderson,
Secretary

Note 23: The Nuclear Installations Inspectorate is a part of the Health and Safety Executive, with special responsibility for the safety of design and operation of nuclear installations. Their offices were recently moved to Bootle, and since then they have been about 20 down on their full complement of 90 inspectors. Since their salaries are several hundred pounds per annum less than the equivalent grades of nuclear engineer/scientist employed within the nuclear industry, it may not be a very attractive job.

When the Sizewell Inquiry opened, the NII had not been given all the information necessary to carry out safety assessments. Even when two years later it ended, the NII was unable to say that a licence could be granted for a PWR to be built at Sizewell – there was still work to be done on safety.

23 May 1983

To: Mr John Anderson,
Secretary,
Central Electricity Generating Board,
London

Dear Mr Anderson,
I thank you for your letter which Sir Walter asked you to write to me.

You write 'these processes are exceedingly thorough and painstaking'. And so people believe nuclear power is 100% safe: no side effects.

These very same processes which must surely be just as exceedingly thorough and painstaking with continuous monitoring by the Ministry of Agriculture Foods & Fisheries and BNF have failed to prevent the Irish Sea from becoming the Most Radioactively Polluted Sea in the World.

Don't you and Sir Walter feel this is too high a price to pay for so-called cheaper fuel?
Yours sincerely,
Deirdre Rhys-Thomas

Central Electricity Generating Board
London
22 June 1983

Dear Ms Rhys-Thomas
Thank you for your letter of 23 May 1983 in which you seek the CEGB's comments on the environmental implications of nuclear power.

First of all I would like to set in proper context the statement, which you quote in your letter, that the Irish Sea is the 'most radioactively polluted sea in the world'. Radioactive discharges arise from the reprocessing of irradiated nuclear fuel at BNFL's reprocessing plant, at Sellafield in Cumbria, as well as from CEGB nuclear power stations. All releases are strictly controlled, and cannot be made without a joint authorisation from the Ministry of Agriculture, Fisheries and Food and the Department of Environment, or, in the case of power stations in Wales, the Welsh Office.[24] Before permission is granted these authorising bodies satisfy themselves that discharges will not endanger members of the public, taking into account every possible way in which released material might affect them, for example through water supplies, food, and air. Additionally, each installation has to demonstrate that every practicable step has been taken to minimise discharges.

Because these precautions are taken the amount of radioactivity in the Irish Sea is very small. The highest individual doses occur in the Sellafield area and these vary depending upon individuals' consumption of locally-caught fish and shell-fish. Even so, during the 1970s the highest estimated individual dose, based on pessimistic assumptions, ranged from 15 to 130 millirem per year, well below the International Commission on Radiological Protection (ICRP) recommended limit of 500 millirems per year, for members of the public. This figure constitutes only one-tenth of the limit accepted as safe for power station workers, whose health and working conditions are regularly and closely monitored.

95

You suggest in your letter that the public has been encouraged to believe that nuclear power is 100 per cent safe. The CEGB has never made this claim, and in fact has never tried to conceal that nuclear power, like any other method of generation, or indeed any modern industrial process, has certain attendant risks. The development of nuclear power in the UK has been accompanied by an awareness of the radiological hazards, and every effort is made to ensure that the risk to the public and the environment is minimized. For example, staff in nuclear power stations undergo specific training to acquire a thorough understanding of the way the plant works; the highest quality of materials and designs are employed; and the safety rules and procedures are continually updated to account for scientific and technological advances. Furthermore, the Acts of Parliament relating to the nuclear industry are far more embracing and restricting than those for any other modern industry. As a result of these stringent measures, no accident involving a significant release of radiation to the environment has occurred in nearly twenty years of operation of CEGB stations.[25]

It is the Board's view, supported to date by the public, that the very small risks associated with nuclear generation are acceptable in return for the economy, reliability and security offered by nuclear power.

Yours sincerely,
John Anderson
Secretary

Note 24: Although 'all releases are strictly controlled', a glance at the accompanying chart makes you wonder. (See Black, Sir Douglas, *Investigation of the Possible Increased Incidence of Cancer in West Cumbria*, HMSO, London, 1984.) Discharges from Sellafield have been traced as far as the Arctic Circle, and fish caught off the coast of Sweden have contained a higher level of contamination from Sellafield discharges than from the wastes of local nuclear reactors.

Note 25: While it is true that in general discharges of radioactive wastes from the nuclear power stations pale into insignificance if they are compared to the environmental pollution from Sellafield, the factory run by British Nuclear Fuels Limited, it is also true that no health study of the effects on the local population has been carried out in this country. A study done in the US on infant mortality before and after new nuclear power stations started working showed that the rates rose in accordance

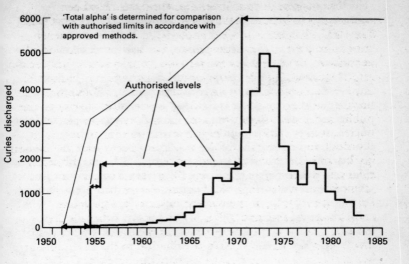

with the direction of the wind. Among the people living downwind of the stations more babies died in their first year of life, especially if they were of low birth weight. A similar study in Bavaria confirmed this observation.

There is disagreement among scientists and doctors about what kind of release should be called 'significant'. See Bertell, Rosalie, *No Immediate Danger*, The Women's Press, London, 1985, pp.207, 209, 231.

To: Mr John Anderson
Secretary, CEGB
London

10 October 1983

Dear Mr Anderson,
You wrote to me on 22 June 1983, replying to my letter to you of 23 May. The correspondence was about the environmental implications of nuclear power, and the opinion that the Irish Sea is the 'most radioactively polluted sea in the world'.

I have discussed your letter with several people, including some scientists of repute. They confirm my first impression when I got your letter – that you would appear to be ill-informed of the case against nuclear power.

This criticism – of the apparent ignorance of those whose career is in the nuclear energy field – is widespread, and is reinforced by letters such as yours.

My attention has been brought to a number of books, Government Statements, Debates in Parliament, and disclosures at the current Sizewell Inquiry. All these lead many people, including myself, to the conclusion that many spokesmen for the nuclear industry have lost their intellectual integrity.

Let me suggest that you read or maybe re-read the speech by Baroness White in the House of Lords, 23 December 1976. She was a member of the Royal Commission on Environmental Pollution and was one of the signatories of their sixth report (Cmnd. 6618). I give a few quotations from this debate, which was about that report:

'. . . we felt that the attitude of those concerned with the administration of our nuclear endeavours in this country was simply not geared to the quite understandable apprehensions of the general public. I found this the most disappointing aspect of our investigations; and, my Lords, one does not have to be a nuclear physicist to judge the quality and attitude of mind of some of those who are in charge of our nuclear activities.'

'. . . some of us, at least, were often depressed by what we felt was the blinkered outlook which could preclude adequate consideration of matters not directly in the line of vision. We were depressed by a certain rigidity of mind, and in some cases by what I have called the impenetrable complacency of those in high places. A Micawberish attitude does not go well with a substance as potentially risky as plutonium.'

'Bland assertions are the least convincing of all, and they usually indicate that the respondent has not adequately understood the question.'

The whole Debate would be worth reading – it might do something to mitigate the 'blinkered outlook' which appears to be the norm among 'those in high places'.

I suggest you also get and read the recently published book – *Rationality and Ritual: The Windscale Inquiry and Nuclear Decisions in Britain*, sponsored by the British Society for the

History of Science and published by them. The book seems to indicate how the Windscale Inquiry into BNFL's application to construct their THORP plant was rigged.[26]

Walter Patterson's new edition of *Nuclear Power* (Pelican, 1983) brings up to date the first edition, 1976, and describes the many disasters near disasters which nuclear power stations in several countries have suffered.

Your letter, and comparable statements by your colleagues in the nuclear industry, assume that the permissible limits laid down by authority are correct, and that compliance with these – as far as economics and practicability allow (the 'ALARA' principle) is sufficient. This is an office boy approach: comply with the rules and that suffices. But those rules are devised by biased and narrowly experienced experts in the ICRP and the NRPB.[27] Furthermore, the ICRP is a self-elected body, and membership of both bodies is interlocked. All have a vested interest in setting the standards and interpreting them in such a way that what is practical (the 'ALARA' principle) is decided to be what is conformable with the continued existence of the nuclear power industry. That industry is now under a cloud, any confidence in it that still remains being rapidly reduced by disclosures at the Sizewell Inquiry, and by the tortuous argument with which, over the last two decades and more, the CEGB has tried to make out that such power stations will give cheaper electricity than power stations of other kinds, and that they are safe.[28]

Your letter shows a misconception of the role of an employee of a nationalised industry. You are a *servant* of the public, not an instructor of the public. You and your colleagues since the mid-fifties have served that public badly. After spending many thousands of millions of pounds on trying to develop a British type reactor, you are now hoping to get permission to switch to an American type.

If you have not already read the paper Lord Bowden has submitted to the Sizewell Inquiry you should do so – Inquiry Document VBO1 (Rev) (ADD 1). He ends his Paper with these words:

'It has become notorious in the U.S.A that none of the big utilities is likely to buy another PWR set, and that the failures of many sets which have been built are resulting in very expensive difficulties for suppliers of electric power who depend on them. Furthermore the export market has suffered, and is unlikely to recover until the PWR sets are selling again in the home market. For this reason Westinghouse is terribly anxious to make sure that we should build a PWR set in this country, and thereby do something to rehabilitate the design in the whole World. However successful we are we shall not be able to export any ourselves – the American industry has huge unused capacity; they have recently scrapped a big factory in Florida which was built to manufacture PWR sets.

'I believe that the British authorities are being exploited and used by the Americans. We shall be building another prototype, but they will represent it as a triumph for their PWR, and try to use it to revive their vanished industry.

'Why, Oh Why, have we fallen victims to this propaganda? Why are we such suckers?'

Yours sincerely,
Deirdre Rhys-Thomas

Note 26: The Windscale Inquiry in 1977 examined the case for granting BNFL planning permission to build a new factory, to be called THORP – Thermal Oxide Reprocessing Plant – on their site in Sellafield. Without such a factory the plutonium that builds up in the fuel rods from the Advanced Gas-Cooled Reactors, and in nuclear reactors abroad where the fuel is uranium oxide, could not be separated out. France is the only other country in the world where reprocessing is a business, and they have had a lot of trouble trying to meet their targets for reprocessing oxide fuel. In spite of detailed and spirited arguments against granting permission presented at the Inquiry by a number of opponents, the Report when it came out barely acknowledged their arguments, and recommended that permission be given.

Copeland Council held out against BNFL for several years, insisting that the roads to the site needed to be widened and the substructures strengthened to take the heavy traffic involved in constructing and then using such a factory, but in 1985 work on THORP at last began. There are many tonnes of imported oxide fuel stored at Sellafield, among them some from Sweden, and some from Japan. The radioactive wastes created by reprocessing this type of fuel are even more unmanageable than the wastes currently giving so much trouble to BNFL. So far, in spite of years of research, the answers to the problem of how to fix high level wastes in a form that would enable them to be buried, or kept in dry storage, have not been found. At present, hundreds of gallons of liquid high-level waste are kept in double-walled steel tanks surrounded by thick concrete, perpetually stirred to prevent the plutonium clumping together into an explosive mass, perpetually cooled to prevent them boiling from the heat of the radioactive breakdown which will not end for thousands of years. At least one of the tanks has been leaking since 1976.

Note 27: The National Radiological Protection Board (NRPB) at Harwell is the body responsible for researching and advising on the standards of safety in exposure to radioactivity of workers and general public. Sometimes people have suspected that they more often protect the nuclear industry than the general public, but recently there have been signs of disquiet among some of the staff.

At the time of the Chernobyl disaster they were quite unable to carry out the work of analysing the data which was being collected at various points of the UK – mainly at nuclear facilities, who had the appropriate monitoring equiment – and providing the general inquirer with advice as to what they should do to protect themselves. In the House of Commons during a meeting with MPs at the end of May, a spokesperson from the NRPB said, 'It would have been a precaution to have kept children inside on Saturday when it rained . . . but that is in retrospect. Try not to put that statement out because people could be frightened by it.'

The International Commission on Radiological Protection (ICRP) grew out of the organisation set up to monitor what was happening to the health of the early radiologists and people who worked with radiation. The recommended 'safe' levels have come down a lot since the early days:

1925	52 Roentgen per year
1934	36 Roentgen per year
1945	15 rem per year (rem = Roentgen adjusted for outside the body or taken into lung or gut, etc.)
1959	5-12 rem per year depending on age

The dose for workers in the UK is still 5 rems per year, although it is less in most other countries. Dr Bertell points out that 'the ICRP has never taken a public position in favour of protecting public health in any of the controversial radiation-related problems encountered (since 1950).'

Note 28: Whatever you do to reduce the risk of exposure to radioactive material involved in the nuclear industry, there are always accidents where some gets out, the range and quantity of man-made radioactivity is constantly increasing, and the routine operation of a nuclear facility depends on some of the radioactive gases and contaminated water being poured out of the building into the air or water nearby. If the gases that build up inside a nuclear power station were not expelled to the air, the levels of exposure for workers could not be maintained.

It is possible to adopt a policy of keeping to levels of exposure 'as low as technically achievable' – ALATA – but the filters, resins and equipment to extract the radioactive gases and dust from air and water in the nuclear facility buildings would be very expensive. To keep costs down, the principle of 'as low as reasonably achievable' is generally used instead. To decide what is reasonable a balance is struck, with on the one hand the electricity supplied to industry and the public, plus the jobs for nuclear employees, and on the other the deaths from leukemia and cancer that any increase in radiation exposure will cause. Both the workers and people living in the vicinity of a nuclear facility run an increased risk of getting a disease caused or made worse by radiation. If there is an accident even people living 800 miles away run extra risks! It has been suggested that up to 500 cases of thyroid cancer may have been set in train by the cloud from Chernobyl that rained over the UK. In a population of 56,000,000 where at least one person in five can expect to suffer from cancer some time in their lives, this will not be 'socially significant', because only those families afflicted will notice.

It seems that even ALARA varies from one country to another:

Country	maximum alpha discharges to sea
Japan	0.2 curies
France	90.0 curies
Britain	6,000.0 curies (before 1 January 1985)
Britain	600.0 curies (since 1 January 1985)

Central Electricity Board
London
8 November 1983

Dear Ms Rhys-Thomas,
Thank you for your letter of 10 October addressed to my predecessor Mr John Anderson.

I cannot accept that the CEGB is ignorant of public concern about nuclear power – in fact nothing could be further from the truth. The Board is well aware of the anxieties aroused by nuclear energy, and makes considerable efforts to reduce fears and dispel misapprehensions by publishing factual information on all aspects of nuclear generation; an example of this is the booklet *Nuclear Power: Questions and Answers*, a copy of which is enclosed for your information.

In this connection, I believe that you may have misunderstood the role of the Public Inquiry now in progress into the Board's proposal to build a pressurised water reactor at Sizewell in Suffolk. The Inquiry has been set up, under an independent Inspector, to consider evidence from bodies and individuals who oppose the project, as well as its supporters, and will have every opportunity to examine the economic, environmental and safety implications of the proposed power station. The Inspector, Sir Frank Layfield, has drawn attention to the 'unprecedented volume of information' which the CEGB has made publicly available, and has commented in particular on the Pre-Construction Safety Report, which he described as 'a unique document to be presented to a local Public Inquiry'.[29]

Turning now to your remarks on the economics of nuclear power and the selection of the PWR system, I should point out that the CEGB's Magnox and AGR reactors have made a safe and valuable contribution to the UK's energy supply, and have helped to hold down the price of electricity because of their economy and reliability. The CEGB now wishes to establish the option of the PWR, which is a proven and economic system with a successful world-wide operating record. The design proposed for Sizewell 'B' incorporates improvements made in the light of operating experience, and has been further modified to meet stringent UK safety standards and operating requirements. You quote at some length the evidence given to the Sizewell Inquiry by Lord Bowden, who incidentally is a well-known proponent of the Canadian-designed CANDU reactor system: in his comments on the American nuclear industry, Lord Bowden fails to mention that the highly-successful French nuclear programme is based on the PWR, and that the USA has the largest PWR construction programme in the world.

You quote in your letter Baroness White's remarks in the House of Lords in 1976, in which she criticised 'bland assertions'. That description could I think be applied to many of the remarks in your letter. The CEGB would not claim to have a monopoly of truth. But the Board does make a point of basing its policies on carefully researched facts, hard evidence, and a thorough study of alternative options.

Yours sincerely,
Graham Hadley
Secretary

Note 29: The financing and conduct of the Sizewell Inquiry are very interesting. The CEGB presented mountains of evidence, 80 copies of each document, in all 55 tons of paper. They spent an estimated £15 million of public money (provided by electricity consumers). Forty organisations took part in presenting objections, and there were an additional 112 written objections, and 4,000 letters of objection from individuals.

The opponents requested that at least some of their expenses be met from public funds, so that they too would be able to hire lawyers to cross-question on their behalf, but this request was not granted. Friends of the Earth spent £130,000 and found it very frustrating that even though the CEGB had spent two years preparing their evidence, they kept changing their case as the Inquiry went on, and even changed their minds over the type of design they would use for a PWR, so the safety arguments changed.

In addition to having to raise money to present their objections, many small groups found that the amount of time spent on the research and writing were exhausting, as this was something they did in their spare

103

time, unlike the CEGB officials for whom it was all part of the job. Even so, the information that was published in connection with the Inquiry will be valuable to anyone keen to gain better understanding of the problems of nuclear power, as seen from several different points of view.

To: Mr G.H. Hadley
Secretary
Central Electricity Generating Board
London

21 November 1983

Dear Mr Hadley,
I am surprised you draw my attention to Sir Frank Layton's comment on the 'unprecedented volume of information' which the CEGB has made publicly available. To my mind that is not the least of the CEGB's responsibilities to the public.

I am a hard-headed businesswoman so, of course, I understand the CEGB's enthusiasm for PWRs in so far as £100 million will have been spent on Sizewell whatever the outcome of the public inquiry (Business News/*Sunday Times* 13.11.83).

Thank you for your glossy Brochure which I had already read. Having had the ALARA principle explained to me by a Government Scientist one would have thought that the CEGB's application of the ALARA principle would have appeared in the Brochure so that we 'the public' can understand how it is used in decision-making by the CEGB.

And pages 10 and 11, nuclear waste flasks, I am glad to know they have been recently withdrawn from railway services by the CEGB after they have been found to be liable to crack.[30]

I hope you watched the television programme 'Windscale – the nuclear laundry': you may now better understand my concern about radioactive contamination of the environment. Or as my children see it 'their World'.
Yours sincerely,
Deirdre Rhys-Thomas

Note 30: The fuel rods that have become too contaminated with fission products to be efficient at giving out energy are withdrawn by robot from the reactor core and placed in ponds of deep water to cool. The water absorbs the radioactivity and prevents the workers being exposed. After at least 90 days the rods are piled under water into a basket and loaded into a 'nuclear waste flask'. These flasks are huge boxes weighing 48 tonnes, with walls of mild steel 14 inches thick. They used to be welded, but tests showed that they could develop cracks along the weld lines. A new type of flask was developed from forged steel, and 27 old flasks were rapidly taken out of service.

The flasks are transported by British Rail on passenger lines from the nuclear power stations to Sellafield, and carrying them through densely populated areas such as London is the cause of a great deal of controversy. The CEGB claim that the chance of an accident is so remote as to be virtually impossible – they used to say they were as safe as houses before the Ronan Point collapse, then they said it was as remote as two jumbo jets colliding until that happened. The GLC opposed the plan for Sizewell 'B' because it would mean that PWR-irradiated fuel rods would be transported though London, and bring even greater risks.

There are over 500 journeys a year made by trains carrying nuclear waste flasks, and each flask may contain up to 5 million curies of radioactivity. Although the old flasks were taken out of service, the volume of traffic with the new ones is increasing as new nuclear power stations start up.

To: Mr Ian MacGregor
Chairman,
National Coal Board
London

14th March 1983

Dear Mr MacGregor,
A really dumb question coming up: if there are stockpiles of coal all over Britain today why do we need more nuclear power stations?[31]

I realize you're not responsible for the nuclear industry but when putting the case for coal you must take into account your competitors' costs?

Nuclear energy costs of
   – nuclear power stations – maintenance
   – administration
   – guarding and transporting nuclear waste containers by rail and road to Windscale
   – private nuclear police force
   – £100 million paid out for Sizewell PWR even if it is never built
   – storage of high level radioactive waste under the safest conditions
   – radioactive pollution of the Irish Sea to which the CEGB

105

has contributed: how one works the cost of that out, I don't know? No doubt the next generation will?

When all the hidden costs of nuclear energy are lumped together how can coal be more expensive? And if less than half the money to be spent on Trident were to be spent on scrubbers the pollution disadvantages of coal-burning would be overcome.
Yours sincerely,
Deirdre Rhys-Thomas

P.S. My late Grandmother — Alexandrina Malloch, of Kinghouse Rannoch Moor, knew a MacGregor who left Kinlochleven before the Second World War for America. Would you be the same MacGregor?

Note 31: The CEGB often say that nuclear power is cleaner than coal power because burning coal releases sulphur to the environment, and leads to acid rain, which is killing forests all over Europe and the United States and Canada. If the chimneys through which the surplus steam from the coal fired power stations escapes into the air are fitted with 'scrubbers' up to 98 per cent of the sulphur gases can be removed.
It is really extraordinary that the heat obtained from burning coal, oil or uranium to generate electricity is largely lost through those chimneys — only one-third of the potential energy of the original fuel gets turned into electricity and two-thirds goes up the chimney or out to sea. Small coal or oil-fired stations built near industrial premises or housing can send that heat into pipes used to heat both the rooms and the water while at the same time supplying them with light and electric power. Nuclear power stations are not built near large centres of population in this country, although of course, because the British Isles is so small what we consider a fair distance may be thought near in a larger country. For instance, 984,000 people live within a 19-mile radius of Oldbury power station, and judging by the Russian experience they would all have to be evacuated if there was a serious accident.

National Coal Board
Grosvenor Place
London

29th March, 1984

Dear Ms. Rhys-Thomas,
Thank you for your letter of the 14th March, in which you raise the question of the need for nuclear power.
I would say that the current stock piles of coal are not

really relevant to the need for additional power stations. The next nuclear power station to be ordered could not be working fully much before the mid-1990s and we would hope to get the coal industry into a reasonable balance of supply and demand well before then.

Our analysis of the relative costs of coal and nuclear power indicates that the comparison is between the very capital intensive nuclear system which has low operating costs, and the coal system which is more modest in its capital requirements but which has relatively higher continuing operating costs over the life of the station.

The French Government have opted for a programme of substantial investment in nuclear power with the contraction of their coal industry, because of their belief this will provide France with the lowest energy costs in Europe and thus support and attract industry.

The price of coal in the UK will increasingly be influenced by the international coal prices. In our view, these will have to increase significantly above current values before there will be a clear overall economic benefit in favour of new nuclear power stations.

With regard to the postcript I was born in Kinlochleven in 1912 but my family moved first to Edinburgh in 1918 and Glasgow in 1920. I did have some relatives, an uncle and cousins who remained in Kinlochleven and may have left there before World War II.
Sincerely,
Ian MacGregor
Chairman

22 September 1983

To: Sir Kelvin Spencer
Seaton
Devon.

Dear Sir Kelvin,[32]
I would like to thank you for your letter which I read in the *Guardian*:[33] your letter helped me understand a letter I had from the CEGB. Learning of the Government scientists' mandate known as ALARA I was able to comprehend the reasoning of the CEGB and apply this to the UKAEA and BNFL.

I am not a scientist, Sir Kelvin, just a concerned Mother – concerned for my sons' futures and even more concerned since learning from a British scientist that with all the Government safeguards laver (seaweed) growing in the Irish Sea has become radioactively contaminated. I ask myself what confidence can I have in these safeguards? Does this not also mean that other sea products can be similarly contaminated via the food chains?

I enclose copy/letter from the CEGB.

Yours sincerely,
Deirdre Rhys-Thomas

Note 32: Sir Kelvin Spencer was for many years before his retirement Chief Scientific Advisor on Energy to the government, and over a period of time he became convinced that nuclear power technology is intrinsically harmful and should be dropped. He gave a lot of encouragement to objectors at the Sizewell Inquiry, and introduced a note of humour by offering a weekly prize of one guinea for the 'silliest' quotation sent in to the journal *Sizewell Reactions* which was published throughout the Inquiry summarising the events and arguments as they were presented.

Note 33: *Guardian*, 29 September 1983, p. 14.

From: Sir Kelvin Spencer
Seaton, Devon
Sunday, September 24, 1983

Dear Ms Rhys-Thomas
Thank you for your letter of 22 September, with copy of letter to you, dated 22 June 1983, from John Anderson, secretary of the CEGB. I'm glad my *Guardian* letter had some impact! I write few letters to the Press as whether they get published is such a chancy business. So when one evokes a response it gives encouragement.

You have every reason to distrust the whole nuclear energy industry, and statements defending that industry by members of the Government and by MPs. The fact is that so much money is now tied up in nuclear energy, and so many reputations are at stake, that no one so far in the industry has had the guts to come clean. But the sands are running out.

You don't tell me whether you replied to Anderson's letter. Reading it made me so angry that I dashed off the attached draft reply for you to send if you thought it seemly – it needs toning down a bit. Writing it released some of the rage that would be better out than gnawing at my entrails.

I enclose an article which I wrote for the *Contemporary Review* that may interest you.

Yours sincerely
Kelvin Spencer

23 June 1983

To: Dr Nick Christofi,
Napier College,
Edinburgh,
Scotland.

Dear Dr Christofi,
I understand research is being done today on the safety of deep geological disposal of radioactive nuclear waste, *vis-à-vis* the effect of microbes living deep under the earth's surface and their effect on nuclear waste containers?

Please tell me, Dr Christofi, in all honesty do you think radioactive nuclear waste should be buried anywhere in Great Britain until all doubt concerning the containment of this nuclear waste has been removed?

I thank you most kindly for your prompt reply.
Yours sincerely,
Deirdre Rhys-Thomas

Napier College of Commerce and Technology
Edinburgh, Scotland
5 July 1983

Dear M/s Thomas
Thank you very much for your letter dated 23 June 1983 which was obviously prompted by an article which appeared in the *Guardian* on the same day.[34]

Please can I make it clear that the aim of my research on the effect of microorganisms on nuclear waste is to determine whether it would be safe to dispose of high level waste in deep geological containments. The disposal of high level waste in deep crystalline rocks is only an option and I can honestly say that if microorganisms are shown to have a negative effect on

109

containment then this option will no longer remain one.[35]

I have enclosed a recent publication of ours which shows that we are extensively researching the 'microbial connection' in deep subterranean environments.

Yours sincerely,

Dr N Christofi

Lecturer

Department of Biological Sciences

Note 34: Judy Redfearn, 'The Bugs in the Nuclear Bin', *Guardian*, 23 June 1983, p.13.

Note 35: For every substance that is buried in the ground, there exists a microbe that will break it down and bring it back into circulation; this is nature's recycling programme — nothing is wasted, it is simply transformed, as we know from the folk song 'On Ilkley Moor baht 'at' with the memorable line: 'Then't worms'll come and eat up thee.' This is even true of such stuff as stainless steel drums and radioactive wastes packed into them. The question is, how long does it take, and will the microbes carry atoms of plutonium, caesium, etc. away from the drums so that they get into groundwater? Groundwater, the water that collects under strata of rock beneath the soil, is a precious resource that cannot be replaced. In some areas of high rainfall it rises almost to the surface, and it could happen that if it is contaminated by microbes carrying bits of nuclear waste around, then the contamination would be recycled into the soil nutrients and absorbed by plants to be eaten by humans or their farm animals.

The Nuclear Industry Nuclear Waste Executive (NIREX) was set up in 1982 by BNFL, the CEGB, the South of Scotland Electricity Board (SSEB) and the United Kingdom Atomic Energy Authority (UKAEA) to implement the government's strategy for disposing of some of the low and intermediate-level radioactive wastes from the nuclear industry, hospitals, industry, research and defence. NIREX is at present trying to gain entry to three sites where they want to carry out geological surveys to see whether they are suitable for shallow or deep burial of nuclear waste. The people who live in the immediate neighbourhood do not want nuclear waste buried near them, because they do not consider that enough research has yet been done to prove that the waste will not get out of the containers.

10 August 1983

To: Dr N. Christofi
Napier College
Edinburgh Scotland

Dear Dr Christofi,
Thank you for your letter of 5 July, and for sending me a copy
of the Report January 1983. As I am sure you realise I am not
a scientist but I have read the Report and I would like to ask
you the following, so please bear with me!

It states, 'Alternatively, intermediate level waste might
consist of ion exchange resins or evaporator sludges
incorporated into a bitumen, resin or cement matrix in stacked
steel drums in a mine or cavern at a depth of ~0.5 km. In such
cases, a wide range of microbes would be expected to inhabit
such environmental niches naturally and, in addition, further
contamination with foreign microbial populations would result
from the repository mining and waste emplacement operations.
For any type of nuclear waste, the main purposes of the total
waste package is to prevent or minimise groundwater
penetration and retard any subsequent radionuclide removal.
Such containment may be considerably affected by the influence
of microbes on component materials.'
'. . . Finally it must be noted that the chemical speciation and
physical form of output nuclides will greatly affect behaviour in
the food chain and thus final uptake mechanisms and
consequent doses to man.'

As I understand research is still being carried out surely
doubts remain until all research has been completed? Aren't
NIREX and the UKAEA premature in their applications to be
made this year for planning permission for sites in Britain for
the underground storage of intermediate level nuclear waste?

How can they anticipate the results of research that is in its
infancy? The Report: 'A factor which has, to date, been largely
ignored in high/intermediate level nuclear waste management
research is the possible perturbation of "inorganic"
geochemistry caused by microbial populations.'
Yours sincerely,
Deirdre Rhys-Thomas

111

Institute of Geological Sciences[36]
Harwell Laboratory
Oxfordshire

8.9.83

Dear Ms. Rhys-Thomas,

Dr Christofi has passed your letter of 10th August to me for reply as the work Napier College is doing is under contract to the National Environment Research Council and he himself is not involved in the broader implications of the work to the waste management field.

As far as I am aware NIREX have stated that they hope to announce preferred sites for detailed evaluation later this year and not that they will be seeking planning permission for sites as you suggest in your letter. The NIREX evidence to the Sizewell Public Inquiry states that, for a shallow burial site, it is their intention to seek and have authorised new sites by 1990 (paragraph 78). For cheap underground burial they state that the initial selection of potentially suitable sites will be made on the basis of existing geological information and availability of sites. Final selection of a deep burial site in the UK will then be dependent upon the results of the detailed investigation of site geology (paragraph 87).

Thus for both the shallow and deep repository there will be a period during which detailed site evaluation will take place in order to provide the data needed for radiological safety assessment. This will provide time for research, such as that being undertaken by Dr Christofi and his group, to be completed.

Yours sincerely,
Dr J.D. Mather

Note 36 (Deirdre's note): I would have thought this would be an independent body with no links with the nuclear industry. That's what it sounds like. I now find that it shares the same telephone number and telex number as the Atomic Energy Research Establishment at Harwell.

30 May 1983

To: Mr W.E. Price,
Chief Executive,
Radnor District Council,
Llandrindod Wells, Powys.

Dear Mr Price,
I understand that in the event of a nuclear war you will be
designated District Wartime Controller. From the Government's
booklet *Protect and Survive* it looks as if the only place in our
house to make into an Inner Refuge is our downstairs
cloakroom. In no way will it accommodate 2 adults + 2
children + bedding + food + water containers.
    I have established that my building society does not grant
loans for the provision of nuclear shelters and there are no
government grants available for the provision of same.
    My family's best protection against radioactive fallout will
be in the ground floor/basement area of the Radnor District
Council offices at Llandrindod Wells which will double as a
nuclear shelter during a nuclear war.
    Many people will be in the same situation so I suppose it
will be 'first come, first served'. May I reserve my family's places
in your nuclear shelter?
    I am given to understand that we (the British people) will
have advance warning of a nuclear war of 3 weeks to 1 month,
or 7 to 10 days, or at the very worst 3 to 4 days so my family
will be able to get to Llandrindod Wells in plenty of time.
Yours sincerely,
Deirdre Rhys-Thomas

Radnor District Council
Llandrindod Wells
Powys
3rd June 1983

Dear Mrs Rhys-Thomas
I thank you for your letter of the 30th May.
    There are no proposals for using the basement of this
building as a shelter in the event of a nuclear war. In any event

113

it is totally suitable for that purpose and will offer little
protection against nuclear fall out.
      Yours sincerely
W.E. Price
Chief Executive Officer

                                                              6 June 1983

To: Hugh Richards,
Technical Adviser,
Central Wales Energy Group,
Llandrindod Wells,
Powys.

Dear Hugh Richards,
I have read that Sir Peter Hirsch, the new Chairman of the
Atomic Energy Authority, has said that underground sites will
be used for the disposal of intermediate radioactive nuclear
wastes. Apparently he said that local authorities must eventually
agree to this, 'I suspect there are ways of doing this by offering
them something' he said.
      Remembering that parts of Wales (Mid Wales?) were
considered for nuclear waste underground sites how concerned
should farmers, or anyone, or everyone living in Mid Wales be?
Yours sincerely,
Deirdre Rhys-Thomas

                                          Central Wales Energy Group
                                                  Llandrindod Wells
                                                             Powys

                                                       June 8th 1983

Dear Deirdre,
      The Disposal of Radioactive Waste
      The Government's new nuclear waste disposal agency, –
NIREX, is about to apply for planning permission for three sites
in Britain to dump all the intermediate and low level waste
resulting from the civil and military nuclear programmes.
CWEG's excellent 'guide to nuclear waste' leaflet (still available
from the above address) made it clear that it was the
intermediate waste that was the 'BIG' problem. There is already

114

over 35,000 cu metres of it, and there will be a great deal more once the decommissioning of old Magnox reactors starts, in a few years time.[37]

The Central Wales Energy Group has always maintained that the Government's geological investigations in Mid Wales have been directed to finding a site for the dumping of 'intermediate level' nuclear waste, rather than the 'high level' waste which was the supposed subject of their concern. The evidence for this is to be found in the Atomic Energy Authority's own (April 1979) booklet *Radioactive Waste*, which states that there are disadvantages in using clay-type rocks, such as those of Mid Wales, for high level waste because of the large amounts of heat emitted by that type of waste. The booklet goes on to say that clay-top rocks are very promising for the disposal of intermediate waste.

When overwhelming public pressure caused the Government to abandon its test drilling programme for high level waste disposal, in December 1981, the Minister for Local Government said that 'Appropriate provision will be made for the surface storage of vitrified waste. At the same time', he stated, 'priority will be given to the early disposal of those wastes with a lower level of radioactivity for which there is no technical advantage in delaying disposal.'

NIREX acknowledge that they may be forced to abandon the cheap option of burying the waste in existing mines and excavate deep repositories for intermediate level wastes. These involve a labyrinth of concrete-lined tunnels, 300 metres below ground, reached either by vertical shafts or by railway tracks in sloping tunnels. The repositories would be sealed with concrete, section by section, as they are filled, and the ILW would therefore not be retrievable.

By the year 2000 there will be at least 67,000 drums of intermediate nuclear waste containing large amounts of plutonium-239 and -240 and americium-241. The isotopes give off long-lasting alpha radiation and will remain dangerous for at least 3,000 years. The plutonium content of intermediate level waste is ten times greater, at the time of disposal, than that of high level waste at the same time. Although the total beta and gamma radioactivity of intermediate level waste is one thirtieth that of high level waste, some containers of ILW will have about the same amount of beta/gamma radioactivity. (Beta/gamma radioactivity, although it decays more rapidly than alpha, penetrates further, and requires greater shielding.)

A NIREX design study makes it clear that suitable sandstone areas are to be found in South Wales, and that the hard argillaceous rocks of Mid and North Wales are suitable for inland repositories. NIREX said in mid May that it intends to announce a short list of sites for waste disposal by the end of the summer.

The July 1982 White Paper 'Radioactive Waste Management' confirmed that the disposal of intermediate level radioactive waste was the immediate priority and also stated that 'there must be proper scope for public discussion.' The Association of County Councils recognising 'the intense public concern on all matters which touch upon radioactivity' have expressed considerable disappointment that the Government has included no local authority representatives on the Radioactive Waste Management Advisory Committee to reflect public concern.

Summary
(a) Unlike the long-term research into high level waste for disposal in the next century, the intermediate level waste is for 'early' disposal, with sites being announced within a few months.
(b) Although not as hazardous as high level waste, intermediate level waste must be isolated from mankind for at least 3,000 years. Some containers of intermediate waste *will* be as dangerous as high level waste.
(c) As with the proposals for high level waste disposal, the intermediate waste will be sealed in, and will not be retrievable should anything go wrong.
(d) The transport of enormous quantities of intermediate level waste is itself a hazard.
(e) Enormous quantities of rock (over 1M tons) would have to be excavated in order to create the underground radioactive waste dump. That would be roughly equivalent to the spoil from the Vale of Belvoir coalfield over its whole lifetime. It is doubtful whether this aspect alone would be acceptable in Mid Wales.
(f) It is difficult to see any objectors, including local authorities, being successful in blocking any proposal for intermediate level waste dumps, as Government approval for the detailed

waste management strategy will have been given before planning permission is applied for.

Having said that, we know that public opinion halted the high-level waste disposal programme, and forced the Government to take a more common sense attitude to its responsibilities.

Intermediate level waste should be stored at or near the surface, in the same way as high level waste, where it can be monitored, and dealt with in the event of a mishap.

Yours sincerely,

Hugh Richards MA BArch MRTPI
Technical Adviser

Note 37: Classifying nuclear wastes as 'low' or 'high' level is easier than deciding on a precise definition of 'intermediate'-level waste. Low-level waste comes from the nuclear power stations, hospitals, research laboratories, industry — anywhere that has a use for radio-isotopes, small quantities of radioactive materials used in a variety of ways. When the rubber gloves, overalls, dishes, bits of broken equipment and so on have a measurable degree of radiation, they are packed separately from ordinary rubbish, and sent to Sellafield for disposal in the special concrete trench at Drigg, Cumbria. This is the kind of waste that used to be dumped at sea, although sometimes intermediate-level waste was packed into drums of concrete and thrown overboard. Drigg is nearly filled to capacity, and the need for a low-level dumping site is pressing.

High-level waste is intensely hot and radioactive liquid, and at present comes only from reprocessing spent fuel rods. The plutonium is separated out, except for traces, but the remaining liquid contains equally toxic and more unstable chemicals. The plan is to mix this type of waste with glass, in small blocks, and keep it in a gas-cooled store where it can be guarded for several thousand years. If the fuel rods were not stripped down and dissolved in acid for reprocessing, they themselves would be classed as high-level waste. They can be kept in dry stores, as has been shown at Wylfa nuclear power station. In the US the fuel rods are stored without reprocessing, as uranium is cheap, and plutonium from them is not at present of any use.

The storage of radioactive waste containing plutonium is a hazardous business, as it takes only a small quantity of the stuff to form a 'critical mass' that can explode. There was a terrible accident at a Soviet military plant in the Urals in the winter of 1957/8 when a nuclear waste store exploded caused so much contamination that 30 small towns disappeared from the maps of the region, and to this day anyone driving a car through the area is told to keep the windows closed and not stop.

A similar accident in the United States was narrowly avoided by a clean-up operation costing $2 million. Drums of low-level waste had been buried in a trench at Hanford, Washington, where there is a big military nuclear complex. Scientists thought that the plutonium would stay where it was, in the drums, but with time the drums corroded, the plutonium seeped out and when the dump was flooded after heavy snow plutonium gathered in clumps. It is a mistake to think that objects buried in the ground stay where they are put.

See Medvedev, Zhores, *Nuclear Disaster in the Urals*, W.W. Norton, New York, 1979. See also Chudleigh, Renée and William Cannell, *The Gravedigger's Dilemma*, obtainable from Friends of the Earth, 377 City Road, London EC1, from which the accompanying illustration is taken.

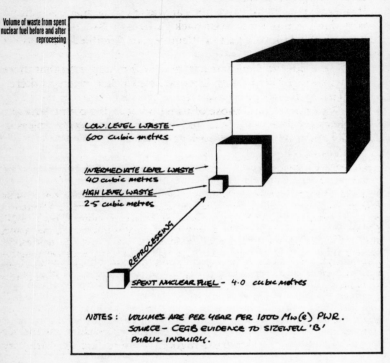

Volume of waste from spent nuclear fuel before and after reprocessing

LOW LEVEL WASTE
600 cubic metres

INTERMEDIATE LEVEL WASTE
40 cubic metres

HIGH LEVEL WASTE
2·5 cubic metres

REPROCESSING

SPENT NUCLEAR FUEL - 4·0 cubic metres

NOTES: VOLUMES ARE PER YEAR PER 1000 Mw(e) PWR.
SOURCE - CEGB EVIDENCE TO SIZEWELL 'B'
PUBLIC INQUIRY.

6 June 1983

To: Sir Peter Hirsch,
Chairman,
Atomic Energy Authority
London

Dear Sir Peter Hirsch,
If intermediate radioactive nuclear waste can be made so safe
why don't you put it in your back garden, or No. 10's, or
beneath the hallowed turf of Wembley, or Wimbledon, or
Lord's.
    Have not the *New Scientist* and *Atom*[38] reported that there
are as many problems with intermediate nuclear waste as there
are with high level nuclear waste?
    Why then should those of us who live in the country have
our back gardens made into nuclear dumping grounds, unless it
is your intention to use city/urban areas?
Yours sincerely,
Deirdre Rhys-Thomas

Note 38: *ATOM* is the monthly magazine of the United Kingdom Atomic
Energy Authority, and is available free from: Paul Fielding, Information
Services Branch, UKAEA, 11 Charles II Street, London SW1Y 4QP.
Although it is pro-nuclear it is a very readable and interesting magazine,
and invaluable for its reporting of conferences, and inquiries such as the
present Inquiry at Thurso into the plan to build a European Demonstration Reprocessing Plant to deal with fuel rods from French and German
Fast Breeder Reactors. There is also a summary of debates in the Houses
of Parliament.

AERE Harwell, Oxfordshire
United Kingdom Atomic Energy Authority

21st June 1983

Dear Ms Rhys-Thomas,
Sir Peter Hirsch has asked me to reply to your letter of 6th June.
    The technology for disposing of low and intermediate level
waste is comparatively simple and can be summed up as burying
it at a sufficient depth within a suitable container. Present
technology can guarantee the safety of such an operation. There
is no technical reason why intermediate level waste repositories
should not be located at any site where the geology is suitable.

No sites for such repositories have yet been chosen. The Nuclear Industry Radioactive Waste Executive (NIREX) expects to make proposals later in the year for the detailed geological investigation of a few preferred sites.[39]

Yours sincerely,

L E J. Roberts
Director

Note 39: Anyone reading this bland reply would think that low and intermediate level waste could very well be buried under Wembley or Wimbledon provided the geology was suitable. We need to ask —

1 Simple compared to what?
2 what is a sufficient depth?
3 what is a suitable container?

This answer completely ignores the migration of radioactive chemicals in burial sites, the influence of water, and the work of microbes in their recycling of nature's building blocks, the atoms of which everything living or dead is made and constantly re-made.

21 November 1983

To: Mr. J.H. Harvey-Jones,
Chairman of ICI,
International Chemical Industries
London

Dear Mr Harvey-Jones,

I want you to promise me that as the Chairman of ICI you will not store nuclear waste in the ICI Billingham mine until the research on the microbiological aspects of nuclear waste disposal is completed.

This is a factor which has, to date, been largely ignored in high/intermediate level nuclear waste management research (ref. Progress Report, Jan.1983, Institute of Geological Sciences, Harwell). This crucial research is as yet in its early stages.

Why you may wonder am I so concerned? Because for several years I have been concerned about the radioactive discharges from Windscale into the Irish Sea.[40] Letters from the CEGB etc. assuring me of the reliability of NCRP and Dept of Agriculture monitoring and controls did not allay my instinctive fears as a Mother that my children's World was not in safe-keeping.

Yesterday I read – front page of the *Observer*[41] – that for all the Government controls the state-owned BNFL standards are inadequate.

That is why I need your promise, Mr Harvey-Jones, that there will be no parallel in the storage of nuclear waste underground.

Yours sincerely,
Deirdre Rhys-Thomas

Note 40: On 14 November 1983 at 10.00 a.m. members of Greenpeace in a small boat were attempting to plug the end of the pipeline through which Sellafield wastes are pumped out to sea. The reprocessing plant was closed for its annual maintenance and washing down of the pipes and equipment. During the year 'crud' – lumps of sticky high-level waste – builds up in the pipes, and solvents used to extract some of the radioactive isotopes accumulate in the tanks. The level of radioactivity inside the buildings would reach unacceptable heights if the equipment was not cleaned thoroughly, but the solvents and the solid lumps of crud are not supposed to be flushed out to sea, they should be separated and transferred to the high-level waste tanks.

This year the operation was performed very carelessly, and the Greenpeace boat found itself in contact with a slick coming up from the pipelines, which they monitored for radioactivity. The contamination was so high that later that week when a second slick was blown towards the shore, the beaches became so 'hot' that they had to be closed to the public for six months. BNFL were prosecuted for failing to keep the discharges to 'as low as reasonably achievable', and fined £10,000. Greenpeace was prosecuted for attempting to sabotage the pipeline and were fined £50,000 but they were let off after paying £36,000.

The discharge of solvent to sea could be responsible for the build-up of plutonium found on shore, where it dries out into dust and is blown into people's houses.

Note 41: Geoffrey Lean, 'Windscale Crackdown', *Observer*, 20 November 1983, p.1.

Imperial Chemical Industries
London
29th November 1983

Dear Mrs Rhys-Thomas,
Thank you very much for your letter relating to the NIREX proposal to store nuclear waste in the Billingham mine. As you will know from recent press comments, ICI has no wish to use this mine for this purpose. This, you will notice, is confirmed in the attached copy of the Company's statement of 25th October.

121

We intend to satisfy ourselves on a number of factors relating to safety and we are aware that there has been reference recently in some learned journals on the relationship between microbiological activity and nuclear waste. This is one of the aspects which, if NIREX proceed with the proposal, we shall take into account when ICI makes its own assessment.

I trust that this gives you the assurance which you require.

Yours sincerely,

J.H. Harvey-Jones, MBE

Chairman

6 June 1983

To: Mr Denis Chamberlain,
The Editor,
Farmer's Weekly,
Sutton,
Surrey

Dear Mr Chamberlain,
Living in a sheep-rearing area, where most sheep graze on hills,
could the *Farmer's Weekly* advise me on how to protect
livestock from radioactive fallout should there be a nuclear
accident: we have at least two nuclear power stations here in
Wales.
    I was interested to hear recently, I think it was the Minister
of Agriculture, say on the radio that to protect livestock from
radioactive fallout they should be driven into a valley and a
tarpaulin covering should be erected over them.
    I thank you.
Yours sincerely,
Deirdre Rhys-Thomas

Farmer's Weekly
Sutton
Surrey
June 14 1983

Dear Ms Rhys-Thomas
Many thanks for your letter of June 6.
    I cannot give you any details at the moment, but we will be
running an article on this subject during the next few weeks and
I hope you will find it useful.[42]
Yours sincerely,
Denis Chamberlain
Editor

Note 42: See 'The Grim Reaper', *Farmer's Weekly*, 30 September 1983,
pp. 166-7.

14 June 1983

To: Kelvin McKenzie,
The Editor,
The Sun,
London

Dear Mr McKenzie,
I do not buy *The Sun* as my local knacker uses it to wrap up meat for my Beagle puppy.

In yesterday's wrapping the front page story was of an attack made on Mr Heseltine by the peace women at Greenham Common.

Now I am sure that as a well-informed editor you are well aware of the eye-witness accounts made by the Ministry of Defence and the Chief Inspector that Mr Heseltine was 'certainly not pulled down' and certainly not attacked by the women of Greenham Common.

Why then, Mr McKenzie, did you print such an untrue story?
Yours sincerely
Deirdre Rhys-Thomas

The Sun
News Group Newspapers Ltd
A Subsidiary of News International Ltd
London

20 June, 1983

Dear Ms. Rhys-Thomas,
The *Sun*, like other newspapers, received several letters about the demonstration at Newbury in February and all of them were answered at the time.

These exchanges of correspondence were monitored on two occasions by the Press Council.

They may be able to assist you. I do suggest, however, that you show more courtesy in your letter to them than you did in your cheap shot at us.
Yours sincerely,
Kenneth Donlan
Managing Editor

22 June 1983

To: Kenneth Donlan
Managing Director,
The Sun,
London

Dear Mr Donlan,
I thank you for your letter of 20 June.
      I do not understand your cheap shot remark.
      Is it my reference to my local knacker using the *Sun* to wrap up my dog's food? I'm sorry but it's a fact. I do not go in for distortion.
      Or is it my request for an explanation as to why the *Sun*'s account of an alleged attack by Greenham Common women on Mr Heseltine and the first-hand eye witnesses accounts of what happened were so different?
      I would hope that an Editor accepting responsibility for the story would be prepared to justify its printing.
Yours courteously,
Deirdre Rhys-Thomas

The Sun
News Group Newspapers Ltd
A Subsidiary of News International Ltd
London

July 5th, 1983

Dear Mrs Rhys-Thomas,
      Your letter of June 22nd, 1983, was a better presentation. I am now prepared, however, to respond to your point as well as repeating that the Press Council members have already monitored your belated complaint.
      The coverage of the demonstration against Mr Heseltine caused controversy by the nature of the event. The Minister tripped and fell because of the unpleasant scenes arising from the large crowd of demonstrators.
      I have no more to add to our correspondence.
Yours sincerely,
Kenneth Donlan,
Managing Editor

125

22 June 1983

To: Mr Morgan
Director,
The Press Council
London

Dear Mr Morgan,
I would be most grateful for your help.

At the suggestion of Mr Kenneth Donlan, Managing Editor of the *Sun*, I enclose letters.

I would be the first to admit that I don't fully understand the workings of Fleet Street, but I had hoped that a newspaper having printed a story would have seen fit to justify it.

I thank you.
Yours sincerely,
Deirdre Rhys-Thomas

The Press Council
London

24 Jun 83

Dear Ms Rhys-Thomas,
Thank you for your letter of 22 June 83 with enclosures regarding coverage of Mr Michael Heseltine's visit to Newbury on 7 Feb 83 in *The Sun*.

I am bound to tell you that any complaint about this would now be out of time as there is a two month time limit for the presentation of a complaint to the Council.

However, you will be pleased to know that the Council is investigating a complaint made by another complainant about this matter, and that investigation is now well advanced.

Yours sincerely,
[illegible signature]
Assistant Secretary

16 May 1983

To: Mr William Rees-Mogg,
Chairman,
The Arts Council of Great Britain,
London W1

Dear Mr Rees-Mogg,
Why would Britain become an ineffective member of the
Western Alliance if she rejected her nuclear weapons and
unilaterally disarmed?

Canada has unilaterally disarmed, has no nuclear weapons
and I think would take great exception to being told she is 'an
ineffective member of NATO'. Canada takes a conventionally
active part in NATO.

As for your criticism of the Soviet Union in using
biochemical weapons after the 1976 Biological Weapons
Convention came into effect. Did not America use defoliating
chemicals, e.g. Agent Orange, spread indiscriminately from the
air gallon by gallon, causing massive environmental damage and
genetic damage to newborn babies in Vietnam? Prohibited by
the 1925 Geneva Convention?

Surely it's about time we all made an honest attempt to
look at all our shortcomings, of friends and foes alike? There is
absolutely no chance of disarmament if we continue as we are.
Yours sincerely,
Deirdre Rhys-Thomas

Arts Council of Great Britain
London W.1
1 June 1983

Dear Miss Rhys-Thomas,
Thank you very much for your letter. Canada has remained a
part of the NATO defence system in which different countries
have adopted different roles, some effective, some ineffective.
Britain has at present an effective role, and for Britain to reject
American bases would inevitably have a severely disruptive
effect on NATO. The difference between the biological weapons
that have been used by the Soviet Union and the defoliating
chemicals used by the United States is that the biological

weapons were designed to kill people; defoliating agents were
designed to kill leaves.
Yours sincerely,
William Rees-Mogg
Chairman

14 June, 1983

To: Anthony Tucker,
Science Correspondent,
The Guardian,
London

Dear Anthony Tucker,
I have been informed by Sir William Rees-Mogg that 'The
difference between the biological weapons that have been used
by the Soviet Union and the defoliating chemicals used by the
United States is that the biological weapons were designed to
kill people; defoliating agents were designed to kill leaves.'
    I had understood from reports that since Agent Orange had
been used in Vietnam by the United States many Vietnamese
children had been born with severe handicaps?
    And regarding the biological weapon, yellow rain, I seem
to remember hearing an American scientist say, only last week,
something about bee excreta and yellow rain/U.S.S.R./Indo-
China?
    Perhaps I am not alone in having doubts when the Super
Powers indulge in their tit-for-tat dialogue.
Yours sincerely,
Deirdre Rhys-Thomas

The Guardian
London
July 7 1983

Dear Deirdre Rhys-Thomas,
    It seems that Rees-Mogg has either failed to examine the
issues properly or is simply voicing a politically expedient
position. The defoliating agents, as everyone knows, were
designed to keep tracts of forest cleared of natural growth and
people. By depriving the Vietnamese people of their food crops
and, incidentally creating conditions in which badly

contaminated foodstuffs were eaten by humans and by wildlife or stock, enormous harm was wrought. We do not know how many humans died through direct or indirect effects, but the numbers are probably very large.

In contrast the 'yellow rain' accusations appear to have no authenticated basis and may, in fact, be no more than fabrication. The article I said that I hope to write for the *Guardian* on this subject came to nothing because we had already carried a news story from the US. However I am enclosing a copy of a note on the subject which I wrote for the journal *Doctor* together with a copy of a rather more recent 'round up' of the bee excrement theory from the US journal *Science*. The bee theory does not, of course, exclude the possibility that biological agents have been used by the USSR in Southeast Asia. It is to me rather significant, however, that British attempts to recover toxins on foliage, analysed at Porton, have all been negative.

Yours sincerely,
Anthony Tucker
Science Correspondent

30 June 1983

To: The Prime Minister, The Hon. Mrs. Indira Gandhi,
The Prime Minister's House,
New Delhi,
India.

Madam Prime Minister,
In spite of elaborate communications – satellites, telexes – the peoples of the World seem to be becoming more insular and nationalistic.

Instead of releasing the Doves of Peace we release the Hounds of War. No longer is offered the olive branch: we offer nuclear weapons.

Madam Prime Minister, if India acquired nuclear weapons do you think it would make the people of India feel more peaceful? And does the number of people dying of starvation decrease in proportion to the number of nuclear weapons?

I thank you.
Yours sincerely,
Deirdre Rhys-Thomas

Dear Miss Rhys-Thomas,
Your letter of the 30th June shows astounding lack of knowledge about India's policies and attitudes.

Apart from Japan, India is the only country which has taken a firm stand against nuclear warfare and has been consistently working for disarmament.[43]

We use nuclear energy for energy, for agriculture, for medicine. Our policy and our intention is to use it only for peaceful and developmental purposes. However, you are right in saying that in spite of sophisticated communications, nations are becoming more insular in their outlook. The advanced ones want to use their technological supremacy to dominate others.

Yours sincerely,
Indira Gandhi

Note 43: During the period when Indira Gandhi was at the height of her powers as Prime Minister of India, an atomic device was exploded. The fissile material had been developed from the fuel used in civil nuclear reactors, and the device was claimed to be for 'peaceful' uses. Some political observers thought that it might also warn Pakistan that India could build nuclear weapons.

10 July 1983

To: His Holiness, The Pope,
The Vatican,
Rome,
Italy.

Your Holiness,
Though I am not a Roman Catholic I still treasure the times I spent wandering and resting in St Peter's Square. (For months in the late 1960s I lived in Piazza Risorgimento, near to The Vatican.)

I remember joining the crowds on Sundays to receive The Blessing, so many people, from so many countries, not speaking the same language but smiling at each other, standing closely together at Peace.

Now as the Mother of two sons – 14 and 10 years – I question the values I have given them – of caring, loving, reasoning with others, not fighting, thinking of the world's peoples, not being nationalistic.

My sons tell me they only see adults bullying, threatening each other, countries solving their arguments not by reasoning but fighting, so why shouldn't they follow in these adults' footsteps?

After all, they say to me, is there a magic age – 15, 16, 17, 18 – when a child should put away their childhood values?

Their greatest fear is nuclear war. For my sons and the frightened children of the world, Holy Father, could you not invite Mr Andropov and President Reagan to openly speak with each other keeping this thought uppermost in their minds to the exclusion of their Communist/Capitalist conditioning?
Deirdre Rhys-Thomas

Secretariat of State
From The Vatican,
1 August 1983

Dear Mrs Rhys-Thomas,
His Holiness Pope John Paul II has received your kind letter and he has directed me to reply in his name.

His Holiness wishes you to know that he appreciates the sentiments which prompted you to write to him, and he invokes God's blessings upon you and your family.

Yours sincerely,
Mgr R. Marsiglio
Department Head

15 July 1983

To: Dr David Owen, M.P.
Leader of the SDP,
The House of Commons,
London

Dear Dr David Owen,
Why do you belong to the Chorus of Cruise Supporters?
The NATO Chief of Staff, the President of the USA, the

Prime Minister all sing the praises of Cruise. Where is it written 'Thou Shalt Have Cruise', on Tablets of Stone?

Are not the dictats of pro-nuclear deterrence nothing more than people's personal opinions?

Yours sincerely,

Deirdre Rhys-Thomas

From The Rt Hon Dr David Owen MP
House of Commons
London SW1A 0AA
9th August, 1983

Dear Deirdre Rhys-Thomas,

You wrote to me about Cruise missiles. It is a pity that you didn't take the trouble to find out my views before labelling me rather offensively as belonging to the 'Chorus of Cruise Supporters'.

What I have supported and continue to uphold is the 1979 NATO decision to deploy Cruise and Pershing, if there had been no agreement in the INF talks in Geneva by the end of 1983. I don't want to deploy Cruise and I still hope we shall see some kind of interim agreement along the lines of the informal package put forward by the US negotiator Paul Nitze in his now famous 'walk in the woods'. But I don't believe the way to get concessions from the Soviet Union on their own deployment of SS20's, which was after all the original purpose of the 1979 NATO decision, is to announce before the INF talks have failed that we renounce totally any deployment of Cruise.[44]

Even in the event of the INF talks failing to produce an outcome, the SDP would still not automatically deploy Cruise. We went into this in some detail in the SDP White Paper on Defence and Disarmament in Europe and I am sending you the relevant extract. I do hope this will enable you to more clearly understand my position.

Yours sincerely,

David Owen

Note 44: In 1979 NATO agreed to 'modernise' the armed forces in Europe by taking delivery of new missiles, Cruise and Pershing, which because they were able to be used to destroy military targets in the USSR, made it possible for NATO to think about a first use in case of war. Cruise missiles fly low and are difficult for radar to detect, and they fall within 300 feet of the selected target — in theory, that is, but in practice they have been found to have a high failure rate. They can be launched from huge lorries parked anywhere in the country, hidden by trees so invisible to enemy satellites.

The USSR are more worried about the Pershing missiles being deployed in West Germany, because they are capable of reaching Moscow in four minutes.

While Cruise and Pershing were being developed, arms talks between the US and USSR went on intermittently. They were the Indetermediate Range Nuclear Forces Talks (INF) and the United States Arms Control and Disarmament Agency's representative was Paul Nitze, who had long been associated with diplomacy between the two superpowers. At one point in the negotiations, Nitze and his Russian counterpart left the formality of the negotiating table and went for 'a walk in the woods', where they were able to approach a basis for agreement, only to be pulled back to their respective capitals by their Governments.

In fact, soon after the deployment of Pershing missiles in West Germany the USSR withdrew from the INF talks in protest.

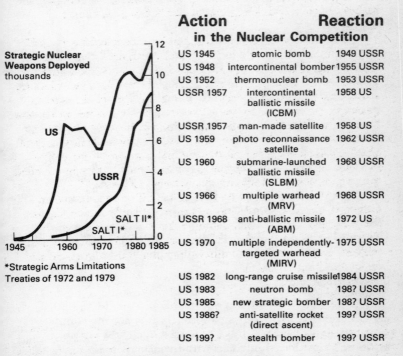

Action   Reaction
in the Nuclear Competition

Strategic Nuclear Weapons Deployed thousands

US 1945	atomic bomb	1949 USSR
US 1948	intercontinental bomber	1955 USSR
US 1952	thermonuclear bomb	1953 USSR
USSR 1957	intercontinental ballistic missile (ICBM)	1958 US
USSR 1957	man-made satellite	1958 US
US 1959	photo reconnaissance satellite	1962 USSR
US 1960	submarine-launched ballistic missile (SLBM)	1968 USSR
US 1966	multiple warhead (MRV)	1968 USSR
USSR 1968	anti-ballistic missile (ABM)	1972 US
US 1970	multiple independently-targeted warhead (MIRV)	1975 USSR
US 1982	long-range cruise missile	1984 USSR
US 1983	neutron bomb	198? USSR
US 1985	new strategic bomber	198? USSR
US 1986?	anti-satellite rocket (direct ascent)	199? USSR
US 199?	stealth bomber	199? USSR

SALT II*
SALT I*

*Strategic Arms Limitations Treaties of 1972 and 1979

(Source: Ruth Leger Sivard, *World Military and Social Expenditures 1985*, World Priorities Inc., 1986.)

24 April 1984

To: The Foreign Minister of the U.S.S.R, Mr Gromyko,
The Foreign Ministry,
The Kremlin, Moscow,
U.S.S.R.

Dear Mr Gromyko,
Today there is a promise of summer – of sun-filled days, of days lying in the sun switching the brain off. No thinking. But always in the back of one's head, like a cancer, is the threat of nuclear war.

There is no promise of a stop to the nuclear arms race. No promise for my sons, no promise for Russian children, no promise for your grandchildren, Mr Gromyko? For American children, for all children?

I am so weary of megaphone rhetoric of today's leading politicians. I ask you Mr Gromyko to think of my 2 sons, Theo and Toby, who fear nuclear war.

I know in my heart that other Mothers like me, in those dark moments that won't go away, fear for their children's futures.

I send my concern to you and your family.
Yours sincerely,
Deirdre Rhys-Thomas

St John's Wood Park
London NW8

3rd May 1984

Dear Deirdre Rhys-Thomas,
Thank you for your letter. I am afraid you took a wrong way of channelling your letter to Mr. Gromyko. I think that the address which is on it, is correct, and there are a lot of English-speaking people in the ministry.

As you sent the letter to me, may I make some comments on it. It seems to me that you put the blame equally on both sides, and it is a totally wrong approach. It is not my country that started nuclear race. If we produced nuclear weapons it was only to be able to catch up with the newest weapons, invented by the U.S.A. And the sole reason of having them is to be able to deter nuclear blackmail and to defend ourselves. If

134

you look carefully at the history of nuclear race, you will understand, that the U.S.A. were always to be the first in introducing of new kinds of nuclear armaments. And it is not my country which refuses for nuclear freeze and for a treaty for no first use. In fact, the U.S.S.R took a unilateral obligation for no first use, but unfortunately N.A.T.O.'s strategy in Europe is based on the idea of using nuclear armaments.

Yours faithfully,
Vladimir Skossyrev
Izvestia Correspondent in U.K.

P.S. I would like to add, that I fully understand your anxiety for the future of your children.

10 July 1983

To: Group Captain Leonard Cheshire, V.C., D.S.O., D.F.C.,
The Leonard Cheshire Foundation,
London

Dear Group Captain Cheshire,
I understand you were an official British observer when the atomic bomb was dropped on Nagasaki, in 1945.[45]

Would you be so kind as to tell me were you as an official observer told beforehand what kind of damage the atomic bomb would do?

Or did it come as a complete surprise to you to see that the civilian population of Nagasaki – inevitably children, pregnant women, doctors, old and disabled had been killed in such great numbers, and so many others permanently damaged by the radioactive dust?

Yours sincerely,
Deirdre Rhys-Thomas

Note 45: From 1943 on the development of fissile material to make the atom bomb followed two different paths of research in a joint US, British and European programme called the Manhattan Project. One group of scientists worked to build a plant that would separate the heavy, stable isotope U238 from the fissile and fractionally lighter form of the metal – U235. This uranium was made into the first device exploded at Los Alamos to test the theory, and into the bomb called 'Little Boy' that was dropped on Hiroshima on 6 August 1945. Another group worked to produce plutonium in a nuclear reactor built under the football stadium of Chicago; at that time the reactor was called an atomic pile, but the basic technology was the same. The plutonium, about 4½ kgms, was made into another bomb, called 'Fat Man' that was dropped on Nagasaki on 9 August 1945.

From the beginning of the Manhattan Project all nuclear information was 'born classified', and the secrecy persists. The US occupation forces used over 85,000 feet of 16mm film to document the effects of the bombs, but this film only became public in 1980, following the Freedom of Information Act. On 19 September 1945 an American research team moved into Hiroshima and set up the Atomic Bomb Casualty Commission (ABCC). They collected data on injuries, deaths and all other health factors experienced by the irradiated population. They did not set up medical centres to treat the sick or wounded, and many of their early pronouncements have since been found to be wrong. Although similar research was officially prohibited to the Japanese, a few surviving doctors carried out their own studies of the people's health. For example, a small book containing the stories of 164 survivors was published in 1950, but it was immediately suppressed by the occupation forces and not rediscovered until 1981. The ABCC was reorganised in the late 1970s with the Japanese assuming overall direction of the work, and renamed the Radiation Effects Research Foundation, but it is still partly funded by the US National Academy of Sciences.

In practice, the data from the two bombs has provided a fruitful field of research and many careers have been constructed on it. See Burchett, Wilfred, *Shadows of Hiroshima*, Verso, London, 1983.

London SW1
19th July, 1983

Dear Miss Rhys-Thomas,

Yes, it is quite true that I was one of the two official British observers at the dropping of the atomic bomb in 1945.

Before answering your question, however, may I ask you one so that I know what common ground there is between us. Do you think that Britain was right in using armed force to oppose Hitler's plan for the conquest of Europe and Russia and for the elimination of whole sections of society, such as Jews, gypsies, the entire Polish nation and others whom he considered unfit to be members of the human family? Going to war would inevitably cause enormous loss of civilian life, whilst not going to war would allow Hitler to fulfil his terrible plans. Between 1933 and 1945 he exterminated more than 20 million people in his concentration camps.

The point is that one needs to determine one's moral stance in respect of the rights and wrongs of a conventional defence before moving to the still greater moral dilemma of nuclear weapons.

I would appreciate hearing your considered comments on this point and will then write to you further.

Yours sincerely,
Leonard Cheshire

9 August 1983

To: Group Captain Leonard Cheshire, V.C., D.S.O., D.F.C.,
The Leonard Cheshire Foundation,
London SW1

Dear Group Captain Cheshire,
Thank you for your letter of 19 July.

I think it was inevitable but not right that Britain used armed force to oppose Hitler. Man has conditioned himself to war-making.

I think it was not right and not inevitable that the atom bombs were used on Japan. Knowing now that the Prime Minister of Japan sent a cable to Stalin expressing the desire to end the war quickly; this cable was shown to Truman at the Potsdam Conference on 18 July, having already been intercepted and decoded by the USA.

Also learning that there was quite probably an experimental element in the dropping of the atom bombs by the Allies, in so far as in the second atom bomb plutonium was used instead of uranium.

I would like to read all those papers recording the events and build up to the Second World War (from 1933 to 1939) to better understand how the good men let Hitler grow in power.

I can't help wondering what would have been the course of events if the Allies had agreed to a cancellation of reparations — temporarily stopped by the Hoover moratorium?

People who defend the nuclear stance always harp back to the Second World War as a means of justification for nuclear preparedness but surely this logic should be examined more carefully: is it not likely that Hitler would have used the atom bomb in spite of nuclear parity, deterrence, on the basis that he was mad?

Yours sincerely,
Deirdre Rhys-Thomas

London SW1
16th August, 1983

Dear Miss Rhys-Thomas,
I was pleased to receive your letter of 9th August and appreciate the sincerity with which you write and the obvious thought that you have given to this most difficult and distressing issue.

I wholeheartedly agree with the question you raise about how it was that the 'Allies', if I may call them this, allowed Hitler to grow in power and bluff his way into a position where he was able to reverse all the military odds in his favour. Undoubtedly the fact that there was an unjust element to the Versailles Treaty gave him a power base which otherwise I personally do not think he would have had. Lord Home has just written an excellent book, *Letters to a Grandson* which record in a very personal way some of the factors that contributed towards the tragedy of World War II.

However, I wonder whether you are really convinced that once Hitler had set about the armed conquest of Europe it was wrong to attempt to stop him. The basic problem is that man has conditioned himself to use armed force in pursuit of his goals, knowing that only superior force will stop him. Would the world really be a better place if arms were left to the sole possession of those who had evil and aggressive intentions against their neighbours? It is a great dilemma, I know, but one that we need to face and answer as honestly as we can.

A little while ago I was asked to give a talk at a City church on this question and I am taking liberty of enclosing a copy with this letter. You may well not want to read such a lengthy document but it sets out my own views as I have struggled to form over the past 40 years. I would be very interested in your comments on it.

I don't think there is any question that Hitler would have used an atom bomb, had both he and the Allies possessed an atomic capability of approximate parity. Perhaps one can say that he was mad in respect of what he wanted to do to the world around him, but he was very rational and logical in the steps he took to attain his goal. Witness the way he got the better of the rest of us until finally defeated on the battlefield. Witness also the fact that he used gas to destroy his helpless victims (in the concentration camps) but never used it when there was the possibility of retaliation. In my own view no

138

nation would ever deliberately take a step that they knew would bring about their own destruction, however fanatical they might be. My own belief is that war of any kind between major powers is no longer possible because of the danger of escalation to all out nuclear war which inevitably means self destruction. I have just completed a paper on this subject, which is to be published by the Catholic International Justice and Peace Commission later in the year, and should you wish I would be happy to send you an advance copy.

Regarding the atom bomb against Japan, I can assure you that there was no experimental element of any kind: I know at first hand the agonising that went into the decision as to whether to drop the bomb in the hope that it would bring the war to an end or to proceed with the frontal assault on the mainland of Japan, at a probable cost of 3 million lives, most of them civilians. It is not strictly true that the Prime Minister of Japan cabled Stalin saying that he wanted to end the war quickly. The Japanese Ambassador spoke to Molotov at about the time of Potsdam to see if there were favourable terms under which Japan could disengage, but Molotov never passed the message on. In any case by this time the Japanese military command was in control of the politicians and had made up its mind to fight to the last man rather than surrender. You may recall that when, after the second atom bomb, the Emperor surrendered, the military high command rebelled against the decision – in Japanese terms an almost unbelievable act.

With kind regards.
Yours sincerely,
Leonard Cheshire.

1 August 1983

To: The Rt Hon. Sir Harold Macmillan, FRS,
London

Dear Sir Harold,
My sons have been looking at press cuttings of their Grandfather as Chairman of The Thomas Hardy Festival Council and as the 'Mayor of Casterbridge'. Several photos showing him with you, Sir Harold, The President of The Thomas Hardy Festival.

My eldest son has just read a book about Britain's

involvement in the nuclear arms race, *Overkill*. Words you wrote as Prime Minister to President Kennedy about nuclear weapons are quoted –

> If all this capacity for destruction is spread around the world in the hands of all kinds of different characters – dictators, reactionaries, revolutionaries, madmen – then sooner or later, and certainly I think by the end of this century, either by error or insanity, the great crime will be committed.

My son and I share your views. Do you have any words of comfort for us as unwilling participants in this nuclear race? The sweet voice of reason seems to fall on deaf ears, today.
Yours sincerely,
Deirdre Rhys-Thomas

From the Rt Hon. Harold Macmillan, O.M.
1st September 1983

Dear Mrs Thomas,
    Mr Macmillan, who is presently resting in the country, has asked me to write and apologize for the delay in replying to your letter of the 1st August.
    The words you quote were, of course, addressed to President Kennedy by him when he was urging the negotiations which led to the Test Ban Treaty. This, at least, was a partial contribution to the problem. Meanwhile Mr Macmillan feels that the West must continue its nuclear defence but it should be ready to enter into and promote further negotiations at any time for the reduction of nuclear weapons and looking into the far future for their final abolition.
Yours sincerely,
Rosemary Annetti
Personal Secretary

11 August 1983

To: Mr Kevin McGinley, Chairman, British Nuclear Tests
Veterans Association,
Dunoon,
Argyll.

Dear Mr McGinley,
Last week I saw a news item on Channel 4 News about the
present circumstances of some of the men who were in the
British Forces and present at the nuclear tests conducted by the
British on Christmas Island, in the Pacific, and in Australia, and
who now believe they are suffering medical effects from
radiation. I understand a Nuclear Test Veterans Association has
been started.

On the off-chance that you have not heard of it, but I
expect you have, I recently read of a recent Congressional
hearing held in America at which it was reported that the Safety
Chief at the first post-war atomic bomb test warned in 1946
that the health of 42,000 servicemen could be jeopardised by
radiation fallout. The report said he was ignored.[46]

Obviously as the British nuclear tests were conducted after
1945 the British Servicemen were given full advice on safety
precautions to be followed?
Yours sincerely,
Deirdre Rhys-Thomas

Note 46: Among books published about the experiences of the
servicemen who took part in the British programme of nuclear tests, are:
Robinson, Derek, *Just Testing*, Collins Harvill, London, 1985; Smith,
Joan, *Clouds of Deceit: The Deadly Legacy of Britain's Bomb Tests*,
Faber & Faber, London, 1985; Blakeway, Denys and Lloyd-Roberts, Sue,
Fields of Thunder, London, 1985; Milliken, Robert, *No Conceivable
Injury*, Penguin, Australia, 1986. The information on which these books
are based came to light during the Royal Commission set up by the
Australian Government to examine the events connected with the British
atomic tests carried out in Australia between 1952 and 1958. One of the
documents declassified in 1984 and made available to the Royal
Commission was a hitherto top secret report by the Defence Research
Policy Committee dating from May 1953. The report spelled out what the
military and civil service departments in Britain wanted to know about
the effects of atomic weapons on ships, aircraft, tanks, and men: 'The
army must discover the detailed effects of various types of explosion on
equipment, stores and men with and without various types of protection.'
Some newspapers interpreted this 'shopping list' as a demand for
experiments involving human guinea pigs, although witnesses at the

141

hearings pointed out that at no time were unprotected troops placed close to any British atomic blasts – the information was obtained by using dummies and animals.

Treasurer: Rita Dale
Committee Advisers: Mrs. R. Dale,
Mr R. Tarrant, Geraldine
Semke (Widow), Dan Brown,
Mike Doyle
Solicitor: Mark Mildred Q.C.
Scientific Adviser: Dr. Alice Stewart

British Nuclear Tests
Veterans Association
Dunoon
Argyll

18 August 1983

Dear Deirdre,
If you don't mind me calling you by your christian name!
Thank you for your letter which I received and appreciate your interest shown.

We sent two members of our Association to Washington on May 24th 1983 to attend, at the invitation of NAAV (our American Test Veterans) the Congressional Hearing. We also have copies which are known as the 'Warren Papers'.

I also have the knowledge that the tests held after 1945 conducted in Nevada 1957, Monte Bello 1952, Maralinga 1956, Malden Isles and of course Christmas Island 1956-58, were followed by 27 Nuclear Tests on Christmas Island this time conducted by the U.S.A. As a veteran of 3 H bombs and 2 A bombs I also can confirm that at no time was I issued with protective clothing. I served on Xmas Isle for one year and have had a terrible history of illnesses.

We are a non-political association and not connected with any pro- or anti organisations.

We are only 600 ex-servicemen who wish to know the truth about our illnesses.
Yours sincerely,
Ken McGinley
Chairman
British Nuclear Tests Veterans Association

142

14 March 1984

To: Mr K. McGinley,
Dunoon, Argyll.

Dear Ken McGinley,
Reading again your letter to me of last August, this week's news
must have shattered you. I don't know how one comes to terms
with accepting that with other British soldiers you were
deliberate 'guinea pigs' during the nuclear tests.

What frightens me, Ken, is that such a decision having been
made how can ordinary people be certain that a decision similar
to this will not be made again?

The radioactively contaminated beaches around Windscale
have again been sealed off, and the authorities say people living
nearby will not be affected but I cannot help wondering?

I am so angry for you.
Yours sincerely,
Deirdre (Rhys-Thomas)

21 September 1983

To: Professor Joseph Rotblat,[47]
Emeritus Professor of Physics,
University of London,
London WC1

Dear Professor Rotblat,
Having watched *Panorama*'s programme 'Cloud over Christmas
Island' I am left ever more confused. Can you explain to me,
please, how the official bodies like the UKAEA, the Ministry of
Defence, and the CEGB are so certain, so confident, so sure that
they know the exact amount of nuclear radiation a person can
receive without suffering any harm, when I know that scientists
are divided amongst themselves concerning the 'safe' amount?

As a Mother I know I would be failing my children if I did
not question this. I can recall chemicals, products which have
had successive Government 'O.K.s' only to be found to be
harmful, dangerous, even fatal.
Yours sincerely,
Deirdre Rhys-Thomas

Note 47: Professor Rotblat was a member of the British team of scientists, many of whom had fled Europe as Hitler grew in power, who worked on the development of atomic weapons, the Manhattan Project. He left Los Alamos before the first weapon was tested, since he believed that when Hitler was defeated, there was no longer any need to fear that Germany would build and use such a bomb. In 1950 Professor Rotblat took the seat of Professor of Physics at St Bartholomew's Hospital Medical College. He is a founder member of the Pugwash Council, set up in 1957 in response to the appeal started by Bertrand Russell and Albert Einstein for abandonment of the nuclear arms race, and the cold war. He was President of the British Institute of Radiology in 1971-2.

Some of the major breakthroughs in arms control, and some of the most important lines of trustworthy communication between east and west have been the fruit of work done at Pugwash meetings, which are held alternately in the eastern and western blocs.

Professor Rotblat is the author of several books, including *Nuclear Radiation in Warfare* (1981) for the Stockholm International Peace Research Institute.

From: Professor J. Rotblat
4 October 1983

Dear Mrs Rhys-Thomas,

Thank you for your letter of 21 September. You are certainly right in questioning the arrogance of those bodies which claim that there exists a safe dose of radiation. There is too much that we do not know about the effects of radiation for anyone to make categoric statements.

The trouble is that many effects of radiation, for example cancer, also occur in unirradiated people, and therefore it is impossible to establish a causal link and we have to resort to statistics.

I can assure you that many of us scientists share your anxieties.

Yours sincerely,

J. Rotblat

22 July 1983

To: Mr Stephen Reed,
Mayor of Harrisburg,
Harrisburg, Pennsylvania,
U.S.A.

Dear Mr Reed,
I was shocked while watching a recent BBC television
programme to learn that the Controllers of the Three Mile
Island PWR were totally unaware that the core was
approaching 'melt-down' and radioactive steam was being
emitted into the atmosphere.

Until this programme I had thought, along with many
others, that although the incident was potentially very
dangerous the Controllers were fully aware at all times of what
was happening. Now I know otherwise.

I know I am on the other side of the Atlantic but it still
concerns me to think that the people around Three Mile Island
have been put at risk by this incident.

Please tell me is the nuclear reactor at Three Mile Island
now working again?

And have people who were living near the nuclear reactor
at the time of the incident sought compensation?

Thank you.
Yours sincerely,
Deirdre Rhys-Thomas

Office of the Mayor
City Hall
Harrisburg, Pennsylvania 17101

August 22, 1983

Dear M. Rhys-Thomas:
This is to acknowledge and thank you for your correspondence
regarding Three Mile Island. The BBC program indicating that
the TMI control room operators were entirely unaware of the
fact that the core was approaching a meltdown is completely
correct.

What is more, it has been learned since that there were
several previous more minor incidents when the same control
room operators unsafely operated the plant and failed to make

145

required reports to the U.S. Nuclear Regulatory Commission about unsafe conditions about which they did have knowledge.

Further, it has also been proven that cheating on examinations for licensing as control room operators routinely occurred involving TMI staff during the late 1970's and even as recently as last year. The TMI owners have received a variety of large fines for each of these facts but they continue to own Three Mile Island and have not had their license to own and operate a nuclear power plant revoked, incredibly.

TMI is not yet functioning. Unit Two, the damaged reactor, will take years to clean up and it is not certain whether it can ever reopen. Unit One, the undamaged reactor, has undergone a great deal of testing and the TMI owners certainly wish it to be reopened and the U.S. Nuclear Regulatory Commission is considering their petition to do so. Their petition is opposed by various persons, including myself.

Yours sincerely,
Stephen R. Reed
Mayor

6 October 1983

To: Sir Peter Green,
Chairman,
Lloyds of London, EC3

Dear Sir Peter,
I wish to consider insuring against nuclear war in the next 5-10 years. I require cover for my family, 'a nuclear family' – 2 adults + 2 children + 1 Beagle dog.

Without provisions of a purpose-built nuclear shelter but following the instructions in the Government's *Protect and Survive* we will make our own domestic nuclear shelter.

I had thought my small town would be far from nuclear conflict but it transpires that that would not be so, in so far as the American Sonar Surveillance Submarine Tracking Station at Brawdy would be a first target by the Russians as apparently its main purpose is to send information direct to mainland America.

I have read the Report of the British Medical Association's Board of Science and Education *The Medical Effects of Nuclear War* so I hope I will recognize the symptoms of radiation sickness, etc.

146

I appreciate that the premium I would have to pay will increase if and when Cruise missiles are deployed having read the statements by retired NATO Generals who state that their deployment will make the World a less safe place.

Finally, I have been given to understand that request for insurance against nuclear war received the response from the Insurance Company

'As regards material damage insurance, we have contacted several syndicates in the Lloyd's market who deal with the "trickier" risks and, while initially they say it would be difficult to find an Underwriter who would be prepared to give this cover, we feel that, if granted, the premium would be so high that it would not be attractive to you.'

In that respect I would like to mention that a letter I received from the Ministry of Defence read

'First, let me say that I entirely appreciate your concern over nuclear weapons, but reassure you and your son that the Government does not for one moment hold that nuclear war is inevitable, or even likely. There has been considerable discussion in the media about the prospects of a nuclear war, but despite relations between East and West, being far from ideal there is no reason to believe that a war is imminent.' I await details of premium and cover.

Yours sincerely,
Deirdre Rhys-Thomas

Lloyd's
London EC3
12th October, 1983

Dear Mrs Rhys-Thomas
Thank you for your letter.

I am afraid that the cover you seek is not available whether against war risks arising from nuclear events or more conventional weapons. Lloyd's and the British insurance companies, with the agreement of the British Government, signed an Agreement in 1936 that they would not insure persons or property on land against war risks.

Yours sincerely,
Sir Peter Green
Chairman

19 October 1983

To: Mr Jim Slater,
General Secretary,
National Union of Seamen,
Clapham, London

Dear Mr Slater,
Sometime ago I heard someone talking on the radio about the Melbourne Communique and as I was driving at the time I wasn't able to get down the details.

I wrote to the Attorney General of Australia, Senator Gareth Evans, but he has not replied, and to the Australian High Commission in London. They replied and seem to know nothing about the Melbourne Communique and suggested the London Dumping Convention.

Can you give me the background to the Communique, what it says, and the signatories?

I would like to thank you and your members for stopping the dumping of yet more radioactive waste into the Atlantic. Thank you also from my 2 sons.

Ironically, Wales was democratically declared a nuclear free country 18 months ago through the County Councils and yet washing our shores is the most radioactive sea in the World – the Irish Sea. The only grain of comfort being that the jury of the International Water Tribunal has advised BNFL to stop discharging all plutonium and americium into the Irish Sea. Who knows if they will heed this advice?
Yours sincerely,
Deirdre Rhys-Thomas

National Union of Seamen
Clapham
London SW4

3 November 1983

Dear Ms Thomas
Thank you for your letter of 19 October. I am sorry I could not reply earlier but I have been out of the country most of the time since then. In fact, I have been busy successfully persuading other unions abroad to agree an international boycott of nuclear waste to be dumped at sea.

In reply to your question about the Melbourne Communique, this was signed on 3 October 1981 by the 41 Commonwealth heads of government (or representatives) present.

Paragraph 37 of the communique states: 'Heads of Government noted the opposition in the South Pacific region to the proposals for dumping and storage of nuclear waste in the Pacific Ocean and the deep concern at the serious ecological and environmental dangers to which member countries could be exposed. In this regard the resolution adopted at the recent meeting of the South Pacific Forum was strongly supported.'[48]

The resolution of the South Pacific Forum which was held at Port Vila, Vanuatu, on 10/11 August 1981:

'urges the United States of America and Japan to store and dump their nuclear waste in their home countries rather than storing or dumping in the Pacific'

and

'reaffirms its strong condemnation of testing of nuclear weapons or dumping or storage of nuclear waste in the Pacific by any government, as having deleterious effects on the people and environment of the region.'

I hope this answers your question. Thank you for your kind words of support for our action to prevent nuclear waste dumping at sea.

Yours sincerely,
Jim Slater
General Secretary

Note 48: The Pacific Islands have been favourite sites for testing nuclear devices since the end of the Second World War. Bombs have been exploded by the US, British and French using islands retained from colonisation of the area. Naval manoeuvres are practised by many countries, including the US and the USSR, and there are many military installations for surveillance and storage of dangerous weapons.

Vanuatu is near the island of Fiji.

22 September 1983

To: The Attorney General, Senator Gareth Evans,
The Department of The Attorney General,
Canberra
Australia.

Dear Sir,
I write to you from Wales, sincerely hoping that you will have
the time to give me details I most anxiously require.

Sometime ago I heard a reference on BBC radio to a
Treaty (?), I think the Melbourne Treaty, which concerned
nuclear dumping in the Pacific, and at the same time the names
of the signatories were mentioned.

I have not been able to seek out this information and look
to you for help.
Yours sincerely,
Deirdre Rhys-Thomas

Attorney-General's Department
Australia
6 December 1983

Dear Ms Rhys-Thomas
The Attorney-General has asked me to reply to your letter to
him of 22 September 1983.

You seek information regarding a conference which you
heard on BBC radio concerning nuclear dumping in the Pacific.
I think that the program would have referred to the so-called
'Melbourne Communique' of October 1981 (rather than to the
'Melbourne Treaty') issued by the Commonwealth Heads of
Government who met in Melbourne from 30 September to 7
October 1981.

Paragraph 37 of the Final Communique of that meeting
reads as follows:

> '37. Heads of Government noted the opposition in the South
> Pacific region to the proposals for dumping and storage of
> nuclear waste in the Pacific Ocean and the deep concern at
> the serious ecological and environmental dangers to which
> member countries could be exposed. In this regard the
> resolution adopted at the recent meeting of the South Pacific
> Forum was strongly supported.'

150

The full text of the Final Communique has been published by and may be obtained from:

The Commonwealth Secretariat,
Marlborough House,
London SW1Y 5HX

I trust that this information will be of assistance to you.
Yours sincerely,
(G.P.M. Dabb)
for Secretary

20 October 1983

To: The Hon. John Glenn, Senator for Ohio,
The Senate,
Washington, D.C.
United States of America.

Dear Senator Glenn,
I thank you for publicly speaking out against the deployment of Cruise missiles in Britain around Christmas because you think they are amongst the most destabilising elements in the nuclear arms race.

Please will you come to Britain and say this on television and on the radio?

Do not be put off by the fact that the Conservative Government was re-elected to Parliament with a large majority, it was with considerably less than 50% of the votes of the British people.

And the support of the silent majority much quoted by pro-nuclear politicians – I can't help wondering if they are silent because they are so ignorant about Cruise?

My love for my sons and my concern for their future – a future they can think of in three score years and ten – triggered off my interest in Cruise.

What a macabre celebration of Advent – 'the arrival of Cruise' – would that there was no room for them at the Inn.
Yours sincerely,
Deirdre Rhys-Thomas

Dear Ms. Rhys-Thomas,
Thank you for sharing your thoughts with me about the
intermediate-range nuclear force.

I am afraid the Intermediate-Range Nuclear Forces (INF)
Talks in Europe are in grave jeopardy. And, even if the talks are
stalled, I believe it is vital that we continue to press the Soviets
for agreement. Frankly, I liked the first idea the President put
forth for an agreement in which neither side would have
intermediate-range missiles in Europe. This is consistent with
my long-standing concerns about verification, because there is
no arms control agreement easier to verify than a total ban. If
you see a prohibited weapon, you have your adversary cold; it
is a clean and simple approach.

Unfortunately, absolute zero proved to be unattainable.
And if zero is not possible, the smart thing to do is to get the
next best deal. But, we may have lost our best opportunity
when Ambassador Paul Nitze tried to negotiate a deal last
summer and was publicly repudiated by his own Administration
for his efforts. Now the Soviets have dug their heels in and may
be unwilling to discuss limitations even after the deployment of
U.S. missiles begins later this year.

What we seek in an INF agreement is rough force
equivalence at reduced levels. A halt in the arms race and a
reduction of super-power tension serves the interest of both
sides and, indeed, the whole world. I believe that it is most
unfortunate that an agreement linking intermediate range
nuclear forces in Europe appears highly unlikely prior to the
NATO deployments in December, and both the U.S and the
USSR, share the blame, in my view, for the failure of the INF
talks to date.

I recommend we break the deadlock by combining the
intermediate-range weapons talks with the START strategic
weapons negotiations. Two years of inconclusive discussions at
Geneva should convince us that the arbitrary approach we have
taken, based on the range of a weapon, has not worked. A
weapon's range alone fails to define adequately its role and
mission. Moreover, comparing nuclear forces East and West in
this fashion assumes a weapon comparability that does not
exist.

I believe, for example, that ground-launched cruise missiles could be extremely destabilising, given the difficulties of verification and thus the great difficulty of capturing them in an arms control agreement once they are deployed in significant numbers by both sides. Thus, despite the difficulties I acknowledge it would raise, I have proposed that the U.S. temporarily delay deployment of GLCM's in Europe in order to see if there is the possibility of an agreement which would keep this new and destabilising weapon from contributing a new level of complexity to the already formidable challenge we face in controlling nuclear weapons.

I believe we must rededicate ourselves to achieving real arms control based upon a reduction in the total number of nuclear warheads possessed by both sides. We should seek an agreement to establish a ceiling at lower levels on strategic and intermediate range warheads, thus reducing the destructive potential of both sides while allowing Washington and Moscow to choose the mix of weapons they wish to retain in their inventory. If we are really serious about arms reductions, such an approach gets at the real problem – warheads – in a sensible but flexible way.

I appreciated hearing from you on this important issue.
Best regards.
Sincerely,
John Glenn,
United States Senator

2 November 1983

To: Professor Andrew Mathews,
Head of Clinical Psychology Department,
St George's Hospital Medical School,
Tooting Bec,
London

Dear Professor Mathews,
It has caused me considerable confusion and fury over the years how so many of my friends and relations can be so completely apathetic towards nuclear weapons and their possible use. It seems to me as if they have a mental blind they pull down over this 'horrible subject', or follow the ostrich's head in the sand habit.

153

How, I wonder, can they be so concerned with the 'whiter than white window wash test' exhorted by TV commercials and vacuuming the house be content to sweep the nuclear dust under the carpet?

I love my children passionately. And with a Calvinistic Scottish heritage I don't gamble. I am not going to gamble with my children's lives in the nuclear lottery.

But yesterday I read that research shows that there are two reactions to the possible use of nuclear weapons: some people (the silent majority?) deal with it by 'denial and apathy' and others by seeking to remove the threat.

Tell me please, Professor Mathews, have the military powers and the nuclear weapons manufacturers known of this psychological response to nuclear weapons for sometime, and laughing behind our backs know that they could always count on the apathy of the silent majority?

I thank you.

Yours sincerely,

Deirdre Rhys-Thomas

St George's Hospital Medical School
University of London
9th November, 1983

Dear Mrs. Rhys-Thomas,

Thank you for your letter of 2nd November, presumably concerning a newspaper report of the Greenham Common trial.[49] Unfortunately I didn't see this article myself, so I am not quite sure what impression it gave. The affidavit that I submitted to the Court,[50] simply outlines the usual cognitive coping strategies that people use in dealing with any frightening threat, as shown by research. Obviously the possibility of a nuclear war is very much more frightening than most other possible threats, but it would appear that most of the population deal with this in the same way as they cope with other threats, namely by avoiding thinking about it too much. However, I think we can be fairly certain that those responsible for nuclear weapons are not particularly interested in the precise mechanics of psychological coping strategies, but have simply found in practice that the majority are content to leave any thinking about possible disasters to others. Hopefully this usual situation is in the process of change.

Yours sincerely,
Andrew Mathews,
Professor of Psychology

Note 49: Jean Stead, 'Why Cruise may land in Court', *Guardian*, 1 November 1983, p.17.

Note 50: The Greenham Common Women Against Cruise took President Reagan and Secretary of State Caspar Weinberger to court in New York to seek an injunction against the deployment of Cruise missiles at Greenham Common. They collected a great deal of evidence to show that the deployment of Cruise in the UK was against the interests of the majority, and would interfere with the democratic process. They maintained that the deployment of nuclear weapons was in contravention of several international laws, and had a number of documents from legal, medical, philosophical, scientific and political experts in defence of their case. The preliminary hearing took place on 9 November 1983, and a further hearing in a higher court in New York was held the following year. The case fell when the judge decided that he was not the appropriate level of judiciary, and the women decided against spending any more money on this particular trial.

The case attracted a lot of publicity in the USA, but was not well reported in this country.

11 November 1983

To: His Excellency Mr Shridath S. Ramphal, O.E.,A.C.,Kt,
    C.M.G.,Q.C.
Secretary General,
Commonwealth Secretariat,
Pall Mall, London

Your Excellency,
Thank you for giving me a glimmer of hope yesterday when I heard you speaking on the radio about the need for the Super-Powers to be less aggressive and use more restraint.

I just cannot understand how a dialogue of reason can be reached when quite frankly the Super-Powers indulge publicly in slanging matches with each other. (Oh yes, some diplomats may say that restrained talk is going on behind the scenes: if so, it is even more insidious as publicly they reinforce the cliche-ridden attitudes of the silent majority.)

I am neither anti-American, nor anti-Russian, but I am

155

anti-Super Powers and the military might they wield.

May I trust that at the forthcoming Commonwealth Conference to be held in the presence of Her Majesty The Queen that Your Excellency will endeavour to get the Commonwealth Heads of Government to shed their political attitudes and think only in terms of survival of the human race in line with the feelings of the late Earl Mountbatten of Burma with respect to the nuclear arms race.[51]

I have friends and family throughout the Commonwealth and I know as parents we are desperately concerned because we know that the threat of the nuclear arms race is having a destructive effect on the hopes of our children in that they feel they may not live to become adults – 'the Bomb' will go off.
Yours sincerely,
Deirdre Rhys-Thomas

Note 51: Earl Mountbatten, a most distinguished military gentleman and diplomat, said in a speech delivered on the award of the Louise Weiss Foundation prize in Strasbourg, 11 May 1979, that he saw no military use for nuclear weapons. He concluded his speech:

'The world now stands on the brink of the final abyss. Let us resolve to take all possible practical steps to ensure that we do not, through our own folly, go over the edge.'

Office of the Commonwealth Secretary-General
Pall Mall London SW
15 November 198.

Dear Mrs. Rhys Thomas,

The Secretary-General is absent abroad at the moment but I know he will read your very thoughtful letter of 11 November with great interest. I need hardly say that we here entirely share your thoughts on the nuclear arms race.
Yours sincerely,
Christopher Laidlaw
Assistant Director
Secretary-General's Office

To: Dr Philip Day,
Department of Chemistry,
University of Manchester,
Manchester

2 November 1983

Dear Dr Day,
You were very kind several months ago to answer my obviously
unscientific questions but important to me as a concerned
Mother. Last night my husband and I watched 'Windscale the
nuclear laundry' and were shattered when we heard that you
had found plutonium dust in Mrs Merlin's vacuum cleaner.

The BNFL man in trying to minimise the significance of
plutonium in the house dust talked as if the only source of
contamination was from imbibed dust and you would have to
eat so many ? ozs to be harmful. But surely, Dr Day,
contamination from all other radioactive sources has to be
added – inhalation, intake through food and drink, contact
through skin, contact when playing in the garden, playing on
the beach, paddling in the Irish Sea? in view of the high
environmental radioactivity. Could not these all add up to the
equivalent of eating x ozs of dust containing plutonium?

Tonight on the *PM* programme the Environment Secretary,
Patrick Jenkin, spoke reassuringly of BNFL's forthcoming £10
million programme to reduce discharges by 80% (why the need
if it is already so safe I ask myself?) but he made no mention of
the advice then given by the Jury of the International Water
Tribunal to BNFL to stop *all* discharges into the Irish Sea. As a
Jury Member said, 'The addition of any fraction of plutonium
into the environment is incomprehensible.'

Yet again I thank you.
Yours sincerely,
Deirdre Rhys-Thomas

Department of Chemistry
The University of Manchester

17th November 1983

Dear Mrs Rhys-Thomas,
Thank you for your letter following the Yorkshire TV film
'Windscale – the nuclear laundry'. Although, clearly, the

157

producer was making his points as dramatically as possible, I think the programme was factually correct, certainly in so far as radioactive contamination of the environment is concerned. I was pleased to hear that the Department of the Environment is to set up an enquiry into the cancer issue, although I doubt if their conclusions will be definitive.

On the issue of the ingestion of dust, yes of course the point at issue is the total intake of radioactive materials, not just plutonium by an individual from all sources (ingestion and inhalation, and all routes leading to these). The method used by the official bodies concerned (the National Radiological Protection Board, etc.) is called the 'Critical Pathway' approach, which sets out to determine the most important pathway to the most 'exposed' group of people. Other pathways to the same group are then evaluated so that the total exposure for the group can be estimated. The drawback to this is that it depends on identifying *all* possible pathways which contribute.

In the present case, dust seems to have been ignored. The purpose in measuring plutonium and other particles in dust was to discover whether this could be a significant *additional* route to a group of people (the inhabitants of the coastal villages) who are already exposed to additional radiation from the Windscale source. As you rightly point out, the British Nuclear Fuels Ltd response to the television programme was not helpful, and tended to cloud the issue. If house dust was the only source of ingested radioactivity, the amount needed to reach the present (arbitrary) safe 'limit' would be quite large – say around 1 kg a year (just a guess). This sounds a lot. But 10% of this, 100g per year or 1/3g per day, would be a significant amount to someone already receiving a large proportion of the permitted intake from other sources. Also, 1/3g per day would, in my estimation, be quite feasible for, say, a child who spent a lot of time scrabbling about on the floor.

Now that the house-dust pathway has been established as *possible*, the next step is to work out its relative importance, and to add it to the other routes of exposure. I'm no expert in that field, but I'm quite sure that this will now be done – indeed, a team from the Department of the Environment is already taking samples. British Nuclear Fuels Ltd's bland approach, although very annoying, can be ignored as I think the issue will now have to be taken to a proper conclusion. It will be interesting to see what this is, but we'll not allow it to die of neglect!

I hope this answers your questions. Thank you for writing, and please get in touch again if I can help in any way.

Yours sincerely,

Philip Day

15 December 1983

To: Mr Con Allday,
Chairman,
British Nuclear Fuels Ltd., Windscale, Nr Sellafield, Cumbria

Dear Mr Allday,

I heard you speaking on the radio about the mistake which led to the radioactive contamination of beaches near Windscale.

Your words of reassurance do not reassure me. I am not a scientist, I am a Mother who has no confidence in those people who control my sons' futures.

Dr Polk, Jury Member of the International Water Tribunal, kindly sent me a copy of the IWT casebook on Windscale, and I know my concern is not ill-founded.

'Company and Ownership   British Nuclear Fuels Limited, 100% owned by U.K. Government

It is charged that

1   the discharges are not necessary. Adequate treatment technology exists, and if built in at the design stage does not significantly affect processing costs.

2   although BNFL had accepted that its past discharges have been unacceptably high (and is installing treatment technology at great cost), the treatment plant under construction will not deal with those nuclides which present the most intractable problem in terms of environmental contamination – the long lived transuranics such as plutonium-239 and americium/241

3   past discharge practice has been the result of mismanagement and failure in design, as well as poor judgement in terms of ecological effects. Present policy is unduly influenced by past commitments and judgements and is not in line with either best practice technology or discharge philosophies of other states, especially with regard to transuranics,

159

4   on the basis of current dosimetric models, the present
discharges will lead to cancer deaths and hereditary damage,
and to a total estimated health detriment 1.5-15 million
pounds sterling, depending on the detriment costs ascribed to
deaths and other health effects, for each year of operation,
5   however, the range of uncertainty is high and damage
may be greater (or less) than this, depending upon the
accuracy of modelling. There is some epidemiological
evidence of statistically significant excesses of radiosensitive
cancers in the coastal region.'

I never forget the time I stood beside the cradle of my Mother's
friend's baby. A flaxen-haired, picture-book baby girl, lying
quietly: a soft lambswool shawl framing her face. Without a
word her Mother unwrapped her – there was a freak of science
not nature, without ears, legs, arms – only flesh. Thalidomide.
Yours sincerely,
Deirdre Rhys-Thomas

British Nuclear Fuels plc
Risley Warrington Cheshire WA3 6AS
11 January 1984

Dear Mrs Rhys-Thomas
My Chairman, Mr Allday, has asked me to reply to your letter
to him of 16 December. I do so with apologies for the delay.
     Your letter refers to the recent incident at Sellafield which
caused radioactive contamination of the beach and then goes on
to quote comments by a participant in the recent so-called
'International Water Tribunal'. May I deal with these matters
separately?
     The incident which led to contamination of the beach was
an isolated occurrence which we regret. The circumstances have
been investigated by Government regulatory bodies and their
reports are now awaited. You may have seen from the Press
that we have already taken significant action to ensure that such
an incident cannot recur and for your information I attach a
copy of a recent Press statement by BNFL.
     On the matter of our routine discharges of low-level
radioactivity I should say that the 'International Water
Tribunal' to which you refer was an entirely unofficial event,
unrecognised by Government and with no status. On the advice

of the British Government BNFL declined an invitation to participate.

You should know that our discharges of radioactivity from Sellafield are within authorised limits imposed by Government regulatory bodies which take account of public health and are based on the recommendations of the appropriate international advisory[52] body, the International Commission on Radiological Protection.

As well as complying with these absolute limits BNFL is also required to observe the ALARA principle that discharges shall be kept as low as reasonably achievable. To that end we have already achieved at great expense substantial reductions from the peak levels of the 1970s and plan further reductions. Contrary to the allegations you quote these reductions do include the long-lived transuranics including plutonium. Our discharges of these types of radioactibity have been cut to one-fifth of the peak levels and in the near future will be cut again to one-fifth of the present levels, thereby achieving reduction to one twenty-fifth of the peak levels of discharges in the 1970s.

Yours sincerely

J A Preece

Director Information Services

Note 52: Some nuclear experts think it is possible that the release of plutonium solvent and 'crud' during the washing-out of the pipes and equipment at Sellafield reprocessing plant was not an isolated incident, but that this was the first year the practice was detected. At the time, November 1983, the six High Active Plant Washout tanks were not fitted with equipment to detect the presence of either solvent or crud, and only the activity of the water solution could be measured.

On 11 November, assuming that all solvent and crud had floated to the top of the tank and been pumped out, Sea Tank 1 was flushed out to seal. Pumping was halted just after midnight when activity levels at the discharge pipe rose sharply, and the rest of the contents were diverted to an intermediate-level storage tank. On 13 November the sea discharge pipework was flushed out, taking with it some solvent and crud. Workers at the sea pipeline valve had to be urgently evacuated when radiation levels rose. On 17 November Sea Tank 2 was emptied more completely than usual, and a second slick of solvent and crud washed out to sea, later being blown back to shore. Although a Department of the Environment inspector was working at Sellafield at the time, and was told of the two slicks, resulting from the discharge of high-level wastes to sea, neither he nor the BNFL management considered it serious enough to warrant a formal report.

See 'An Incident leading to Contamination of the Beaches near to the BNFL Windscale and Calder Works, Sellafield November 1983', a report of the DoE Environmental Radiochemical Inspectorate.

161

4 March 1984

To: Sir Douglas Black,
The Royal College of Physicians,
London N.W.1

Dear Sir Douglas,
I understand that the World Health Organisation Report states
that no health service in the world would be able to cope with
the casualties caused by a 1 megaton nuclear bomb. 'Hospitals
and other care centres would be reduced to rubble, fires would
rage, survivors would be panic-stricken, or as in Hiroshima,
reduced to a state of stupor.'

Why is it then that politicians and the military ignore the
World's medical experts, or so it appears to me when I read that
NATO/USA intends building hospitals in Britain 'to be put in
mothballs' until the nuclear need arises?
Yours sincerely,
Deirdre Rhys-Thomas

London NW1
7th March 1984

Dear Mrs Rhys-Thomas,
Thank you for your letter of 4 March. I was convinced by all
the evidence which the WHO Committee heard that the
statement which you quote is substantially correct. The only
purpose which I can see in building hospitals in the way you
describe is to create employment. Regrettably, I cannot account
for the beliefs or actions of politicians and the military.
Yours sincerely,
Sir Douglas Black

14 March 1984

To: Professor Paul Matthews,
Chairman of Management Committee
National Radiological Protection Board,
Harwell,
Didcot,
Oxfordshire

Dear Professor Matthews,
Has a Report by the NRPB been published recently stating that natural radiation should not be used to justify exposure to the public from other sources?

'The existence of one source does not provide a basis for the justification of a different source.'

I can't help feeling having seen several CEGB and UKAEA exhibitions that we (the public) are being given a distorted understanding of radiation — bearing in mind that few of us are nuclear scientists — as so much emphasis is made in these exhibitions on natural radiation with beautiful, glossy blow-up photos of buildings, like Aberdeen Cathedral?
Yours sincerely,
Deirdre Rhys-Thomas
(not a nuclear scientist, but concerned Mother of 2 sons — concerned that the out-of-date radiation levels used will not protect my sons.)

University of Cambridge
Department of Applied Mathematics and Theoretical Physics
Cambridge
23.3.84

Dear Mrs Rhys-Thomas,
    Your letter of 14th March has been forwarded to me here. You are evidently referring to an NRPB report which was the subject of an article by Anthony Tucker in the *Guardian* 29th Jan. '84. You may have missed my reply, a copy of which I enclose. I hope this answers your questions though I am not clear why you refer to 'out of date radiation levels'.

    Yours sincerely,
    Paul Matthews

Enclosure:

Sir, – In an article (January 26) based on a report from the National Radiation Protection Board (NRPB) your Science Correspondent quotes as follows: 'The existence of one source (of radiation) does not provide a basis for the justification of a different source, so that natural radiation doses or their variations cannot be used to justify doses from waste disposal.'

This is not, as he suggests, a new idea being put forward by the NRPB in conflict with current practice but, as the report itself makes clear on an earlier page, it is one of the 'fundamental underlying principles' on which international (ICRP) standards of radiation dose limitation are based. In arriving at these limits, levels of natural background radiation have been used as a general standard of comparison. In doing this, obviously broad averages over wide areas have been used; not situations where the natural background is exceptionally high, like down a uranium mine.

What the report interestingly points out is that in certain circumstances, the natural background radiation in some ordinary houses in granite-based areas can lead to doses to the occupants as much as 10 times the legally allowed limit to the critical group of the general public from manmade sources – the limit relevant, for example, to copious fish and mollusc eaters living in the area at Sellafield.

As your correspondent correctly reports, the NRPB concludes that even at this level it would be extremely difficult to relate variations in cancer incidence to variations in natural radiation. This indicates rather clearly the stringency of the existing regulations, but is certainly not an argument for their relaxation. – Yours faithfully.
P.T. Matthews
(Chairman, Radioactive Waste Management Advisory Committee).
University of Cambridge.

23 March, 1984

To: Professor Paul T. Matthews,
Chairman, Radioactive Waste Management Advisory
   Committee,
Department of Applied Mathematics and Theoretical Physics,
University of Cambridge,
Cambridge

Dear Professor Matthews,
No, it wasn't from the *Guardian* it was from a CEGB official
who quoted the NRPB report to me during a heated discussion.

You don't know why I use 'out of date radiation levels', for
God's sake I'm no nuclear scientist but I understand that
America uses limits which are now 20 times more stringent than
those we live with in Britain. British levels were recommended
by an International Commission over 25 years ago.

No doubt you can come back at me with some nuclear nit-
picking statistics. I don't care, I have no confidence in the
nuclear industry radiation levels, I don't want my children
exposed to any man-made radiation.[53] Put it down to gut
reaction, maternal instincts — these have not let me down in
looking after my children and I don't want it.

Good God, we've got on our doorstep what must be the
most radioactive sea in the World — the Irish Sea — can you tell
me of another sea which has 2.2 million gallons of water
containing nuclear isotopes pumped into it daily?

Quite safe we've been told for years, now reductions must
be made. So much for the levels?

Yes, I'm angry, I make no apology, I cry with utter
frustration that I cannot safeguard my children.
Yours sincerely,
Deirdre Rhys-Thomas

Note 53: Professor Sadao Ichikawa, Professor of Genetics at Saitama
University in Urawa, Japan, points out that man-made radiation is in fact
more dangerous than natural radiation. It has been widely assumed that
because man-made and natural radionuclides decay in the same way (by
giving off gamma rays, and alpha or beta-particles with the same amount
of energy) they would have the same health effects. However, man-made
radionuclides have a tendency to accumulate in living tissues while
natural ones do not. Ninety-nine per cent of internal exposure is due to
potassium-40 which occurs abundantly in nature, but which moves
through the tissues and organs of the body without building up. During

165

the long history of evolution, plants or animals that *did* accumulate potassium-40 would have disappeared.

Some of the fission products of uranium such as Iodine-131, Caesium-137 and Strontium-90 (all of which were present in the Chernobyl cloud) concentrate in different organs; iodine in the thyroid, especially in young children, can be found at $3\frac{1}{2}$ to 10 million times the concentration in air. Once inside the body the accumulated doses of radiation can be extremely high for the surrounding tissues. Caesium is drawn to the organs of production, and can cause sterility or damaged gene cells.

It is therefore rather misleading to imply that because we have evolved in a radioactive world, a bit more won't do us any harm. The *natural* background radiation itself may well contribute to the onset of cancer and genetic defects.

See Ichikawa, Sadao, 'Responses to Ionizing Radiation' in *Encyclopaedia of Plant Physiology*, New Series, Volume 12A, Springer-Verlag, Berlin, 1981.

11 March 1984

To: Mr Brian Thetford,
Chief Executive,
Newbury District Council,
Newbury,
Berks.

Dear Mr Thetford,
You are doing your job with such enthusiasm I can only take it that you have complete confidence in Cruise.

The first cruise missile convoy has got out of Greenham Common: can you tell me how the Russians are going to know when it's a dummy run, or not?
Yours sincerely,
Deirdre Rhys-Thomas

PS There were 167 nuclear alerts in the U.S.S.R. between January and October 1983. Dummy runs might increase them??

To: Mr Brian Thetford,
Chief Executive,
Newbury District Council,
Newbury, Berks.

Dear Mr Thetford,
The other day I spoke on the phone to your Secretary who was really splendid. She told me you are getting so many letters about Cruise, you are not answering them but having them all filed by your Legal and Administration Dept: only answering those from Newbury Ratepayers.

Saying that I had hoped you would have recognised that I want a personal explanation of why you personally endorse Cruise – other than my thinking you think it is just part of your job and so long to any thought of Armageddon – she said that Newbury Ratepayers might object to you replying to me in their time.

I ask you again, Mr Thetford; to recognize the concern of

one human being and answer me. To overcome any inconvenience I enclose s.a. envelope, paper, and £1.00.
Yours sincerely,
Deirdre Rhys-Thomas

copy letter enclosed

P.S. I'm terribly glad the American military are wheedling out those American servicemen at Greenham Common who have been taking drugs. Must be a bit frightening – puts one in mind of the Dr Strangelove film.

Newbury District Council
Chief Executive B.J. Thetford, A.C.I.S., D.M.A.
2nd April 1984

Dear Mrs Rhys-Thomas,

Greenham Common, Newbury

Thank you for your letter referring to your earlier correspondence of 11th March 1984.

I do not propose to engage in any correspondence on the wider subject of the stationing of cruise missiles at RAF Greenham Common as this is a matter for Parliament. I would suggest that, if you wish to discuss the matter at this level, you should write to your local Member of Parliament.

I am returning your £1.00.
Yours sincerely,
B.J. Thetford

2 May 1984

To: The Bishop of Salisbury the Right Rev. John Baker,
Salisbury,
Wilts.

Dear Bishop,
I have the greatest difficulty allaying my children's fears of nuclear war. No sooner do I deal with a question about living in a designated limited nuclear war battlefield, or an 'unsinkable aircraft carrier' than they read President Reagan saying nuclear

war is inevitable, perhaps in his lifetime, because it's written in Revelations.[54]

In the last 18 months I have done everything I can democratically to help reduce my sons' nuclear fears but I have become frightened because it has become apparent to me from reading an article by Sir Martin Ryle that anyone expressing anti-nuclear views could be subjected to phone tapping, interference of mail, surveillance.

Why, Bishop, should people who are anti-nuclear be so persecuted?

Yours sincerely,
Deirdre Rhys-Thomas

Note 54: In an article originally printed in the *Washington Post* and reprinted in full in the *Guardian*, 21 April 1984, Ronnie Dugger drew attention to at least five occasions when Reagan referred to his beliefs that Armageddon may well occur during the present generation and could come in the Middle East.

There are 43 million Christian fundamentalists in the USA, whose beliefs are typified in sermons such as those delivered by the Rev. Chuck Smith:

'We are living in the last days. At any moment the Middle East could erupt into a conflict that will be the war of annihilation – this time of Russia and her allies by the Israelis. Then the Lord will take us out of the whole, mad scene and into the heavenly glories of the Father.'

During the campaign for the 1980 presidential nomination, in the course of a TV interview, Reagan was discussing the need for a 'spiritual revival' when he said, 'We may be the generation that sees Armageddon.' Caspar Weinberger, the Secretary of Defence, shares that view: 'I have read the Book of Revelation, and yes, I believe the world is going to end – by an act of God, I hope – but every day I think the time is running out.'

The Bishop of Salisbury
10th May, 1984

Dear Mrs Rhys-Thomas,
Thank you so much for your letter of May 2nd. I am glad you felt able to write to me about your anxieties.

It is becoming increasingly widely recognised that many children in our society are worried about the prospect of nuclear war. A collection of essays and lectures under the title *Lessons Before Midnight* will be published before long by the University of London Institute of Education and this topic is handled in this book though not perhaps centrally.

I think I would stress, however, that one of the main factors in reducing children's anxiety on such matters is that we ourselves should not have anxieties which get out of hand and which we then communicate to them. Certainly the very anxious tone of your own letter suggests to me that you may unconsciously be making things worse for your boys.

I think it is important to try to learn to distinguish between real dangers and imaginary ones. My own view as a result of the close study I have been able to give to this question is that neither the Government of the United States nor that of the Soviet Union are going to plunge the world recklessly into nuclear war. They are both very sophisticated in the political sphere and well understand that the rhetoric which is used in public exchange has little relation to reality. Moreover both countries are technologically advanced and can do everything humanly possible to prevent conflict by accident. This is not to say there are not dangers but that the kind of Dr Strangelove scenario of madmen recklessly plunging the world into nuclear holocaust has no foundation in fact.[55]

As regards your feelings that those who oppose nuclear weapons may be subjected to official persecution, all I can say is that I have never experienced this myself. I am quite sure that no one in Government has either the time or the facilities to conduct a phone tapping, interference of mail and surveillance of the million or so people in this country who are taking an active part in the Peace Movement. I do not say these things never happen but I am quite sure they do not affect ordinary citizens like yourself.

Finally, I think it is important to inform ourselves carefully and correctly about what is said and done so that when scaremongering rumours get round we can contradict them. For instance I do not believe it to be correct that President Reagan has ever said what you mention in your first paragraph. If somebody has told your children that this is the case then it is important that you should be in a position to contradict it.

I hope these few practical suggestions may be of some help. Obviously it is of the greatest importance that all those concerned with peace should do everything in their power to promote the reduction of nuclear weapons all round and to encourage policies which will help this forward. But I do not myself believe that the Day of Judgment is just around the corner. Not yet.

    With every good wish,
    Yours sincerely,
    † John Sarum

Note 55: The findings of two large surveys to investigate the extent of drug and alcohol abuse in the American services were presented to the US Congress in 1981. Commenting on the results of these surveys, General Louissell said:

> 'We have looked at the consequences of substance abuse in the armed forces. The results are not reassuring: 7% of the armed forces reported they were alcohol dependent; 4% reported themselves drug dependent. This (means) . . . there were at least 170,000 soldiers, sailors, marines and airmen on the firing ranges, in the manoeuvre areas, on the decks and in the maintenance shops, who were high or drunk 40 or more times last year.'

There are no comparable figures for the USSR, but they may well be similar, and since drug abuse may contribute bad judgment to dealing with the unexpected, say an accident or a crisis, then the risk of nuclear war being started inadvertently is high. Is this a real or an imaginary danger? It is a common characteristic of human beings to deny dangers even when they can be clearly foreseen, and since the possible results of a nuclear war are so horrendous, the majority resort to strong denial.

    See Thompson, James, *Psychological Aspects of Nuclear War*, British Psychological Society, 1985.

19 May 1984

To: The Bishop of Salisbury the Right Rev. John Baker, Salisbury

Dear Bishop,
I would like to thank you for being so kind in taking the time to answer my letter so fully. I am 100% confident I do not communicate my anxieties to my sons, I am only too aware that their well-being is the most important thing in my life. Indeed I am reassured by psychologists who say that children who see their parents actively doing something, however small, to stop the nuclear arms race are better able to cope with it.

    Theo, my eldest son, reads and hears nuclear comments and thence comes his anxiety. Perhaps what I do communicate to my sons is my utter frustration and, yes, anger at those leading politicians who are supposed to have the best interests of all children at heart and yet are doing nothing other than indulge in obscene political rhetoric. According to Mr Heseltine deployment of Cruise would bring the Russians back to the conference table and instead the Russian response is to deploy more of their own nuclear weapons.

How can my sons be expected to understand that the rhetoric used in public exchange has little relation to reality when so many adults can't? If politicians didn't indulge in this we wouldn't have so many of the Better to be Dead than Red, Reds under your Beds clichés which reinforce our prejudices. Without doubt the Russians have theirs about us. Remember the response at the Tory Conference to Kenny Everett's 'Let's Bomb Russia'?

As far as I recall, President Reagan's remarks, linked with Caspar Weinberger, were reported in an article in the *Washington Post* which was reprinted in the *Guardian* several weeks ago.[56]

I thank you again, Bishop, and I thank you for openly speaking out against nuclear weapons because I have to confess that I am appalled at the lack of urgency shown by the Church of England as a whole, over the nuclear arms race.

Yours sincerely,
Deirdre Rhys-Thomas

Note 56: 'I turn back to your ancient prophets in the Old Testament for the signs foretelling Armageddon and I find myself wondering if we're the generation that's going to see that come about' – President Ronald Reagan, quoted in 'Sayings of the Week', *Observer*, 4 December 1983, p.7.

To: Mr Terry Turbitt,
Head of the Global Seismology Unit,
Institute of Geological Sciences,
Edinburgh,
Scotland.

Time of Earth Tremor: felt around 10.10 while watching
'*Spitting Image*' on Sunday, 15 April 1984.

Dear Mr Turbitt,
I've read in my local paper that scientists are asking for first-
hand accounts of the earth tremor, apparently one of the
highest recorded in Britain for many years.

Toby and I were sitting on the floor watching television
when it felt as if we were being lifted up by a big wave – just
like when swimming – and as if the house was going to go on
sliding down our steep hill. With it there was a noise which
sounded just like a tube train passing underneath us.

You ask what damage was done?[57] Well as this took place
in an area never before noted for land movement can you tell
me how 'the experts' can ever be certain any site in Britain will
be free from similar geological activity?

Thank goodness for those people in Powys who objected to
test borings by scientists considering Powys for disposal of
nuclear waste.

Just imagine if this had happened several years hence and
disposal of nuclear waste had gone ahead. After all the first
nuclear reactor containing intermediate nuclear waste is due to
cease operation in 1987 and as Wales is a watershed, what
consternation it would cause in Birmingham and Liverpool if
they had to drink radioactive water!
Yours sincerely,
Deirdre Rhys-Thomas

Note 57: The earthquake that shook Powys on 15 April 1984 cracked a
gantry at Trawsfynydd nuclear power station. This meant that the huge
crane used to lift nuclear waste flasks out of the cooling ponds when they
have been loaded with 'spent' fuel rods cannot be used as the gantry in
question is the concrete track along which the crane travels.

This incident may have been the cause of nuclear engineers having
another look at the designs of the older stations, to check whether they
would withstand earthquake shocks.

British Geological Survey
Edinburgh
31 May 1984

Dear Mrs Rhys-Thomas

POWYS EARTHQUAKE OF 15 APRIL 1984

With reference to your enquiry of 7 May to Mr T. Turbitt the simple answer to your question is that, with the present state of our knowledge, we cannot say that any place in Britain will be free of small earthquakes.

Thank you for your report of the way the event was experienced in your house. We have collected 150 macroseismic reports from people in the affected area, in addition to the instrumental records from our seismographs in England and Wales. Our latest assessment based on these data is as follows:

Time of occurrence:	21.05:34 sec GMT
Date:	15 April 1984
Grid reference:	315.6 East 280.3 North
Depth of focus:	8km approximately
Magnitude:	3.3 ML (Richter Local Scale).
Felt area:	2700 sq. km max.
Max. Intensity:	V on Modified Mercalli or MSK scales.

Yours sincerely
Dr C.W.A. Browitt
cc. Mr T. Turbitt

Y Swyddfa Gymrsig Welsh Office News
Adran Hysbysrwyyd Information Division
Crown Building, Cathays Park, Cardiff
16 May 1984

Survey of Environmental Activity in Wales
The Secretary of State for Wales, the Rt Hon. Nicholas Edwards MP, announced today the funding of a survey to establish background levels of radioactivity in Wales. The work will be carried out by the Environment and Medical Sciences Division of Harwell and is planned to last for three years.

The main purpose of the study is to establish the concentration of radioactivity in environmental samples and to study the extent

174

of sea to land transfer of radionuclides. It is proposed to analyse a wide range of soil types from regions of high and low rainfall and the accumulation of radionuclides in some agricultural crops will be examined.

Sewage sludge will be sampled at a number of urban locations in order to determine the amount of radioactivity passing through the body. The transfer through the air of certain radionuclides from sea to land will be assessed by exposure of muslin screens around the coast during the period of onshore winds.

The purpose of this research is to establish the levels in soil and certain crops in Wales, and that coming from the sea and in sewage sludge, so that the baseline can be established against which future changes in the radioactivity in our environment can be assessed.

---

20 May 1984

To: Dr L.E.J. Roberts, CBE, FRS,
Director,
Atomic Energy Research Establishment
Harwell,
Oxfordshire

Dear Dr Roberts,
Please be so kind as to tell me why Scientists at the Atomic Energy Research Establishment (Harwell) are going to conduct a 3 year survey into the levels of background radioactivity in Wales? Our family lives in Wales so you will certainly understand our interest.

By the way, you may be interested to know that Powys, which was being considered for disposal of intermediate radioactive waste until public pressure caused the Government to abandon its test drilling programme, had a severe earth tremor – one of the highest recorded in Britain for many years.

What I am sure will be of particular interest to you, Dr Roberts, is that this earth tremor took place in an area never before noted for its land movement – so stated by the experts.
Yours sincerely,
Deirdre Rhys-Thomas

United Kingdom Atomic Energy Authority
AERE Harwell, Oxfordshire
Date 5th June 1984

Dear Mrs Rhys-Thomas,

Thank you for your letter of 20th May enquiring why scientists from this laboratory are going to carry out a survey of background radioactivity in Wales. The short answer is that the Welsh Office have asked us to undertake this study and are paying us to carry out a specific series of measurements. However, it may be helpful if I outline a little of the background.

We have been measuring radioactive fallout from atmospheric weapon tests at two locations in Wales (Milford Haven and Snowdon) since the 1950s as part of our world-wide monitoring programme. We regard Milford Haven as our master station because it is free from the influence of industrial activity and in the prevailing westerly winds from the Atlantic; measurements elsewhere in the world are commonly normalised to the observations at Milford Haven. More recently we have included two locations in north and south Wales in our national survey of radioactivity in soil. We have also been making measurements of stable (non-radioactive) trace elements in Wales since the early 1970s, originally at locations near Swansea and near Aberystwyth, and last year this developed into a study focussed on lead and cadmium at six widely distributed urban and rural locations. Certainly Wales is one of the most closely monitored areas in the world.

The widespread public interest in radioactivity in the environment has resulted in the more detailed study now proposed by the Welsh Office. We are able to measure radiation levels in all environmental media down to very low levels, far below those of interest for health reasons. Such measurements have to be made against the background of natural radioactivity which has existed since the earth was formed – the soils and rocks, the atmosphere, plants, even the human body are naturally radioactive – and of weapon test fallout. This background radioactivity varies a good deal from place to place so that in order to make use of the high sensitivity available to detect any change due to industrial activity it is necessary to measure the background levels.

That is the purpose of the study we are undertaking. I

would refer you to the enclosed statement put out by the Welsh Office on 16th May giving more details of the work and the materials to be analysed.

Yours sincerely,

L.E.J. Roberts

Department of the Environment
London SW1
31 May 1984

Dear Mrs Rhys-Thomas

1   Thank you for your letter to the Secretary of State which has been passed to this Division for reply. I apologise for the delay in replying.

2   Unfortunately, I have been unable to obtain a transcript to which you refer in your letter. However, the amount of Sellafield-derived activity in the Arctic waters is of no radiological significance compared to the substantial quantities of radioactivity which are naturally present in seawater.[58] In fact, and as the Secretary of State mentioned, the importance of this man-made radioactivity lies in the information it provides about the movement of ocean currents.

3   You also refer to the 'International Water Tribunal', a self-appointed body set up by Dutch environmentalists which held hearings in Rotterdam on October 3-7 1983. The Government decided that to support an unofficial body, such as the tribunal could undermine the official bodies for such discussions at international level, namely the Paris Convention on Pollution which is concerned with marine pollution from land based sources and which will discuss means of minimising radioactive discharges to marine environments at a meeting later this year, and the London Dumping Convention which is concerned with pollution of the marine environments from the sea itself. It was therefore decided by the Government to advise British Nuclear Fuels and other British companies not to attend the 'International Water Tribunal'.

4   I have enclosed a copy of the recent statement made to the Commons by the Secretary of State which presents the current

situation regarding the Sellafield Coastline. I hope this information is helpful.
Yours sincerely
Mr M Mardell
Radioactive Waste Division

Note 58: The 'substantial quantities of radioactivity which are naturally present in seawater' are spread uniformly throughout the vast expanses of the ocean, unlike the effluence from Sellafield, which, although the scientists in the 1950s thought that it would quickly spread itself thinly over a vast stretch of the sea-bed, has in the event shown an unfortunate tendency to creep back to the shore, and some distance inland. Traces have travelled a fair distance, but the bulk remains in the Irish Sea.

The other significant difference between the radionuclides discharged from Sellafield and the radioactivity of sea-water was discussed in note 53.

4 June 1984

To: Lynn Redgrave
Topanga,
California

Dear Lynn Redgrave,
I remember hearing you vividly describe your frustrating battles with the TV moguls over not allowing you to breastfeed your baby at the studio. How you couldn't make them see sense.

Can you give me any tips on how I can get the defence buffs to understand that to my sons the newly-deployed Russian missiles now targeted for the first time on Britain, in answer to Cruise, make them feel less safe, less secure.

My sons know that we can already blow ourselves up 10 times over so they can't see any sense in this.

Have your children got to the age when they are asking you the most impossible questions about nuclear war?

Best wishes,
Yours sincerely,
Deirdre Rhys-Thomas

The letter was returned with 'EMIGRATE' scrawled, very large, across the bottom . . .

Thames Valley Police

P M Imbert QPM
Chief Constable

KIDLINGTON
OXFORD OX5 2NX
TELEPHONE (08675) 4343

GWJ/AT

Ms D Rhys-Thomas

22 December 1982

Dear Deidre Rhys-Thomas,

Thank you for your letter dated 13 December 1982.

It was very kind of you indeed to write informing me of the kindly and courteous behaviour of the police officers on duty at Greenham Common on Sunday, 12 December 1982.

As you are aware, this was a very delicate situation and I am pleased that all the police officers dealt with it so well. I will ensure that your kind remarks are brought to the attention of the officers concerned.

There is one point I would wish to make, and that is, there are no "riot" police in this Force nor in any other Force in the country. The police officers who were actually based inside the airfield were ordinary police officers and were not riot police. I am sorry to labour this point, but I am anxious that all members of the public realise that those police officers who perform duty at demonstrations, football matches, etc. are the same police officers who normally perform ordinary police tasks in our towns and villages.

Once again, many thanks for writing - I am delighted you thought the demonstration such a success.

I wish you a happy Christmas.

Yours sincerely

CHIEF CONSTABLE

BUCKINGHAM PALACE

From: The Assistant Private Secretary to H.R.H. The Prince of Wales

17th January, 1983

Dear Mrs Thomas

Thank you for your letter of 7th January to The Prince of Wales. Your views on this difficult subject have, of course, been noted and His Royal Highness is very grateful to you for writing.

Yours sincerely

Francis Cornish.

Mrs. Rhys Thomas.

Ladbroke Racing Limited

The retail betting division of the Ladbroke Group

Hanover House, Lyon Road.
Harrow, Middlesex HA1 2ES
Telephone: 01-863 5600 Ext.No.
Telex: 923073

Registered Office: Chancel House, Neasden Lane, London NW10 2XE
Registered in England Number 775867

KWO/RDG

18th April, 1983

Ms. Deirdre Rhys-Thomas,

Dear Ms. Rhys-Thomas,

Thank you very much for your letter of the 2nd April, which was only received this morning.

I regret to advise you, however, that we do not bet on disasters.

Yours sincerely,

K.W. Overton
Managing Director

Ladbrokes leisure

Directors
P M George, K W Overton, C A
B J Dixey, R Ling F C A F C M A

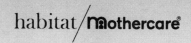

4th May 1983

Ms Deirdre Rhys-Thomas

Dear Ms Rhys-Thomas

Thank you for your letter. I think the colour scheme for
your nuclear shelter should be white with details painted
bright yellow - for optimism!

Yours sincerely

Terence Conran

28 NEAL STREET, LONDON, WC2H 9PH. TELEPHONE 01.240.3474. TELEX 25701.
Registered Office: HABITAT MOTHERCARE PLC, 28 Neal Street, London, WC2H 9PH. Telephone 01 240 3474. Telex 25701
Registered in England & Wales No: 988644.

From: Major The Hon. Andrew Wigram

BUCKINGHAM PALACE

11th May, 1983

Dear Miss Rhys-Thomas

The Duke of Edinburgh has asked
me to thank you for your letter about
his comments on nuclear weapons.

You may like to have the enclosed
copy of the speech he made on 26th April
to the Symposium on the Social and
Cultural Challenge of Modern Technology
organised by the Fellowship of Engineering.

Yours Sincerely

Andrew Wigram

Miss D. Rhys-Thomas,

CYNGOR SIR

POWYS

COUNTY COUNCIL

Chief Executive & County Treasurer/
Prif Weithredwr a Thrysorydd y Sir
S. V. Woodhouse, I.P.F.A.

Emergency Planning Officer/Swyddog Cynllunio Argyfwng
Mr. Mike Dray

Powys County Hall/Swyddfa Sir Powys
Llandrindod Wells, Powys, LD1 5LE.

Telephone/Teliffon
Llandrindod Wells (0597) 3711

To: Deirdre Rhys-Thomas,

If calling or telephoning please ask for/ Os yn galw neu'n ffônio gofynwch am	Extension no./ Rhif ymestyniad
Mr. Dray	385

Your reference/Eich cyfeiriad	Date/Dyddiad	Our reference/Ein cyfeiriad
	15th June 1983	MD

Dear Mrs Rhys-Thomas,

Fall Out Warning

Your letter, dated 20th of April, addressed to the Mayor of Knighton has now been forwarded to me for reply.

First of all I must emphasise that the warning system and matters relating thereto is the responsibility of the Police and they maintain and administer the scheme as well as carrying out the routine tests.

A summary of the information you request is set out in "Protect & Survive" and I have enclosed copies of the relevant pages. You live close enough to Knighton Police Station to hear the maroons (3 bangs) and this could well be re-enforced by whistles soon after to indicate the approach of fall-out.

The All Clear is a long steady note on the siren.

With regard to a "dummy-run" this is entirely a matter for Home Office and the Police but my own view is that any practical exercises involving the general public are not on at this time. War is not imminent and such public involement at this time would, in my opinion, cause un-necessary distress especially to those who still remember the air raids and blitz of the last war.

Yours sincerely,

County Emergency Planning Officer.

PRIME MINISTER
INDIA

New Delhi
July 16, 1983

Dear Miss Rhys-Thomas,

   Your letter of the 30th June shows astounding
lack of knowledge about India's policies and attitudes.

   Apart from Japan, India is the only country
which has taken a firm stand against nuclear warfare
and has been consistently working for disarmament.

   We use nuclear energy for energy, for agriculture,
for medicine. Our policy and our intension is to use
it only for peaceful and developmental purposes.
However, you are right in saying that in spite of
sophisticated communications, nations are becoming
more insular in their outlook. The advanced ones want
to use their technological supremacy to dominate others.

                           Yours sincerely,

                           (Indira Gandhi)

Miss Deirdre Rhys-Thomas,

SECRETARIAT OF STATE

Dear Mrs Rhys-Thomas,

    His Holiness Pope John Paul II has received
your kind letter and he has directed me to reply
in his name.

    His Holiness wishes you to know that he
appreciates the sentiments which prompted you
to write to him, and he invokes God's blessings
upon you and your family.

       Yours sincerely,

       Mgr R. Marsiglio
       Department Head

Mrs Deirdre Rhys-Thomas

From The Rt Hon Dr David Owen MP

HOUSE OF COMMONS
LONDON SWIA OAA

9th August, 1983

Deirdre Rhys-Thomas

Dear Deirdre Rhys-Thomas,

You wrote to me about Cruise missiles. It is a pity that you didn't take
the trouble to find out my views before labelling me rather offensively as
belonging to the 'Chorus of Cruise Supporters'.

What I have supported and continue to uphold is the 1979 NATO decision to
deploy Cruise and Pershing, if there had been no agreement in the INF talks
in Geneva by the end of 1983. I don't want to deploy Cruise and I still
hope we shall see some kind of interim agreement along the lines of the
informal package put forward by the US negotiator Paul Nitze in his now famous
"walk in the woods". But I don't believe the way to get concessions from the
Soviet Union on their own deployment of SS20's, which was after all the
original purpose of the 1979 NATO decision, is to announce before the INF
talks have failed that we renounce totally any deployment of Cruise.

Even in the event of the INF talks failing to produce an outcome, the SDP
would still not automatically deploy Cruise. We went into this in some
detail in the SDP White Paper on Defence and Disarmament in Europe and I am
sending you the relevant extract. I do hope this will enable you to more
clearly understand my position.

Yours sincerely,

David Owen

1st September 1983.

Dear Mrs Thomas,

    Mr. Macmillan, who is presently resting in the country, has asked me to write and apologize for the delay in replying to your letter of the 1st August.

    The words you quote were, of course, addressed to President Kennedy by him when he was urging the negotiations which led to the Test Ban Treaty. This, at least, was a partial contribution to the problem. Meanwhile Mr. Macmillan feels that the West must continue it's nuclear defence but it should be ready to enter into and promote further negotiations at any time for the reduction of nuclear weapons and looking into the far future for their final abolition.

                Yours sincerely,

                Personal Secretary

Mrs Thomas

November 2, 1983

Ms. Deirdre Rhys-Thomas

Dear Ms. Rhys-Thomas:

Thank you for sharing your thoughts with me about the intermediate-range nuclear force.

I am afraid the Intermediate-Range Nuclear Forces (INF) Talks in Europe are in grave jeopardy. And, even if the talks are stalled, I believe it is vital that we continue to press the Soviets for agreement. Frankly, I liked the first idea the President put forth for an agreement in which neither side would have intermediate-range missiles in Europe. This is consistent with my long-standing concerns about verification, because there is no arms control agreement easier to verify than a total ban. If you see a prohibited weapon, you have your adversary cold; it is a clean and simple approach.

Unfortunately, absolute zero proved to be unattainable. And if zero is not possible, the smart thing to do is to get the next best deal. But, we may have lost our best opportunity when Ambassador Paul Nitze tried to negotiate a deal last summer and was publicly repudiated by his own Administration for his efforts. Now the Soviets have dug their heels in and may be unwilling to discuss limitations even after the deployment of U.S. missiles begins later this year.

What we seek in an INF agreement is rough force equivalence at reduced levels. A halt in the arms race and a reduction of super-power tension serves the interest of both sides and, indeed, the whole world. I believe that it is most unfortunate that an agreement limiting intermediate range nuclear forces in Europe appears highly unlikely prior to the NATO deployment in December, and both the U.S. and the USSR share the blame, in my view, for the failure of the INF talks to date.

I recommend we break the deadlock by combining the inter-mediate-range weapons talks with the START strategic weapons negotiations. Two years of inconclusive discussions at Geneva should convince us that the arbitrary approach we have taken, based on the range of a weapon, has not worked. A weapon's range alone fails to define adequately its role and mission. Moreover, comparing nuclear forces East and West in this fashion assumes a weapon comparability that does not exist.

I believe, for example, that ground-launched cruise missiles could be extremely destabilizing, given the difficulties of verification and thus the great difficulty of capturing them in an arms control agreement once they are deployed in significant numbers by both sides. Thus, despite the difficulties I acknowledge it would raise, I have proposed that the U.S. temporarily delay deployment of GLCM's in Europe in order to see if there is the possibility of an agreement which would keep this new and destabilizing weapon from contributing a new level of complexity to the already formidable challenges we face in controlling nuclear weapons.

I believe we must rededicate ourselves to achieving real arms control based upon a reduction in the total number of nuclear warheads possessed by both sides. We should seek an agreement to establish a ceiling at lower levels on strategic and intermediate range warheads, thus reducing the destructive potential of both sides while allowing Washington and Moscow to choose the mix of weapons they wish to retain in their inventory. If we are really serious about arms reductions, such an approach gets at the real problem -- warheads -- in a sensible but flexible way.

I appreciated hearing from you on this important issue.

Best regards.

Sincerely,

John Glenn
United States Senator

JG/dm

16th March, 1984

Dear Mrs Rhys-Thomas

        Thank you for your letter of
the 7th March, 1984.

        NATO is about preventing war,
and I think you will agree, has been
successful in the last 35 years - and
everything that we do and everything
that I shall seek to do in NATO, will
be for that purpose.

                    Yours sincerely

                    Carrington

Mrs. Deirdre Rhys-Thomas,

CHAIRMAN
Ian MacGregor

29th March, 1984.

Ms. D. Rhys-Thomas,

Dear Ms. Rhys-Thomas,

Thank you for your letter of the 14th March, in which you raise the question of the need for nuclear power.

I would say that the current stock piles of coal are not really relevant to the need for additional power stations. The next nuclear power station to be ordered could not be working fully much before the mid-1990's and we would hope to get the coal industry into a reasonable balance of supply and demand well before then.

Our analysis of the relative costs of coal and nuclear power indicates that the comparison is between the very capital intensive nuclear system which has low operating costs, and the coal system which is more modest in its capital requirements but which has relatively higher continuing operating costs over the life of the station.

The French Government have opted for a programme of substantial investment in nuclear power with the contraction of their coal industry, because of their belief this will provide France with the lowest energy costs in Europe and thus support and attract industry.

The price of coal in the UK will increasingly be influenced by the international coal prices. In our view, these will have to increase significantly above current values before there will be a clear overall economic benefit in favour of new nuclear power stations.

With regard to the postscript I was born in Kinlochleven in 1912 but my family moved first to Edinburgh in 1918 and Glasgow in 1920. I did have some relatives, an uncle and cousins who remained in Kinlochleven and may have left there before World War II.

Sincerely,

Ian MacGregor.

4001/3/84/B/35

4 June, 1984.

Dear Lynn Redgrave,

I remember hearing you vividly describe your
frustrating battles with the TV moguls over not
allowing you to breastfeed your baby at the studios.
How you couldn't make them see sense.

Can you give me any tips on how I can get the defence buffs
to understand that to my sons the newly-deployed Russian
missiles now targeted for the first time on Britain, in
answer to Cruise, make them feel less safe, less secure.

My sons know that we can already blow ourselves up 10 times
over so they can't see any sense in this.

Have your children got to the age when they are asking you
the most impossible questions about nuclear war?

Best wishes,

Yours sincerely,

Deirdre Rhys Thomas
Deirdre Rhys Thomas

Lynn Redgrave,

EMIGRATE!

Vladimir Skossyrev
Izvestia Correspondent in U.K.

3. 5 - 84

Dear Deirdre Rhys Thomas,

Thank you for your letter. I am
afraid you took a wrong way of
channeling your letter to Mr. Gromyko.
I think that the address which is
on it, is correct, and there are a
lot of English-reading people in
the ministry.

As you sent the letter to me,
may I make some comments on
it. It seems to me that you put blame
equally on both sides, and it is a
totally wrong approach. It is not
my country that started nuclear race.
If we produced nuclear weapons, it
is only to be able to catch up with
the nuclear weapons, invented by the
USA. And the sole reason of having
them is to be able to deter nuclear
blackmail and to defend ourselves.
If you look carefully at the history
of nuclear race, you will understand
that the USA were always to be the first
in introducing of new kind of nuclear
armaments. And it is not my country
which refuses for nuclear freeze and
for a treaty for no first use. In fact
the USSR took a unilateral obligation
for no first use, but unfortunately
Nato's strategy in Europe is based on
the idea of using nuclear armaments

Yours faithfully, Sven

P.T.O.

P.S. I would like to add, that
I fully understand your anxiety
for the future of your children.

DEC 1 2 1984

Mrs. Deirdre Rhys-Thomas

Dear Mrs. Rhys-Thomas:

This is in response to your letter of 17 September 1984 to Chairman Palladino.

Both the U.S. and the U.K. have established a basic annual dose limit of 500 millirems for the protection of any individual member of the public against radiation. This limit was recommended by the International Commission on Radiological Protection (ICRP) in 1959 and was reaffirmed by the ICRP in 1977. Thus, we believe that there is no difference between the U.S. and the U.K. on the basic dose limit.

We believe that the more stringent levels that you refer to are values applicable to U.S. nuclear power plants and related uranium fuel cycle facilities. These standards implement longstanding recommendations of the ICRP and other international and national authorities that all exposures to radiation and releases of radioactive materials in effluents to unrestricted areas should be maintained as low as is reasonably achievable (ALARA). The ALARA concept is intended to take into account the state of technology, the cost of radiation protection measures in relation to benefits to the public health and safety, and other societal and socioeconomic considerations, in relation to the utilization of atomic energy in the public interest.

At the time the ALARA concept was being incorporated into U.S. regulations (particularly the basic "Standards For Protection Against Radiation," 10 CFR Part 20, and regulations applicable to nuclear power plants, "Domestic Licensing of Production and Utilization Facilities," 10 CFR Part 50), industry representatives requested that guideline values be established for their types of facilities to define the ALARA concept. As a result of rather lengthy considerations specific ALARA guideline values for nuclear fuel cycle facilities were incorporated into 10 CFR Part 50. Standards comparable to these guidelines were incorporated into regulations of the U.S. Environmental Protection Agency (EPA) as 40 CFR Part 190. The EPA value (25 millirem per year) is a factor of 20 lower than the basic annual dose limit of 500 millirems.

Enclosed are copies of 10 CFR Part 20 and 10 CFR Part 50 of the NRC's regulations, and 40 CFR Part 190 of the EPA's regulations. Your special attention is invited to §§20.1(c), 20.105, 20.106, to the concentrations of radioactive materials in air and water listed in 10 CFR Part 20 Appendix B, Table II, 50.34a, 50.36a, and 10 CFR 50 Appendix I.

We suggest that you contact Dr. Roger Clarke, Secretary of the U.K. National Radiological Protection Board, if your wish further information on U.K. practice.

Your questions on ocean disposal specifically referred to the discharge of those radioactive wastes which are produced at nuclear fuel reprocessing plants. There are no plants operating in the US to reprocess commercial spent fuel at this time and there have been no wastes from the reprocessing of commercial spent fuel requiring disposal since 1976. Reprocessing plants related to U.S. military programs are located inland and their effluents are not directly discharged to the ocean.

We sincerely hope that this information is helpful to you and will help resolve your concerns regarding a potential difference in the radiation protection practices between our two countries.

Sincerely,

Robert B Minogue

Robert B. Minogue, Director
Office of Nuclear Regulatory Research

Enclosures:
10 CFR Part 20
10 CFR Part 50
40 CFR Part 190

cc: Dr. Roger H. Clarke, Secretary
    National Radiological Protection Board
    Harwell Didcot
    Oxfordshire OX11RQ
    UNITED KINGDOM

Sailing in Maine
Aug 5 1985

Dear Mrs Thomas

Thank you for writing. I still believe
that citizens can change the course of
government if they will overcome their cynicism
and inertia. (In America only half the citizens
bother to vote.) Of course the answer to not
enough money for school is to stop wasting
it on nuclear arms that only make us
all more insecure.

My answer to children's question about
nuclear annihilation would be, "It could
happen, but it doesn't have to if we would
all vote, write, lobby." Then the parent
can tell what she or he is doing, and
suggest that the child write a letter to
the prime minister or president, MP or MC

It was through political activity
that slavery was ended, child labor was
stopped, and women got the vote.

Sincerely

Ben Spock

Dear Deiot Rhys Thomas,

Being an actress will have no bearing whatsoever on how I confront a Nuclear holocaust. Being a mother — it concerns me greatly.

Yours sincerely

Judi Dench.

ENIGMA

Deirdre Rhys-Thomas   17 March 1986

Dear Mrs. Rhys-Thomas,

I am sorry to have taken so long to reply to your
letter of the 12th December, but I thought you
would be pleased to know that the next major film
I plan to make for Warner Bros. will be the story
of the (malign) creation of the atomic bomb.

I don't know if you will find it satisfying in
terms of a black comedy, but I promise you, if
we do our job properly, it will at least get
people sitting up and talking.

By the time the film is released Theo will have
finished his 'A' levels and hopefully setting out
changing the world from University.

Thanks for writing.

                    Warmest regards,

                    David Puttnam

DP/vk

ENIGMA PRODUCTIONS LIMITED 15 QUEEN'S GATE PLACE MEWS LONDON SW7 5BG 01 581 0238/9 TELEX 888445 ENIGMA G
AND AT 9454 WILSHIRE BOULEVARD BEVERLY HILLS CALIFORNIA 90212 (213) 859 7107/8 TELEX 698702 BNB BVHL

6 June 1984

To: Dr Brian Wade,
Head of Environmental Studies Group
United Kingdom Atomic Energy Authority,
AERA Harwell,
Oxfordshire

Dear Dr Wade,
You are the very man who can tell me: why are scientists from Harwell going to conduct a 3-year survey into the levels of background radioactivity in Wales?

I read your letter in The Observer. It wasn't until I was told about the ALARA Principle that I understood how the nuclear industry calculated their risk factors, so why didn't you mention it in your letter?

You may remember my County was one of those being highly considered for nuclear waste disposal – because there are more sheep than people! Ostensibly it was for high level waste but obviously because of the clay-type rocks here it was for intermediate level. Public opposition, led by the Arch Druid of Wales, stopped test drilling but what may interest you is that last month we had an earth tremor, one of the highest recorded in Britain for many years. This was in an area experts said was previously not known for land movement.

So I do envy you your complete confidence in nuclear energy, and the spin-off of nuclear waste. I am a mere Mother, wanting the best kind of world for my sons to grow up in, so I've always thought it very short-sighted to be so hung-up on nuclear energy when the problems of disposing of nuclear waste have not been overcome.
Yours sincerely,
Deirdre Rhys-Thomas

United Kingdom Atomic Energy Authority
Environmental and Medical Sciences Division
AERE Harwell, Oxfordshire
2nd July, 1984

Dear Mrs Rhys-Thomas,
Thank you for your letter of 6th June. You raise a number of points which I will try to deal with in turn.

Firstly you ask why Harwell is going to carry out a 3-year survey of background radioactivity levels in Wales. I believe you have asked the same question of my Director, Dr L.E.J. Roberts, and that by now you will have received his reply. I hope that provides the information you are seeking, but if you have supplementary questions I will be pleased to answer them.

Secondly, you ask why my letter to the *Observer* did not mention the ALARA principle. Basically the reason is one of space. I tried to cover the points as concisely as I could but the Editor still deleted some of my letter before publication. Thus it was only possible to refer to the high standards of radiological protection adopted in this country in the broadest terms – there was no room to detail important points of principle such as ALARA within the general subject.

Thirdly, you are sceptical about the safe disposal of radioactive waste. In scientific terms we have now reached the position that the problem of safe disposal is solved – we know what has to be done to ensure that the radiation dose to people from disposal is quite negligible. It remains to apply that knowledge to particular disposal sites (involving careful measurement of their properties), to carry out the necessary engineering and to deal with the problem of public acceptability. The last point may well be the most difficult. You have highlighted the fierce emotional response that the subject of waste disposal arouses in Wales, and there have been similar reactions in other places. But I believe that when the general public understand the remarkably high standard of safety proposed then disposal will be acceptable.[59]

Finally, you express the wish for the best kind of world for your sons to grow up in. I can wholeheartedly echo that sentiment. I too have a son, and I am doing everything I can to secure the brightest possible future for him. I am entirely convinced that the advent of nuclear power will benefit his life and future happiness.

Yours sincerely,
Dr. Brian Wade

Note 59: Brian Wynne, who teaches science and technology policy at Lancaster University, points out several interesting facets of the misunderstandings that creep in when laypersons and scientists debate. There is a tendency on the part of scientists to think that they argue from an 'objective' and therefore disinterested standpoint, and that the arguments of the laypersons are based on emotional if not hysterical 'subjective' views. What is missed out of this interpretation, is the area of social expectation and experience of both sides. By and large the scientists go by the rule – if there are regulations which describe perfect control, then they assume that whatever is governed by the regulations is safe and acceptable. The 'woman on the Clapham omnibus' looks at the same things from a very different aspect – she *knows* that however perfect things are on paper, or in intention, the real world is messy, real people cheat on regulations, and if an accident can happen, it will. Thus we have two perfectly sincere people who are not giving the same meaning to words, and whose expectations of events are totally at odds. Each of them is struggling to find security for their children, but they disagree fundamentally on whether it is wise to be certain, when certainty has so often been shown to be misguided.

See Wynne, Brian, *Rationality and Ritual: The Windscale Inquiry and Nuclear Decisions in Britain*, London, British Society for the History of Science, 1982.

21 July 1984

To: Dr Brian Wade,
Head of Environmental Studies Group,
Environmental and Medical Sciences Division,
AERE Harwell,
Oxfordshire

Dear Dr Wade,
Since receiving your letter we have now had our second earthquake and once more experts say they don't know why they're happening in Wales, not known for earthquakes.

How right you are, there was fierce emotional response in Wales over nuclear waste disposal but don't think that it was ill-informed – information was sought from scientists throughout the World.

I follow your reasoning on nuclear waste disposal – and again I stress I am only a Mother not a nuclear scientist – but I cannot understand how you can be so happy about nuclear waste disposal until the research being done today on the safety of deep geological disposal of radioactive nuclear waste, *vis-à-vis* the effect of microbes living deep under the earth's surface and their effect on nuclear waste containers has been completed.

The world you want for your son is not the World I want for my sons. In your World I take it that you are quite happy with the Irish Sea now being the most radioactive sea in the

World. But my sons have to swim, paddle, and sail in it – we
have our boat at Aberdovey. I can't see that it will benefit their
lives and future happiness.
Yours sincerely,
Deirdre Rhys-Thomas

United Kingdom Atomic Energy Authority
Environmental and Medical Sciences Division
AERE Harwell, Oxfordshire
30th July 1984

Dear Mrs Rhys-Thomas.
I felt I should respond to the further questions in your
second letter. Firstly you ask how I can be satisfied with the
safety of nuclear waste disposal when much on-going research
remains to be completed – you specifically mention the effect of
microbes at the deep geological levels but you could have cited
many other topics currently under investigation. Broadly the
answer lies in the multiplicity of barriers to the migration of
radionuclides back to our environment. Even if we assume that
the waste miraculously changes itself into soluble form
immediately after disposal, the radionuclides are still faced with
the absorptive properties of the surrounding packing, the low
rate of ground-water movement and the barrier of the
geological strata. It is this succession of barriers which
engenders confidence in the conclusion that the resultant
radiation dose to people will be quite trivial. Research is
continuing to establish cheaper, more cost effective methods of
disposal and to prove that specific sites have the particular
properties necessary for safe disposal – just as industry generally
continues to undertake research on well-established
technologies. If we can show, for example, that our waste
containers are impervious to all the microbes that may be
present then it may be possible to use thinner containers or
cheaper materials.
Secondly you cannot see any benefit in the Irish Sea being
the most radioactive in the world. From the point of view of
people it does not matter if a particular sea is the most (or the
least) radioactive, or the deepest or shallowest or hottest or
coldest or the most polluted by sewage, etc. What matters is
whether any harm arises as a result of the particular feature.

The radioactivity in the Irish Sea is a quite negligible risk – if its radioactivity was the only hazard then you and your children could paddle, swim and sail in it without concern. But of course there are other hazards which are very much greater than its radioactivity, to the point where people die in easily measurable numbers every year. In the country as a whole some 300 people are drowned each year, some in the Irish Sea. If you sail your boat then you run a risk far greater than that from radioactivity. In return for the trivial radiation risk we obtain an energy source to replace expensive oil, generating electricity with less risk than using oil or coal. We also reduce the cost of electricity – the French, with over 50% of their supply from nuclear stations get their electricity at some 30% lower cost than in the UK. Overall the benefit of cheaper electricity produced with less risk whilst minimising the need for oil far outweighs the radiation risks involved. That is part of the better future I want for myself and my children and my grandchildren yet to be born.

So you can enjoy sailing in the Irish Sea without any worries about radioactivity. But do make sure your sons wear their lifejackets.[60]

Yours sincerely,

Dr. Brian Wade

Note 60: The factor that is omitted from this catalogue of barriers placed between radioactive waste and the environment is the length of time that they must remain intact. A quarter of a million years is a long time, long enough for there to be an ice age, perhaps, with glaciers crushing rocks and gouging out valleys like the Norwegian fiords. Even for less long-lasting radioactive materials, say those classified as suitable for treatment as intermediate-level wastes, the length of time involved is 3,000 years. If the Trojans or Ancient Greeks had invented nuclear power, we would still be guarding the wastes.

The generation of electricity from nuclear power has not been shown to have less risks than coal, unless you ignore the fatalities among uranium miners who are not part of the British workforce, and deny the fact that there is no safe level of radiation exposure. The length of time it takes for cancer to develop after exposure clouds the issue of safety; the nuclear industry is a bare 40 years old, and the levels of contamination arising from it have been slowly increasing throughout that time. The payment in health has hardly had time to become visible, although a number of studies of the health of workers in nuclear facilities in the States led to a reduction in exposure levels to one twentieth of the levels permitted in the UK.

20 June 1984

To: J.P. Kleiweg de Zwaan, Esq.,
Counsellor,
Royal Netherlands Embassy,
London

Dear Mr Kleiweg de Zwaan,
Thank you for informing me that the contents of my letter to
Mr Lubbers have received due attention.
    I wonder if you would be so kind as to clarify the following
for me. Sometime ago, when I was visiting my Dutch cousin, I
heard a high-ranking Dutch Officer openly speak out against
nuclear weapons. When I questioned this with my dinner guests,
I was told that it was quite within the Dutch rules and
regulations for any officer or rank to do so: is this correct?
Yours sincerely,
Deirdre Rhys-Thomas

Ambassade Van Het Koninkrijk Der Nederlanden
Royal Netherlands Embassy
London
26th June 1984

Dear Mrs Rhys-Thomas,
    With reference to your letter of June 20, 1984 I may inform
you that Netherlands military officers as other citizens of my
country have the right to express their own opinion on all
matters. However, if they speak in capacity of spokesman of a
particular governmental organisation, they should express the
view of the organisation concerned.
Yours sincerely,
J.P. Kleiweg de Zwaan,
Counsellor

4 March 1985

To: Brigadier P.F.B. Hargrave, C.B.E.
Director of Army Recruiting,
Empress State Building,
London

Dear Brigadier Hargrave,
Are officers and soldiers serving in the British Army who
disagree with nuclear policies allowed to talk openly about this
without jeopardizing their careers? Not at a public meeting, but
just, say, over a drink with friends/acquaintances?
Yours sincerely,
Deirdre Rhys-Thomas

Ministry of Defence
Empress State Building
London SW6
7 March 1985

Dear Miss Rhys Thomas,
Thank you for your letter dated 4 March.
My responsibility as Director of Army Recruiting is to meet
the annual recruiting targets that are set for me. I am not
responsible for the careers of those officers and soldiers who are
actually serving in the Army.
I have therefore passed your letter to the Department
concerned who will, no doubt, contact you shortly.
Yours sincerely,
[Brigadier P.F.B. Hargrave, C.B.E.]
Director of Army Recruiting

Ministry of Defence
Our reference D/AG Sec 2/16/20/3H, TEJ7
28 March 1985

Dear Mrs. Rhys-Thomas,
I have been asked to thank you for your letter of 4 March 1985
to Brigadier Hargrave, which was passed to this branch of the
Ministry of Defence for investigation and reply.
It has been a long-standing principle that the Army must
always be, and be seen to be, neutral in political matters. Service

185

personnel, in their capacity as such, should not therefore participate actively in matters of political controversy. To this end, the relevant parts of Queen's Regulations lay down that regular personnel are not to take an active part in the affairs of any political organisation, party or movement. There is, however, no restriction upon regular personnel attending political meetings provided that uniform is not worn, that service duties are not impeded and that no action is taken which could bring the Service into disrepute.

It follows, therefore, that the answer to the specific question which you raised is that there can be no objection to a soldier or officer, in his private capacity, expressing his own personal opinion at a private social function or over a drink with friends or acquaintances.

Yours sincerely,
[Miss S Paul]
AG Sec 2c

Your ref: D/AG Sec 2/16/20/3H. TEJ7

1 April 1985

To: Ms Susie Paul,
Ministry of Defence,
London SW6

Dear Susie Paul,
Thank you for your letter. You write 'There is, however, no restriction upon regular personnel attending political meetings provided that uniform is not worn, that service duties are not impeded and that no action is taken which could bring the Service into disrepute.'

I take it therefore that the Ministry of Defence has no objection to a soldier or officer joining the CND?

Yours sincerely,
Deirdre Rhys-Thomas

P.S. I still think it's funny to think that the Director of Army Recruiting is only concerned with counting numbers. It's such a grand-sounding title for the job. I would have thought that Army Recruiting Officers at the UK offices would have told prospective entrants what they could and couldn't do in the Army.

18 April 1985

Dear Mrs. Rhys-Thomas,

Thank you for your further letter dated 1 April, in which you asked whether the Ministry of Defence objected to Army personnel joining the Campaign for Nuclear Disarmament.

Queen's Regulations allow members of the Armed Forces to be members of a political party or organisation, and these rules would apply in the case of the Campaign for Nuclear Disarmament. However, as you are aware Service personnel are specifically precluded from actively participating in such groups; this requirement is part of the general policy that the impartiality of Her Majesty's Forces must not be brought into question.

With regards to the postscript to your letter, every applicant to the Army is given a thorough job-briefing and in-depth interviews before going to the selection centre at Sutton Coldfield. Despite this, with the thousands of applications that the Army Careers Information Offices process, it would be impossible for every 'DO' and 'DON'T' of the Army to be explained to each individual. However, if an applicant has a particular question, this will always be answered.

Yours sincerely,
Susie Paul

12 September 1984

To: Dr Alice Stewart,
The Cancer Registry,
University of Birmingham,
Edgbaston,
Birmingham

Dear Dr Stewart,
It came as a surprise to learn from Dr Roberts of Harwell that Wales is one of the most closely monitored countries in the world for radioactive fallout from nuclear weapons tests, indeed that 'measurements elsewhere in the World are commonly normalised to the observations at Milford Haven.'

I enclose Dr Roberts' letter and a News sheet from the Welsh Office.

I wonder why Wales has been chosen, would Wylfa and Trawsfyndd Nuclear Power Stations, and the Irish Sea have any bearing on the baseline?

Have any studies been done on children in Wales with respect to exposure to low-level radiation? I can't help feeling as a Mother that this would compliment the Welsh Office survey.
Yours sincerely,
Deirdre Rhys-Thomas

Birmingham & West Midlands
Regional Cancer Registry
Queen Elizabeth Medical Centre
Birmingham
9th November, 1984

Dear Mrs Rhys-Thomas,
We are at present engaged in relating all childhood cancer deaths in Britain (1953-84) to levels of background radiation. When we have any results we will let you know but do not expect anything in less than a year from now.[61]

Yours sincerely,
Alice M. Stewart

188

Note 61: Dr Alice Stewart's survey relating all childhood cancer deaths in Britain to levels of background radiation is expected to be published in the autumn of 1986. It will be an invaluable epidemiological study of a rather contentious issue, that is whether background radiation contributes to the incidence of cancer, and if so, to what extent.

Dr Stewart's earlier work, published in 1957, showed that even a single X-ray of the abdomen of a pregnant woman increased the risk that her baby would die of leukemia before the age of five by 40%. Nowadays, women of childbearing age are given a lead apron to hold over their lower back if they have a chest X-ray, and X-rays of pregnant women are avoided wherever possible.

(An 'epidemiological' study is when research is carried out into the health records of whole communities, involving the records of thousands of people, and statistical mathematics.)

6 July 1984

To: Dr Eric Chivian,
Staff Psychiatrist,
Massachusetts Institute of Technology,
Cambridge
Massachusetts

Dear Dr Chivian,
Your studies of Russian and American children – that they don't hate each other and recognize the need to work with people whom adults recognize as enemies – doesn't surprise me. This is what my children feel. And knowing this makes me more sad because my eldest son has no confidence in those very adults who should be looking after him. He is so cynical of our World Leaders.

I try to reassure my children, to underplay the sayings of our paranoid Leaders and their respective military hawks, and yet how can I take away their fear of nuclear war when just now Theo has come into the kitchen and flung a newspaper on the table. In it there is an article about the American Air Force which is going to start building 15 – 200-bed – hospitals at the American military bases in Britain for their troops because the British National Health Service will not be able to cope with the casualties of a nuclear attack.

I tell you, Dr Chivian, it's this kind of pressure on my children that makes me scream and cry with rage and frustration. How I'd like to get Chernenko, Reagan, Thatcher, Mitterand to try and make sense of their deterrence to my children. Deterrence, so my sons tell me, means, 'Not knowing what Peace is because war is only ever minutes away'.

With best wishes,
Yours sincerely,
Deirdre Rhys-Thomas

Harvard Medical School/The Cambridge Hospital
Nuclear Psychology Program
Studies of Psychological Issues in the Nuclear Age
July 27, 1984

Dear Mrs. Rhys-Thomas:
Thank you very much for your letter of July 6th. It touched me
to hear of the pain that you and your family feel in this
unsettled world of ours. I also appreciate your interest in our
project to study the effects of the nuclear war threat on
children.

Enclosed please find more information on this project.[62]
With my regards,
Eric Chivian, M.D.
Research Associate

Note 62: Dr Chivian wrote a chapter about his work on the adverse
effects of the use of nuclear weapons as deterrents which is published in
Farrow, S. and Chown, A. (eds), *The Human Cost of Nuclear War*,
Medical Campaign Against Nuclear Weapons/Titan Press, Cardiff, 1983.

20 June, 1984

To: The President of Tanzania, Dr Julius Nyerere,
c/o The Tanzanian High Commission,
London.

Dear Dr Nyerere,
The way I feel at the moment any crumb of comfort is gratefully
received. So thank you for starting the 'four-continent peace
initiative' which I understand aims to put a freeze on nuclear
weapons production.

I wish you all the luck in the world, all the cunning and
patience in dealing with the Super Powers, Britain, France, and
China.

For my part, I'm fed up with explaining away their
prejudiced paranoid actions to my sons – only so that my sons
may feel less tense about living in this World where they can
already be blown up 10 times over with the nuclear weapons
already stockpiled.
Yours sincerely,
Deirdre Rhys-Thomas

The State House,
Dar es Salaam,
Tanzania.

6th August 1984

Dear Ms Rhys-Thomas,
	Thank you for your letter of encouragement about the
Joint Statement signed by myself and five other national leaders.
The problem you have in trying to explain the present actions of
the nuclear powers to your children is one which we share.
	But all of us who are concerned about the dangers to
humanity which are created by the existence and the threat of
nuclear weapons, and by the destructiveness and waste of the
arms race, have a major task in front of us. We shall only
succeed if everyone plays their part in their own area of
operations; and in this the pressure of public opinion in the
nuclear power states can be especially important.
	Let us encourage each other, for we must keep trying.
Yours sincerely,
Julius K. Nyerere

7 March 1984

To: Lord Carrington,
The House of Lords,
Westminster,
London SW1

Lord Carrington,
I understand you will succeed as Secretary-General of NATO in
1984, and I am sure you are aware of the responsibility you
have taken on – that of safeguarding the futures of children, not
just of the Western Alliance, but of the World.
	As a concerned Mother, totally repulsed by the nuclear
arms race, I wish to know what you intend doing about Cruise
in so far as why is Cruise at Greenham Common when the U.S.
Defense Mapping Agency will not complete the basic working
set of maps for attacking primary targets in the Soviet Union
until 1986? As Cruise cannot function without the TERCOM
guidance system I cannot understand how Mr Heseltine can say
that Cruise is now operational.
	Why is the British Government/NATO happy to accept

Cruise missiles at Greenham Common when the final critical testing of them will not take place until next month in Utah and continue until Summer 1985?

I thank you for your reply.
Deirdre Rhys-Thomas

16th March, 1984

Dear Mrs Rhys-Thomas
Thank you for your letter of the 7th March, 1984.

NATO is about preventing war, and I think you will agree, has been successful in the last 35 years – and everything that we do and everything that I shall seek to do in NATO, will be for that purpose.
Yours sincerely,
P. Carrington

20 March 1984

To: Lord Carrington
The House of Lords,
Westminster,
London SW1

Lord Carrington,
Thank you for your letter. You say NATO is about preventing War and that's what you will seek to do. I have never doubted that for a moment.

But you know as well as I do that the NATO Chiefs did not ask for Cruise, it was a political request.

To my mind there is a contradiction in NATO's acceptance of Cruise; it does not increase my children's safety and that's what I look to NATO for.

Perhaps if my questions are answered I will not be a 'doubting Thomas' but there again my brother's comments made on his return from Argentina during the Falklands War will always make me question everything to do with war.
Deirdre Rhys-Thomas

6 July 1984

To: Leslie Kenton,
Health & Beauty Editor,
Harpers & Queen,
London W1

Dear Leslie Kenton,
There's a touch of irony in Monica Fine recommending the
Sloane Rangers to get their iodine intake from Welsh laverbread
– being one of the foods which protects us from the cumulative
build-up of radiation from all sources. A leading British scientist
advised me that laverbread is best avoided as the seaweed
porphyra from which it is made concentrates radioactive
nutrients from seawater.

So unless the Sloane Rangers want an irradiated glow in
their dimly-lit discos perhaps they had better keep off the
laverbread.

Thank you for your excellent article – Radiation, The
Silent Menace.
Yours sincerely,
Deirdre Rhys-Thomas

Harpers & Queen
August 6th 1984

Dear Ms. Rhys-Thomas,
Thank you so much for your letter. I would be very interested
to meet the British scientist you mentioned and see his research.
Perhaps you could be kind enough to give me a name and
address.

I'm sorry for the delay in answering this but I have been
out of the country and have only just seen the letter.
Yours sincerely,
Leslie Kenton
Health and Beauty Editor

Office of the Mayor
The City of Hiroshima
August 6, 1984

Dear Sir/Madam:
It is my great pleasure and privilege to enclose a copy of the 1984 Peace Declaration which I was honored to read to the whole world at the Peace Memorial Ceremony conducted today at Hiroshima Peace Memorial Park on the occasion of the thirty-ninth anniversary of the atomic bombing in Hiroshima.

I also would like to take this opportunity to renew my profound respect for you who are sincerely devoted to the realization of world peace. This realization would be promoted into a definite form only by cooperation and solidarity of people who are eager for peace. I hope for your continuous effort towards our common goal.

It would be most deeply appreciated if you would fully understand the meaning of the enclosed Peace Declaration and convey the 'Spirit of Hiroshima' to as many people as possible throughout the world.

Praying for your continued success in your efforts,
Yours very truly,
Takeshi Araki
Mayor

10 September 1984

To: The Bishop of Hereford,
The Palace,
Hereford.

Dear Bishop,
My eldest son has just told me a rather confused story about a cherry tree being in police custody because the Cathedral staff, we don't know whether they were gardeners or clerics, refused to accept the tree from Hereford Quakers and CND people on August 6.

Theo can't understand this. I have let him read letters sent to me by the Mayor of Hiroshima, Takeshi Araki, and Theo would very much like those people to read them.

I send you Mr Araki's letters.
Yours sincerely,
Deirdre Rhys-Thomas

The Bishop's House,
The Palace.
Hereford
14th September, 1984

Dear Mrs Rhys-Thomas,
    Thank you very much for your letter of 10th September,
1984.
    The story about the cherry tree is indeed confused and you
are quite right in assuming that none of the clergy were involved
in the incident which took place over accepting the tree from
the Hereford Quakers and members of the CND on 6th August.
    Your eldest son may be interested to know that Canon
Masters is a member of the CND and another of the clergy on
the Cathedral Chapter is a member of the peace movement in
Hereford.
    It was an extremely unfortunate incident and if the clergy
had been approached by the vergers of the Cathedral I am quite
certain that the event would not have taken place.
    Your son may also be glad to know that prayers for peace
are said daily in the Cathedral and at midday on one day of the
week there is a half hour period of prayer for peace to which
everyone is invited, and takes place in the nave of the Cathedral.
    Yours sincerely,
    † John Hereford

4 September 1984

To: His Excellency Mr S.S. Ramphal,
Commonwealth Secretary General,
London

Your Excellency,
Several months ago Mr Jim Slater, of the National Union of
Seamen kindly sent me a copy of the Melbourne Communique
1981 signed by the Commonwealth Heads of Government.
    I read and re-read para 37 of the Communique –

Heads of Government noted the opposition in the South
Pacific region to the proposals for dumping and storage of
nuclear waste in the Pacific Ocean and the deep concern at
the serious ecological and environmental dangers to which
member countries could be exposed. In this regard the

resolution adopted at the recent meeting of the South Pacific Forum was strongly supported.

The resolution of the South Pacific Forum 'urges the United States of America and Japan to store and dump their nuclear waste in their home countries rather than storing or dumping in the Pacific' and

reaffirms its strong condemnation of testing of nuclear weapons or dumping or storage of nuclear waste in the Pacific by any government, as having deleterious effects on the people and environment of the region.

Now I am exceptionally pleased that the people of the South Pacific have been able to get their fears and worries through to the Heads of Government. Just because the South Pacific is on the other side of the World it doesn't make my pleasure at their success any less, as it's becoming ever more apparent that this World of ours is a very small place.

On my doorstep is the Irish Sea which can now be called the most radioactive sea in the World. It amazes me how experts could have thought 25 years or so ago that it would be an ideal place to discharge radioactive waste when it is shallow, has frequent storms and strong bottom currents.

But bringing it down to basics if the people of the South Pacific have this Commonwealth protection how, Your Excellency, can the people of Britain get similar protection?
Deirdre Rhys-Thomas

Commonwealth Secretariat
Pall Mall,
London

5 October, 1984

Dear Ms Rhys-Thomas,
The Secretary-General who is at present out of London has asked me to thank you for your letter of 4th September in which you refer to the Section of the Melbourne Communique dealing with the testing of Nuclear Weapons and the dumping and storage of Nuclear Waste in the Pacific, which was issued by the Heads of Government at the end of their meeting in 1981.

In your letter you asked if it would be possible for a resolution of a similar nature to be adopted in connection with nuclear dumping in the Irish sea. Items for the agenda for Commonwealth Heads of Government's meeting are a matter of Heads of Government themselves and since the Irish sea is within the territorial waters of the United Kingdom and the Republic of Ireland (which as you know is not a member of the Commonwealth) it would be a matter for the British Government to seek to put this on the agenda.

Under the terms of the mandate by which it was established the Commonwealth Secretariat may not intervene in the domestic political affairs of a member government and you may therefore wish to put your enquiry to the British Government.

Yours sincerely,
George Dickson
Assistant Director
International Affairs Division

12 September 1984

To: David de Peyer Esq.,
Secretary-General,
Cancer Research Campaign,
London SW1

Dear Mr de Peyer,
I keep on hearing nuclear representatives speak of the safe low-level radiation dose we can be exposed to without risk, I presume they mean without causing cancer.

I find this totally confusing as surely not everyone's immune system responds in exactly the same way, one person's might be less resistant than another person's and although they were both exposed to the same low level of radiation perhaps one might be more susceptible to cancer?

Could you clarify this for me because as a Mother it is my duty to my children to have their best interests at heart.
Yours sincerely,
Deirdre Rhys-Thomas

Dear Mrs Rhys-Thomas

Mr de Peyer has asked me to reply to your letter of 12 September about the risks from ionising radiation.

As you rightly point out, there is still no agreement on the lowest dose of radiation that might lead to the development of cancer. There is some measure of agreement about high doses based on exposure to radiation for workers in occupations where there is a risk but it is very much more difficult to measure the extent to which exposure at low levels might constitute a danger.

As you rightly say, individuals vary in susceptibility to cancer, whether the risk comes from radiation or some cancer-causing substance or from a habit such as cigarette smoking. It is now known that most cancers require a combination of several factors to initiate and then promote their development. One of these factors will be the individual's own genetic constitution and the fact that this is so obviously greatly complicates the possibility of preventing cancer.

There are three main sources of ionising radiation: occupational, medical, including the use of X-rays for diagnosis and for treatment, and background radiation from the environment and from within our bodies. The background radiation does vary within and between countries and is of low magnitude and there is no evidence that this radiation ever reaches the level that might lead to the development of leukemia or any radiation related cancer. When this source of radiation is augmented by some other source, in particular the nuclear industry, any risk is likely to be slightly increased and that is why there are several studies at present investigating whether there is an increase of cancer in areas where the nuclear industry is based and where there has been some leakage or disposal of nuclear waste. Although the excess of cancers that have developed in certain areas has only been very small, it is highly important that every effort should be made to obtain information about the risks.

It is clear that people vary in the effects that cancer-causing agents have on them but individuals in general appear to have strong resistance to low-level radiation since as I have said, this

199

is universal in the atmosphere. Other man-made hazards are being controlled and doctors are very much more cautious in using X-rays for diagnosis, particularly in early pregnancy. Now that radiotherapy can successfully cure many childhood cancers, the surviving children are being carefully followed up to monitor whether the radiation has any long-term effects in them or in their children. It may be that from this research a clearer picture will emerge about the dose relationship. Even in diagnostic X-rays, there is a difference in the hazards for the embryo at the early stage and at the later stages of the development of the foetus.

Although the evidence is not yet complete, it does appear that the risk of cancer developing from exposure to low-level radiation is very slight.[63] I hope that this goes some way towards answering your query. You may be interested in the enclosed leaflet on prevention.

Yours sincerely,
Miss E D Skinner
Cancer Information Officer

Note 63: At a scientific conference held in Neuherburg in June 1985 to investigate Radiation Risks to the Developing Nervous System, there was some discussion about the effects on the growing brain of the unborn child. It seems that irradiation of a baby between 10 and 17 weeks after the last menstrual period is most damaging, and results in the baby being born with a much smaller brain than is normal. Very low doses seem to have led to a fall in scholastic achievement.

Although most of the argument about radiation effects centres on cancer, especially blood cancer (leukemia), there are other kinds of damage to health that should be kept in mind.

17 September 1984

To: Mr Nunzio J. Pallidino,
Chairman,
Nuclear Regulatory Commission,
Washington D.C.
U.S.A.

Dear Mr Pallidino,
I am sure you get lots of letters so I'm just hoping that my letter will reach your desk for your personal help.

I have two sons who I dearly love and wanting the very

best World for them I'm trying to make sense of the nuclear puzzle so would you please tell me –

I keep hearing here in Britain that the radiation dose levels we use as a reference are based on doses recommended by an International Commission more than 25 years ago and that in America limits have been very much reduced since then – in fact they are 20 times more stringent than the levels we use in Britain. Is this so?

Do you discharge any radioactive waste from nuclear reprocessing plants direct into the seas off the American coast? And if not, why not?

As I say I'm a Mother not a nuclear scientist so I would be very grateful if you could explain this. Thank you.
Yours sincerely,
Deirdre Rhys-Thomas

United States Nuclear Regulatory Commission
Washington, D.C. 20555
Dec 12 1884

Dear Mrs Rhys-Thomas,
This is in response to your letter of 17 September 1984 to Chairman Palladino.

Both the U.S. and the U.K. have established a basic annual dose limit of 500 millirems for the protection of any individual member of the public against radiation. This limit was recommended by the International Commission on Radiological Protection (ICRP) in 1959 and was reaffirmed by the ICRP in 1977. Thus, we believe that there is no difference between the U.S. and the U.K. on the basic dose limit.

We believe that the more stringent limits that you refer to are values applicable to U.S. nuclear power plants and related uranium fuel cycle facilities. These standards implement longstanding recommendations of the ICRP and other international and national authorities that all exposures to radiation and releases of radioactive materials in effluents to unrestricted areas should be maintained as low as is reasonably achievable (ALARA). The ALARA concept is intended to take into account the state of technology, the cost of radiation protection measures in relation to benefits to the public health and safety, and other societal and socioeconomic

201

considerations, in relation to the utilization of atomic energy in the public interest.

At the time the ALARA concept was being incorporated into U.S. regulations (particularly the basic 'Standards for Protection Against Radiation,' 10 CFR Part 20, and regulations applicable to nuclear power plants, 'Domestic Licensing of Production and Utilization Facilities,' 10 CFR Part 50), industry representatives requested that guideline values be established for their types of facilities to define the ALARA concept. As a result of rather lengthy considerations specific ALARA guideline values for nuclear fuel cycle facilities were incorporated into 10 CFR Part 50. Standards comparable to these guidelines were incorporated into regulations of the U.S. Environmental Protection Agency (EPA) as 40 CFR Part 190. The EPA value (25 millirems per year) is a factor of 20 lower than the basic annual dose limit of 500 millirems.

Enclosed are copies of 10 CFR Part 20 and 10 CFR Part 50 of the NRC's regulations, and 40 CFR Part 190 of the EPA's regulations. Your special attention is invited to §§20.1(c), 20.105, 20.106, to the concentrations of radioactive materials in air and water listed in 10 CFR Part 20 Appendix B, Table II, 50.34a, 50.36a, and 10 CFR 50 Appendix I.

We suggest that you contact Dr. Roger Clarke, Secretary of the U.K. National Radiological Protection Board, if you wish further information on U.K. practice.

Your questions on ocean disposal specifically referred to the disharge of those radioactive wastes which are produced at nuclear fuel reprocessing plants. There are no plants operating in the US to reprocess commercial spent fuels at this time and there have been no wastes from the reprocessing of commercial spent fuel requiring disposal since 1976. Reprocessing plants relating to U.S. military programs are located inland and their effluents are not directly discharged to the ocean.[64]

We sincerely hope that this information is helpful to you and will help resolve your concerns regarding a potential difference in the radiation protection practices between our two countries.

Sincerely,
Robert B. Minogue, Director
Office of Nuclear Regulatory Research

cc: Dr. Roger H. Clarke, Secretary
   National Radiological Protection Board
   Harwell Didcot
   Oxfordshire
   United Kingdom

Note 64: At present none of the 'spent' fuel from nuclear power stations
in the US is processed. When they want plutonium they make it and
process it in military factories, from military reactors.

They do have quite a lot of problems with waste, though. For instance,
they have millions of tonnes of uranium tailings near the uranium mines
and mills. Some of the tailings were used as landfill for levelling ground
for roads and building sites, and have led to a lot of health problems for
the people living in these places.

They are also trying to decide what to do with 100 nuclear submarines
that they are currently replacing with bigger models, and suggestions for
burial have varied between sinking them in the middle of the ocean,
dumping them in the desert or paying China to dump them in the Gobi
desert.

16 September 1984

To: Mr Andrew Pomiankowski,
Department of Biology,
University of Sussex,
Brighton,
Sussex.

Dear Andrew Pomiankowski,
To be honest I don't like statistics but I am very interested in the
Black Report on leukemia levels near Sellafield. I think it is my
duty as a Mother to be interested and I can't forget the
uncertainty of those Mothers who appeared in the Windscale —
Nuclear Laundry programme.

So would you explain why you feel there should be serious
doubt over the Report's conclusion that the leukemia level near
the reprocessing plant is 'unusual but not unique' and what
difference did it make not including the 1983 cases?
Yours sincerely,
Deirdre Rhys-Thomas

The Wellcome Institute for the History of Medicine
London
1st October 1984

Dear Ms Rhys-Thomas,

Thank you for your letter to which I reply with a copy of my letter to *Nature*. You may find the statistical argument unintelligible, but the point is simple.

Everyone agrees that the occurrence of childhood leukemia around Windscale is high. But is it abnormally high? To answer this, I'm afraid, one needs a bit of statistics. What this tells us is that the occurrence in Seascale (the village close to Windscale) is very very unlikely to have occurred through chance.

The reason for doubting the Black report's judgement on this is that they used an inappropriate statistical arrangement of the data and only considered the years from 1968-82; 1983 saw two further cases of lymphoma being reported, making the possibility that the occurrence in Seascale was due to chance even less likely.

All this does not *prove* that Windscale is to blame, but from my point of view it does not justify the Report's 'qualified reassurance'.[65]

I hope this will make things a little clearer. Yours sincerely,
Andrew Pomiankowski

PS. I enclose Russell Jones letter to the *Lancet*.

Note 65: Following the Yorkshire TV programme – 'Windscale: The Nuclear Laundry', Sir Douglas Black was asked by the Minister of Health to head an independent inquiry into the number of cases of cancer, especially childhood cancer, that had occurred near Sellafield. The Report said that it was not possible on the evidence given to say that the discharges of radioactive waste from Sellafield had caused the increase. It did recommend that further research be carried out, and that the management of the reprocessing plant be improved. Sir Douglas Black was asked whether he would live near Sellafield, and said not if he had a choice.

The Report made 10 recommendations, including the suggestion that more work should be done on measuring doses of radiation actually received by members of the public in West Cumbria, rather than on guesswork based on what was thought to have been received.

See *Investigation of the Possible Increased Incidence of Cancer in West Cumbria*, Chairman: Sir Douglas Black, HMSO, 1984.

17 September 1984

To: Dr John Dunster,
Director,
National Radiological Protection Board,
Chilton,
Didcot,
Oxfordshire

Dear Dr Dunster,
I find it difficult to put into words my disgust at learning only the other day that for 2 years the amount of radioactive waste discharged from Windscale was deliberately increased in order to find out where it was going because as a spokesman said, 'There was no other way of finding out what happened when radioactivity was released.'

My trust, and my children's, is given to scientists like you on the understanding that experiments are conducted under conditions where any harm done can be undone not to allow you to change the environment because it's my World, my children's World, as much as it is yours, Dr Dunster.

What gives you the right to apply the ALARA principle in such matters where a death or damage to one person is one too many?

That you had Government support for your experiment doesn't reassure me at all: how dare a Cabinet Minister, a Civil Servant, think he has the right 'to play God' and change the environment.

I can only be thankful that Greenpeace was monitoring the Windscale pipeline and picked up the recent radioactive contamination of the beaches.
Yours sincerely,
Deirdre Rhys-Thomas

National Radiological Protection Board
Chilton Didcot
Oxfordshire
27th September 1984

Dear Mrs Rhys-Thomas,
I am sorry that you feel so strongly about decisions such as that at Windscale in the early 1950s, and I am not sure that

anything I can say now will do much to reassure you. Nevertheless, let me try to set the decision in some sort of perspective.

By 1952 a great deal of laboratory and environmental work had been done to establish the limits to be imposed on releases of radioactive waste then planned to take place from Windscale Works at Sellafield into the Irish Sea. Although extensive, this information lacked any direct determination of the way in which radioactive materials would move through the environment and the extent to which they would return to man. We had established limits on the basis of the work already done but it was thought necessary to use the early marine discharges to confirm or modify those limits at an early enough time for it to be possible to introduce changes to the plant should this be shown to be necessary. Our information indicated that the radiation doses to people would be small and the value of the early information considerable. Those who were responsible for managing the plant took the decision that some increase was needed in order to ensure that more dangerous situations did not develop later.

When I say that the decision was taken at a level much more senior to that occupied by myself 30 years ago, I am not trying to evade responsibility because I think, looking back, that it was a sensible and proper decision. I have spent most of my professional life concerned with protecting people and their environment but I cannot accept your argument that there is no right to change the environment. We do not live in a natural environment and, indeed, at our present level of population could not conceivably do so. We do build roads and cities, we do adopt agricultural practices which increase productivity over its natural levels, we do set up experimental road junctions because we do not know whether the change will be for the better or the worse. In the end it is the process of Parliamentary democracy which gives Cabinet Ministers and their staffs the right to take this sort of action and the responsibility to account for the decisions they take. Of course, a death of one person caused by our industrial society is a death too many but there are very few things in that industrial society which do not involve some risk of death to some people. Most of us use electricity and water and private or public transport and, in doing so, we all take our own share of responsibility for the deaths these services cause. At the same time we all share the credit for the overall improvement of standards of health to which these aspects of our society contribute. I would not argue that we always get the balance right but I would like you to believe that we are all trying.

Yours sincerely,
H.J. Dunster CB
Director

9 January 1985

To: Mr John Taylor,
Editor,
'Jane's All the World's Aircraft',
London

Dear Mr Taylor,
While in Palma over Christmas I bought the *Observer* – costs £1.62 there – so imagine my dismay when our maid threw it away before I had finished reading it! But I seem to remember reading in it that you think Cruise is a useless weapon and that it doesn't do anything to improve the defence of the British people.[66] Is this so?

Can you a defence expert explain to me a Mother whose concern is my children's safety why the Government has accepted Cruise into Britain?

Thank you.
Yours sincerely,
Deirdre Rhys-Thomas

Note 66: See Ian Mather, 'Editor Hits at Cruise', *Observer*, 23 December 1984.

Jane's All The World's Aircraft
Jane's Publishing Company Limited
Surbiton
Surrey

24 March 1984

Dear Mrs Rhys-Thomas
Please forgive me for not answering earlier your letter of 9 January, concerning the report in the *Observer* of my warning

207

on the Cruise missile's shortcomings. The reason is that I suffered a coronary thrombosis in December, and am only now returning to work.

Having five small grandchildren myself, I can understand your concern.

Briefly, there is no point in this country maintaining any kind of nuclear *strategic* deterrent. We could never use such weapons against any small nation, such as Argentina, which violated our sovereignty, or we would become outcasts in a world that retains a vestige of civilisation. And how could we ever launch even one such weapon against, say, the Soviet Union? The U.K. would not exist 20 minutes later.

In any case, the Cruise missile is a highly unsatisfactory weapon. There have been many failures in test firings of the various versions. Performance is only marginally higher than the wartime German V-1 flying bomb, which we shot down in hundreds with 1940-vintage defences. It does not possess the sophisticated electronics devices needed to penetrate a modern defence system.

So, to my mind it is utterly wrong to have such missiles based in the U.K., making our nation a more essential target for the nuclear weapons of an enemy.

Having said that, please do not think that I expect a nuclear war. I feel, still, that the Soviet Union – in particular – has far too much sense to start anything that would lead to a 'nuclear winter'. Also, nuclear weapons cannot be uninvented. So, sad though it is, a *very* small number must be retained in the hands of an international (ideally USA-USSR) force to deal with any small 'dictator' who might produce a few such weapons overnight and threaten to hold the world to ransom.

The essential need is for talks of the kind now taking place in Geneva to produce results. I say 'of the kind' because I have no faith in the present negotiators. We need people from each side whose aim is to ensure life, liberty and happiness for their own children and grandchildren. The right people would meet before lunch, talk about arms reduction, and wonder what they could do with their time after lunch as all would have been agreed by then.

I hope that my thoughts make some sense. As you will see, I cannot agree entirely with the views of well-intentioned people in groupings like the CND, as their objectives could not end the overall danger. Nor do they take in the whole gamut of

inhuman weapons that must be reduced or eliminated.
Yours sincerely,
J.W.R. Taylor FRAeS. FRHistS. FSLAET. AFAIAA
Editor

10 January 1985

To: Dr Eric Hamilton,
Institute of Marine Environmental Research,
Plymouth, Devon.

Dear Dr Hamilton,
As a Christmas treat I bought myself the *Observer* — cost me
£1.62 in Palma. To my dismay our chambermaid threw it away
before I had finished reading it! I did however jot down several
notes about an interview with you concerning nuclear wastes.

Would you be so kind as to tell me — have you found that
nuclear waste from Windscale now surrounds the whole of
Britain's coast? And that though the levels are dangerous no one
knows how dangerous it is to be exposed to low doses of
radiation over a long period?

Thank you.
Yours sincerely,
Deirdre Rhys-Thomas

Institute for Marine Environmental Research
Plymouth
29 January 1985

Dear Miss Thomas
Thank you for your letter of 10 January and my apologies for
the delay in replying. The report in the *Observer* was not
accurate. The presence of BNFL radionuclides throughout UK
coastal waters has been known for many years. The levels are
very small. The total dose received by man is mainly derived
from natural sources: 13% come from artificial sources, of
which 11.5% is derived from medical applications. It is
accepted that all ionising radiation is potentially harmful and as
yet we do not know, and possibly never will, the long term
effects from exposure to very low doses simply because we have

always been exposed to them from natural sources and hence any contribution to morbidity or mortality is built into the normal statistics.

Your concern is understandable, but in relation to the Sellafield wastes it is unfounded.[67]

Yours sincerely,

E I Hamilton

Note 67: The biggest difference between background radiation and X-rays as compared with radionuclides from nuclear facilities is that particles of radionuclides become airborne, or are absorbed by fish and vegetables, or get into cow's milk, and they are then swallowed or breathed in by humans. Once inside the body they settle in favoured places (caesium goes for muscle or the ovaries, strontium and plutonium stick to bones). They carry on giving off gamma-rays, which are tens of times more forceful than X-rays as they burst through nearby cells, or they shoot out beta or alpha particles which are like microscopic cannonballs. An X-ray passes through the body; a speck of caesium may stay in the flesh for up to two years, and plutonium will stay in the body for life.

According to a report published in the *New Scientist* on 14 August 1986, Don Popplewell of the National Radiological Protection Board found concentrations of plutonium in the bodies of former workers at the Sellafield plant hundreds, and in one case thousands, of times higher than the general population. Autopsies on the bodies of Cumbrians who did not work at the plant showed concentrations of plutonium from 50 per cent to 250 per cent higher than elsewhere in Britain.

14 January 1985

To: Xavier Pastor,
President of Greenpeace Spain,
Palma de Mallorca,
Spain.

Dear Xavier Pastor,

While we were in Mallorca over Christmas we visited the Exhibition at the College of Architects. Being British we were ashamed to read of the distress caused to the Spanish people by the British nuclear dumping off Galicia.

Had our Spanish been better we would have explained to those Mallorcans, who realised we were from Britain, that we too hated this dumping policy which has been carried out by successive Governments.

I wonder if you have heard of the recent research by the

Institute of Marine Environmental Research which has just found that nuclear waste from Windscale now surrounds all Britain's coast? As traces have been found off Greenland and the Baltic do you think the Spanish people should be concerned about the daily discharge of 2.2 million gallons of water containing nuclear isotopes into the Irish Sea?

The scientist who conducted this research is himself concerned about low level radiation: he says, 'The question of how dangerous it is to be exposed to low doses of radiation over a long period is very difficult to answer. In truth no one knows.'
Yours sincerely,
Deirdre Rhys-Thomas

Greenpeace España
Madrid
4th February 1985

Dear Deirdre Rhys-Thomas,
Thank you for your letter in relation with the Greenpeace and G.O.B. exhibition at the College of Architects of Palma.

We thank you very much for your words related to your feelings about the dumping policy of Great Britain. As you can see, not only the Galician people is worried about this activity. People living in an island in the middle of the Mediterranean sea are also very concerned about the consequences of the radioactive waste disposal at any ocean. In 1983, very strong demonstrations were carried out against the British consulate in Palma, as in many other towns of Spain.

In any case, we know perfectly well that there are millions of British people that are also against this dumping activity. In fact, the help that the British Trade Unions gave, and the special concern of Jim Slater were essential to stop the dumping activities in 1983.

We understand that the problems caused by Windscale to the British and Irish peoples, and especially to those from Cumbria, are of even a greater magnitude than the ones caused by the dumping activity in the Atlantic. Some news have appeared in Spanish press about the possibility of radioactive pollution from Windscale in the coasts of North Spain. But, unfortunately, no strong reaction has followed those news.
Yours sincerely,
Xavier Pastor

1 March 1985

To: Dr Henry P. Coppolillo,
Professor & Director of Division of Child Psychiatry,
University of Colorado,
Health Sciences Center,
Denver,
Colorado

Dear Dr Coppolillo,
I think of you as my friend. Your letter to me was so kind, so caring and understanding.

There are still friends of mine who just won't think that their children's lives may be permanently damaged because of their fear of nuclear war. I can understand their ostrich attitude, thinking of the nuclear arms race is like trying to understand where space ends, it just goes on and on and on.

Would you please, Dr Coppolillo, summarise for me your research describing the symptoms children can show when under the threat of nuclear war.

I send my best wishes to you and your family,
Yours sincerely,
Deirdre Rhys-Thomas

P.S. You know for all their public statements they don't care — Reagan, Gromyko, Thatcher — about 1 Mother who really cares about her children's future in this nuclear infested world, who isn't prepared to gamble the lives of her children on the altar of nuclear rhetoric. I know, I wrote to them: answer came there none. But Indira Gandhi cared: she wrote to me.

University of Colorado Health Sciences Center
Denver, Colorado
March 25, 1985

Dear Mrs Rhys-Thomas,
Thanks so much for your letter of March 1. It was particularly heartwarming to read that you think of me as a friend. In

today's world of technology and profit margins, human exchanges of warmth and friendship become increasingly more precious and rare.

I was sorry to read that our great leaders did not have time to answer a concerned mother. Had you been the head of a state, no matter how insignificant, or the president of a company, who might have contributed to a political campaign, you would have probably received an answer. But being a mother, the only office that we are sure is indispensable for continuing the human race and insuring its future, is not sufficiently important to warrant an answer. I cannot subscribe to the value system that permits this kind of insensitivity as to what is vital for us. When you mentioned that Indira Gandhi had written you, the thought came back of a folk song from the Appalachian Mountains that was popular during the Second World War. The author in it asks why 'the worst of men must fight and the best of men must die.' She was one who spent at least some of her life trying to insure that our children would have a future – and she died.

As far as the work on avoiding the holocaust is concerned, I have largely reported the research of others and will send you a paper in which the research is summarized. I think the important point that people must realize is that the symptoms of children's anxiety can be insidious and well-hidden. Children have learned well that adults either do not want to hear children's worries, or that they will deride them when they are articulated. Therefore children will avoid mentioning certain topics unless they are specifically asked. As you can see from my brief paper, when Sybil Escalona asked about the future, 70% of children mentioned atomic warfare, the atom bomb or a nuclear holocaust. I have had children tell me that not one day goes by that they do not think of a nuclear holocaust more than once. Sometimes, in more vulnerable children we see symptoms such as nightmares, poor school performance and apathy or pessimism about the future. In more well-integrated children the concerns leading to these symptoms are unexpressed, but create fearfulness and sadness from which our children protect us.

In both instances, however, the most corrosive effect is that we humans are gradually losing our ability to look to the future with optimism for a better tomorrow. As a result more humans join the 'now generation' in which immediate gratifications are sought, long-term intimacy is shunned, and an established conviction that goodness and love can be found in our fellow human beings is forsaken. Each generation therefore will have more isolated people in it and with the erosion of human relatedness and basic trust the probability of settling difficulties through destructiveness increases.

None of us wants this for our children, but so many are complacent and disbelieving. My point therefore is that a nuclear explosion may not be the only way that the atomic age is destructive to humankind. The very threat of countries having a nuclear arsenal erodes our children's serenity, their basic trust that the world will protect their tender lives and a belief that their well-being is a sacred trust with which we adults will keep faith. We must undo this erosion of their faith. To live in a world like the one described in *The Clockwork Orange* or Orwell's *1984* may be more horrifying than even those splendid authors imagined.

With my deepest respect for your concerned activism and my best wishes for you and your family, I am
Your friend,
Henry P. Coppolillo, M.D.
Professor of Psychiatry

10 March 1985

To: The Rt Hon. Chrisopher Chataway,
Hon. Treasurer,
ActionAid,
London

Dear Mr Chataway,
Maybe I'm misjudging you, but I have never heard you speak out in public against the purchase of Trident? This wasted money.

Your advert says £95 a year will save Mwende Kamana of Kenya.

As you are the Hon. Treasurer of ActionAid can you tell me how many Mwendes = 1 Trident?
Yours sincerely,
Deirdre Rhys-Thomas

ActionAid
3rd April, 1985

Dear Mrs Rhys-Thomas,
　　Thank you for your letter of 10th March. I am very glad
that you are interested in the possibility of becoming a sponsor
and I enclose an Action Aid leaflet. Having been the Honorary
Treasurer now for a number of years, I can assure you that this
is an extremely effective way to help a a child and its family.
　　I am not sure that my views on defence are particularly
relevant. But since you ask, I should mention that I am not a
pacifist or even a unilateralist. I am inclined to think, however,
that the relatively small proportion of the defence budget spent
on Trident would be better devoted to conventional forces,
where the gap is large and unfortunately growing. Better still, of
course, would be multi-lateral disarmament.
Yours sincerely,
Christopher Chataway.

29 October 1985

To: Mr Trevor Joseph,
Chairman of John Beddoes PTA,
Kinsham,
Powys.

Dear Mr Joseph,
You'll have read about the National Parents Teachers
Association Report that schools are crumbling: children haven't
enough text books. (We should count ourselves lucky that at
least the school had a lick of paint in honour of Princess Anne's
visit last year.)
　　Did the Report come as a shock to you? It certainly didn't
to me. Theo (my eldest son, now in the Lower Sixth taking 'A'
levels) wasn't able to have required 'O' level textbooks because
of the cutbacks.
　　And disturbingly last week's *Mid Wales Journal*, front
page, revealed yet more cuts to come in our children's
education.
　　What does the John Beddoes PTA intend doing?
　　To me, it looks as if the only money which can be diverted
is the £11 billion Trident money. £11 billion! Can you take in

215

that amount, Mr Joseph? I can't all I know is it's a hell of a lot of money. The 50,000 nuclear weapons we've got today don't make us feel safe, so I can't see how more nuclear weapons on Trident are going to make my children any safer.

Yours sincerely,

Deirdre Rhys-Thomas

Kinshan
1st November 198.

Dear Mrs Rhys-Thomas,

Thank you for your letter. I can assure you as Chairman of John Beddoes P.T.A. that we all share your concern for the education of our children. The report by the N.C.P.T.A. is profoundly disturbing. I read, for example, that parents' contributions to schools went up by 200 percent between 1980 and 1984 and that parents are now spending £40 million a year to bolster state provision. The actual sum provided by Powys L.E.A. for text books, stationery etc. is £10,580.84. This works out at about £15.00 per pupil — an amount which is quite simply inadequate. We will do everything we can to campaign for better provision for our schools and the issues you have raised will be fully discussed at our next P.T.A. meeting. My thanks for your letter and for your support for John Beddoes School.

Yours sincerely,

T. Joseph.

10 July 198.

Dear Dr Spock,

I've not had the chance to read your new edition of *Baby and Child Care* but what really interests me is reading yesterday an article mentioning that you've got a chapter on the importance of parents becoming politically active to make a better World for their children and to preserve it from nuclear annihilation.

Four years ago, my son Theo then 12, asked me that question which all Mothers must dread hearing, 'Will there be a nuclear war?'

You know I was totally unable to cope. I mean I was frightened for Theo and myself, it brought up all my own fears, my guilt that I'd let these politicians build up their nuclear weapons, and pure unleashed anger that my child should be burdened with this fear.

All I could rely on and be guided by were my maternal instincts, my intuition.

Theo's now 16 and only the other day he thanked me for visiting Greenham Common, and Molesworth, and having written to the nuclear authorities questioning their attitudes. And although, he says, the World is no safer indeed he feels it is more dangerous – he was quite happy seeing 'Star Wars' on the cinema screen but he doesn't want it up above his head – he feels able to cope because he knows I will do all I can to protect him, and love him. In this my husband, Peter, has been so understanding and supportive.

But, Dr Spock, I don't know about getting politically active. The track-record of successive British Governments on the nuclear issue has been appalling. And I can't make head or tail out of the new SDP/Liberal Alliance – the SDP leader wants Cruise; the Liberal leader doesn't?

We've had a By-Election in our region. It created much media interest because it brought out 'the Thatcher Factor' – a rejection of Mrs Thatcher's dictatorial ways – and yet I wonder how many of these voters were her ardent 'Argie-bashers' round the Falklands War?

What's worrying parents round here is not enough money for their children's school books, schools promised but not built, lollipop school crossing patrols stopped, yet few parents at meetings suggested that the £11 billion to be spent on Trident – a mere £500,000 million each year for the next 20 years so the Defence Minister has said – should be spent instead on these necessary requirements.

You know, Dr Spock, I have a dream. Women, Mothers in the World getting themselves together – never mind the political opinions – but for their children and becoming politically-wise, educating ourselves about all things nuclear, and taking on those over-blown, over-opinionated, over-manipulated negotiators at the Geneva Arms Talks. What's wrong with Mothers of the World sitting in on the talks? We have to answer our children's nuclear fears.

Yours sincerely,

Deirdre Rhys-Thomas

Benjamin Spock, M.D
Arkansas
Aug 5 1985

Dear Mrs Thomas,
Thank you for writing. I still believe that citizens can change the
course of government if they will overcome their cynicism and
inertia. (In America only half the citizens bother to vote.) Of
course the answer to not enough money for schools is to stop
wasting it on nuclear arms that only make us all more insecure.

My answer to children's questions about nuclear
annihilation would be, 'It could happen but it doesn't have to if
we would all vote, write, lobby.' The parent can tell what she or
he is doing, and suggest that the child write a letter to the prime
minister or president, M.P. or M.C.

It was through political activity that slavery was ended,
child labor was stopped, and women got the vote.
Sincerely,
Ben Spock

28 March 1985

To: Sir Walter Marshall,
Chairman,
Central Electricity Generating Board,
London

Dear Sir Walter,
Right, Walt, don't fob me off with your lackeys (as you've done in the past) though that seems to be your style — I ask you, the Chairman of the CEGB not being a witness at the Sizewell Inquiry?

I don't know what % of our family's electricity payments have been spent on your love of PWRs but you keep on about the Sizewell PWR not being the same as the Three Mile Island PWR, that it's been modified/re-designed.

O.K., so why have the Americans stopped building PWRs? Even those already under construction? And not ordered any more PWRs whoever designs them?

If the Americans' technology is not capable of re-designing PWRs to their satisfaction, why should the British tolerate lower standards of safety?
Yours sincerely,
Deirdre Rhys-Thomas

P.S. What's in it for you?

Central Electricity Generating Board
London

10 April 1985

Dear Ms. Rhys-Thomas,
Sir Walter Marshall has asked me to thank you for your letter of 28 March 1985 concerning the safety of PWRs, and to reply on his behalf. I am sure that you will appreciate that Sir Walter receives hundreds of letters and is unable to devote all his time to answering these.

The Americans have not stopped building PWRs as there are currently 42 units under construction of which four have been given full power licences in the last six months and one has been given a licence to operate commercially. It is true that there are no further plans at the moment to construct PWRs in the United States, but this is due to financial and institutional problems rather than technological or safety issues. There has also been a cut-back in building conventional power stations as the American utility structure cannot cope with the finances of new plant whether coal-fired or nuclear. The utilities lack the necessary asset base and are unable to adjust their rates to take account of investment, as these are set by the Regulators. The result is American utilities are forced into inactivity by the varying requirements of the tariff regulations, the safety regulations and the bond ratings, even though the demand for electricity is continuing to grow.

It is worth noting that these circumstances are peculiar to the United States. World-wide nuclear capacity is overwhelmingly based on the technology of the PWR. Already PWRs account for more than half of the world's operational capacity and some two-thirds of the plant under construction or on order. A number of countries around the world are embarking on nuclear generation programmes, and almost all of these are based on the PWR, as a well proven system going back over 30 years.

You mentioned your family's electricity payments and the influence of the PWR. It is because of the economic benefits to consumers that the Board wishes to build the PWR in Britain. If you refer to the evidence presented by the CEGB to the Sizewell 'B' Public Inquiry, which recorded the economic case in great detail, you will see that the PWR presents the best economic option for the future, and electricity generated in a PWR power station would be cheaper than that from coal-fired, oil-fired or AGR power stations.

On the question of safety, the independent UK licensing authority, the Nuclear Installations Inspectorate, act as your watchdog and undertake detailed assessments of all nuclear plant before issuing a licence. The Board is *not* tolerating lower standards, and over the years has developed a code of practice and safety record which is second to none. Again, this is recorded at great length in the evidence presented to the Sizewell 'B' Inquiry.

I hope you find this information useful.

Yours sincerely,

G.H. Hadley

Secretary

Friends of the Earth Limited
London
22/5/85

Dear Mrs Thomas,

Thank you for your recent letter enclosing a copy of a letter sent to you on behalf of Sir Walter Marshall, chairman of the CEGB. I share your concern over the bland statements made in this letter, indeed, I find the inaccuracies and selective nature of the reassurances given somewhat insulting to the intelligence of a member of the public.

Dealing with the CEGB's explanation of the disastrous state of the nuclear industry in America first; it is totally incorrect to say that the Americans have not stopped building PWR's. At least 10 reactors have been literally mothballed at various stages of construction, because it is less expensive to do this than complete the plants. Those PWR's that are still being built are proving extremely expensive for the electrical utilities concerned, and if they are completed will result in large increases in electricity rates for the consumers in these areas. For those who think that these problems have only arisen subsequent to the Three Mile Island disaster, it should be noted that the complete halt in PWR orders occurred in 1977, a full two years prior to this. In the past 11 years, cancellations equivalent to 26 Sizewell 'B's' have taken place.

Whilst accepting that the financial and institutional arrangements for electricial utilities in America are different from those in Britain, this merely points to the lack of any form of a free market in electricity generation in this country. American utilities are suffering because they cannot charge the costs of their PWR to the consumer until it is operating. With average construction delays of *three years*, this has resulted in severe financial stress. In Britain, the CEGB have no such problems and thus were able to charge the consumer for the huge construction delays of the AGR programme before a single kilowatt of electricity was produced.

Dealing with the safety issues raised in the CEGB letter, I take great exception to the assertion that the American problems with the PWR are not related to technical or safety issues. The Managing Director of the largest electrical utility in America, the T.V.A., has stated in an article in the *Washington Post* that 'we went too far too fast in deploying large-scale designs of a reactor type we knew too little about . . . the

221

number of changes required appears open-ended, since many safety issues are still unresolved.' The fact is that outstanding PWR safety issues do still remain. At the end of the Sizewell Public Inquiry, only 32 of the 79 safety issues identified by the Nuclear Installations Inspectorate had been adequately resolved This situation arose because an earlier PWR design by the N.N.C., which had many additional safety features in order to reach British Safety Standards, was rejected on the grounds of cost. The new design, an amended off-the-shelf SNUPPS PWR, does not have many of these safety features, and did not have adequate design detail at the beginning of the Inquiry to allow the N.I.I. to issue a safety licence.

The CEGB's estimates of the chances of an accident at Sizewell were heavily criticised by objectors as being unrealistically low. The Board quoted the probability of a core-meltdown accident at around one-in-a-million. A comparable figure calculated for American reactors which had actually been built, rather than simply on the drawing board, was about one-in-a-thousand — a thousand times greater.

Since the ending of the Sizewell Inquiry, a stream of CEGB press releases have poured from their headquarters at Sudbury House, all asserting that the Board's case at Sizewell had been proven. As an attempt to re-write history, it has few equals. Judging from opinion polls over the past three years, a majority of the British people remain unconvinced.
Yours sincerely,
Stewart Boyle,
Energy Campaigns Director

Hugh Richards BArch MA MRTPl
Llandrindod Wells
Powys

May 20th 1985

Dear Deirdre,
        [Comments on your reply from the CEGB]

Okay, it is financial and institutional problems that have led to the demise of Nuclear Power in the USA. Nationalised industries in Britain are constantly being told that they lack the financial discipline of the private sector. So maybe the answer is to extend the privatisation of 'energy corporations' to the CEGB, so we can see if the private investor will put his money into Nuclear Power.

You are asked to note that financial and institutional circumstances, that have led to the end of orders for new nuclear plant in the USA, are peculiar to that country. This may be so, but something very similar must be deterring the rest of the world from ordering large (1100 MW +) Westinghouse PWRs, because the last order for one of these was in 1973.

The PWR is stated to be a well proven system, going back at least 30 years. The Westinghouse PWR design upon which Sizewell's is based is a 1972 design called 'SNUPPS', but only two SNUPPs stations have survived cancellation, and they are only coming into commercial operation this year. In the last eighteen months Westinghouse have closed their 'offshore power systems' PWR factory, and have entered a 'joint venture' with Mitsubishi to design an 'inherently safe' PWR. Sizewell 'B' thus gives us the bitter irony of an obsolete design with no operating experience.

If the CEGB reckon that this failed technology from a country that has already abandoned it is 'the best economic option for the future', objective outsiders may be forgiven for seeing it as continuing the CEGB tradition of investing in proven failure.

Yours
Hugh

14 March 198

To: The Minister of Agriculture The Rt Hon. Michael Joplin,
M.P.
The Ministry of Agriculture, Fisheries & Food,
London SW1

Dear Minister,
It's getting to be impossible trying to answer the fears of
farmers round here and further afield who seem to have
suddenly woken up to the fact that they don't know anything
about what they should do if there's a nuclear war.

One of them told me he'd heard he should hide all his cow
and sheep under black plastic sheet.

The American Surveillance Station at Brawdy is a first-
strike target and as winds tend to be south-westerly you will
understand the concern of inland farmers.

I'm a director of a farmhouse marketing organisation with
special concern for creating employment and preserving the
environment particularly in Mid Wales. We will be having our
Easter get-togethers quite soon and as I know I'm going to be
asked about this again, could you please tell me – by return –
what you as the Minister advise farmers to do?

I've been waiting in vain for your booklet promised after
Farmers for a Nuclear Free Future met, long overdue as the last
one was published by the Min. of Ag. in 1959.

Thank you.
Yours sincerely,
Deirdre Rhys-Thomas

Ministry of Agriculture, Fisheries and Foo
London SW
21 March 198

Dear Mrs Rhys-Thomas
I have been asked to reply to your letter of 14 March, addressed
to the Minister, seeking advice on what measures farmers could
take to protect their families and livestock from the effects of a
nuclear war.

224

The strength and resolution of the NATO Alliance has maintained peace in Europe for some forty years now and is expected to continue to do so. A nuclear war is not, therefore, considered likely let alone inevitable. However, a prudent Government must consider even the smallest risk a possibility, however remote, and this Department in common with others has a responsibility to plan for this and other contingencies.

In the event of a real threat of war, which might or might not escalate to a nuclear exchange, the general public would be given specific advice on what they should do in the way of preparation; similar advice would be given to the farming community to take account of their special problems with regard to livestock and crops.

The booklet *Home Defence and the Farmer*, to which you referred, was published in 1958 but went out of print following the 1962 edition. The advice it contained remains generally valid and much of it will be included in the updated version which is now being prepared; publication of this has been delayed by the need to take account of certain matters including a recent Home Office review of the blast and radiation damage caused by nuclear explosions.

Obviously I am unable to go into the booklet's content in depth here but, in short, it will recommend protective measures that can be taken to reduce the effects of radioactive fallout. In so far as livestock are concerned advice is given on the need to provide adequate shelter and care, including the prevention of contamination of feed and water. The aim is to keep radioactive fallout as far removed from animals as possible and to stop it coming into contact with their skin, or internal organs by ingestion. Any shelter is therefore better than none and, in the absence of all else, even a cover of thin plastic as you describe would be better than nothing at all. However, metal sheeting, timber, baled hay and straw is usually available to farmers which would enable them to substantially enhance the protection afforded by buildings usually found on farms.[68]

I hope that this will enable you to field any questions raised at your forthcoming meeting.

Yours sincerely,

J W F Frost

Note 68: When the levels of radioactivity recorded in rainwater in parts of Scotland, Cumbria and Wales reached the point at which the animals

should be brought in from pasture, and fed on hay and prepare
foodstuffs, the Ministry of Agriculture gave no advice to farmers. It wa
not until several weeks after the Chernobyl disaster that the Ministr
imposed a ban on the sale of lambs, when the level of caesium in the
bodies was above the limits acceptable even in this country.

The measurements of radiation given out to the public were based o
the average figures for large areas, and the variation from too high t
quite low within those areas was not divulged. A spokesman from th
Ministry of Agriculture said, at the time when some cow's milk ha
dangerously high levels of iodine contamination, 'We don't have th
policy of divulging area breakdowns of the radiation figures for milk. . .
The tendency would be for members of the public to buy their milk from
areas with a less radioactive level and that would be no good for the mil
suppliers.' At the very least, the Ministry should have reacted quickly t
prevent contaminated milk being used for making milk powder fo
babies.

If the Ministry were not able to come up quickly with advice for copin
with the extreme edges of a nuclear accident, how can we rely on them t
cope with nuclear fallout after a war?

4 March 198.

To: Derek Cooper,
The Food Programme,
BBC Radio,
London W1

Dear Derek Cooper,
I only caught the tail-end of your item on putting together a
nuclear shopping list, but it sounded as if you had as much
difficulty as I had when I attempted this.

Cookery experts, Supermarket Directors were unable to
give me a complete nuclear shopping list for 2 adults + 2
children + 1 beagle for 2 weeks in a makeshift shelter – imagine
us packed in our downstairs cloakroom?

The Government obviously has this information – there are
nuclear larders all over Britain for the Forces, the Government
even British Telecom – so I can't understand why Mrs Nuclear
Housewife (me) can't be told, can you? After all we paid for all
their nuclear goodies.
Yours sincerely,
Deirdre Rhys-Thomas

British Broadcasting Corporation
London
March 21, 1985

Dear Ms Rhys-Thomas,
Thank you for your recent letter about our programme on
'Food and Civil Defence'.

As you will have picked up from listening it is very difficult
to get a clear official message about what the ordinary citizen
would be advised to stock in the awful event of some kind of
nuclear exchange. We were particularly concerned about the
rather confused message we received about the logistics of food
'rationing' in a period of growing tension. It seemed to be left to
the retailers to come up with something.

The Conservative MP, Mr Neil Thorne, who spoke on the
programme said he felt there was official ambivalence about
information: on the one hand too much information might
frighten some of the public while others are frightened by too
little.

I hope you have some success in your future enquiries.
Yours sincerely,
John Forsyth
Producer, 'The Food Programme'

10 March 1985

Mr Clarke,
Chief Executive,
Shrewsbury — Atcham Borough Council,
Dogpole,
Shrewsbury.

Dear Mr Clarke,
Toby (my son, he's 12) would like you to tell him if there will
be room for his Granny, who lives in Shrewsbury, in the new
nuclear bunker underneath the Music Hall?

He saw a poster in a shop window in Shrewsbury when
we were visiting his Granny.
Yours sincerely,
Deirdre Rhys-Thomas

P.S. (I'm sure the existing facilities can cope with any emergency

– civil defence or otherwise in Shrewsbury. Indeed you coped with what could have been the Great Fire of Shrewsbury, right next to the Music Hall.

No doubt your employees and you have been issued with your nuclear passcards/key/codes to the bunker, and just in case they haven't read the British Medical Association's Report on *The Medical Effects of Nuclear War* – pages 122 and 123 – perhaps they should.

If you haven't read it, Mr Clarke, I'll willingly drop my copy into you at your office.)

Shrewsbury and Atcham Borough Council
22nd March 1985

Dear Mrs Rhys-Thomas,
Thank you for your letter of 10th March. I apologise for the delay in replying but I have been on holiday and your letter was put on one side for my personal attention.

It was nice to hear of your son's concern for his Granny but I hope that a poster in a shop window in Shrewsbury is not causing him undue worry as to his Granny's welfare. The Council has, of course, no control over this sort of situation.

The fact is that the Council has provided an Emergency Headquarters as part of its legal obligations. The H.Q. is limited in size and is only just capable of coping with those who would be required to man it if an emergency arose. In fact, those who would be required to man the H.Q. would be obliged to leave their spouses and children in their homes. Obviously, therefore, there will not be room for Granny in the event of the emergency use of the H.Q.

Yours sincerely,
M. Clarke

1 May 1985

To: Alan Francis,
The Ecology Party,
Milton Keynes,
Bucks.

Dear Alan Francis,
I had a call the other day from the nuclear man at the
Australian High Commission, he'd just got back from Geneva
and gave me some information I wanted about the Roxby
Downs Project.[69] I had had several letters end of 1983 from the
Prime Minister about it.

He told me that the Australian Government has given the
O.K. to the project to the company concerned – it's a joint-
venture Western Mining Corporation and B.P., subsidiary of the
British parent company. But it is up to the company to decide
whether it will be commercially viable. He says it is a copper
project, but with uranium by-product and gold.

I hate to be cynical but I can't help wondering if it is a
front, you see my brother is General Manager of an American
mining complex in Argentina extracting copper (and silver +
zinc) and he told us this Christmas that the bottom has fallen
out of the copper market, so therefore it won't be commercially
viable?

Also how does B.P.'s involvement fit in with the British
Government's or British companies military/nuclear weapons
programmes? Tridents, etc?

Can you tell me?
Yours sincerely,
Deirdre Rhys-Thomas

Note 69: The Roxby Downs Uranium, Copper and Gold Mine is being
developed on traditional Aboriginal land in South Australia. The mine is
49 per cent 'owned' by British Petroleum and 51 per cent by Western
Mining Company of Australia. The development of the mine is opposed
by the Coalition for a Nuclear Free Australia and the Aboriginal Kokatha
people. In August 1983 the Kokatha people occupied a sacred area to
prevent its destruction, and won. At least ten other sacred sites have
already been destroyed.

229

When Bob Hawke became Prime Minister of Australia he supporte
the moratorium on uranium mining that was a major part of his party'
policy. However, when it came time to pass laws which would prohib
the mining, milling and export of uranium, the government introduced
clause which allowed uranium to be extracted from mines that wer
principally opened for the mining of other metals. Recently, Australi
announced that uranium mining at Roxby Downs would go ahea
because of the difficult economic situation that Australia, in commo
with many other countries is facing. France has signed contracts to bu
some of the uranium.

Uranium ore is slightly radioactive. There is always radium in the ore
and this gives off a gas called radon. When radon is breathed into th
lungs some of it decays into radioactive lead, and is the cause of lun
cancer. Miners who smoke are ten times more likely to develop lun
cancer than those who are non-smokers, but unless good ventilation i
established in the mine (usually open-cast and dusty) up to 1 in 4 miner
will contract the disease. As long as the uranium-bearing rocks remai
undisturbed, the layers of rock, earth and vegetation above them slo
down the passage of radon to the atmosphere, and much of it decays t
lead before it reaches the surface. The mining and milling of the air leav
millions of tonnes of 'tailings' – the rubble – on the surface of the groun
and these tailings release up to 500 times as much radon as th
undisturbed rock.

It is strange that the sacred sites of the Aboriginal people, just like thos
of the North American and Canadian Native Indians, are frequently i
areas where the underlying geological strata are uranium-bearing rock
These are not places where people live, but where they go to dream or t
meditate. Companies intending to mine in such areas are required t
release an Environmental Impact Study for public debate and commen
they are not required to respect the religious practices and traditions c
native peoples.

See Caldicott, Dr Helen, *Nuclear Madness*, Bantam Books, New York
1980.

Ecology Part
Milton Keyne
Buck

6th May 198

Dear Deirdre,

Many thanks for your letter. I didn't get it until Friday evening
because I had to go to the sorting office to collect it.

I have enclosed a draft of a leaflet which the Ecology Party
will be issuing shortly. This answers some of the questions in
your letter.

The Australian Labour Party, which now holds power, has

230

a policy opposed to uranium mining. However when this policy was passed a loophole was deliberately introduced. This allowed uranium to be extracted if it were extracted along with some other ore. It was through this loophole in the policy that the Australian government was able to approve the Roxby Downs project whilst still in theory being opposed to uranium mining. Your comments about the bottom falling out of the copper market may make their excuse look somewhat lame!

I have shown your letter to Brig. Oubridge who was one of the Ecology Party at the Sizewell Inquiry. He will reply to you in more detail but this may take some time. He was one of the Rainbow Fields villagers evicted from Molesworth by 'Mad Mike' Heseltine and his troops, and so is now 'on the road'. He does not have his source documents with him so it will take some days to retrieve them from where they are stored.

I hope that this information helps you and may I wish you the best of luck with your book.
Yours in peace,
Alan Francis.

8 May 1985

To: Sir Peter Walters,
Chairman, BP Group of Companies,
London EC2

Dear Sir Peter Walters,
The nuclear man at the Australian High Commission tells me you've got the Australian Government's go-ahead for the Roxby Downs project because as he says it's a copper project with by-products of uranium and gold. But it's up to BP (49% stake) and Western Mining Corporation to decide whether it's commercially viable.

Now my brother's been in mining for years; at present he's General Manager of a large complex copper, silver and zinc mine in Argentina, before that in Zambia, and the Atacama Desert, Chile. I can't remember a time when he hasn't complained about depressed copper prices, particularly this Christmas.

But to be absolutely certain I understood the copper market today I phoned the London Metal Exchange. A splendid chap gave me chapter and verse about World dealings in copper:

231

about futures, LME settlement prices, hedging, and that today there's a shortage of cash copper sending up the prices – his theory, the Chinese want copper. I asked him about the Roxby Downs project and he said he would back-pedal on that but put me on to John Edwards, Commodities Editor of the *Financial Times*.

I understand from John Edwards that the long-term outlook for copper is not good because the consumption is threatened by optic fibres, etc. and that this present shortage will be short-lived. He said there have been no takers for $\frac{1}{2}$ of the stake at Escondina Chile, potentially the largest copper mine in the World – the holding was previously held by an oil company but they've got out of metals as they've lost so much money in them.

Therefore I trust, Sir Peter, that BP will not go ahead with your Roxby Downs project because it is not commercially viable. Or is it perhaps not the copper you're after? Surely not a 20th century gold rush? So is it the uranium? Will we need it for Trident? Or for the £300 million production line for nuclear warheads being built now, yes today, at the Weapons Research Establishment at Aldermaston (as a businessman, Sir Peter, do you think there is any need for this over-production – we've already got enough weapons to kill ourselves 10 times over?) and due for completion in 1986?

But of no less importance to me is the Aboriginal people. I hope BP's caring image for the British people extends to the Aboriginal people? The land you want to use includes their sacred sites of no less importance to them than Westminster Abbey, St Paul's Cathedral, the hallowed turf of Lord's, Wembley, Twickenham, Cardiff Arms Park, even the White House lawn is to us.

Yours sincerely,
Deirdre Rhys-Thomas

BP
London EC2
22 May, 1985

Dear Ms. Rhys-Thomas,
Thank you for your letter of 8th May regarding BP's involvement in the Roxby Downs Project. Sir Peter Walters has

asked me to reply on his behalf.

Firstly, I should like to respond to your points on the Aboriginal people. As a company we share your concern over the well-being of all people and the environment in which they live. Consequently, we endeavour on all occasions to conduct our business in a manner which reflects this concern and I believe that, as a result of this, BP is regarded as a caring and responsible member of society.

The Roxby Downs joint venturers have worked, and will continue to work, closely with Federal and State governments, for it is they who set the parameters within which our business is carried out. We aim to ensure, in all aspects of the development, that safeguards are met fully and the Aboriginal communities are adequately informed and consulted. In fact, an extensive Environmental Impact Statement which dealt with the management of the matters you have raised has been formulated and approved by both the Government of South Australia and the Federal Government.

On the subject of uranium, let me state immediately that BP has nothing to do with the manufacture of arms. Our involvement in the uranium mining industry stems from a belief that in a world of finite hydrocarbon resources, nuclear power has an important and necessary role to play in meeting energy requirements. As a company we do not ignore the very genuine concern that some people have regarding harnessing the power of the atom to generate electricity and as a result of this we support all moves to ensure that nuclear processes are made safe.

We hope then that BP's involvement in the Roxby Downs project provides a measure of reassurance, and I hope that I have satisfactorily answered the questions raised in your letter. The management of this project is conducted in Australia and so if you wish to find out more about the Roxby Downs venture and its place in Australian society may we suggest that you contact The Manager, Government and Public Affairs, BP Australia Limited, Melbourne, Victoria or the project managers who are Roxby Management Services Pty. Ltd., 168 Green Hill Road, Parkside, South Australia, 500.

Yours sincerely,
N.G.S. Champion
Regional Co-ordinator, Australasia Far East Region

5 May 1985

To: Mr Robert O'Neill,
Director,
International Institute of Strategic Studies,
London WC2

Dear Mr O'Neill,
Your gloomy assessment that 'there is little sign of progress either at the Geneva arms talks or in the overall superpower relationship' makes Reagan, Gorbachev and their camp-followers' flowery words and media-conscious gestures of – 'we're doing all we can, honestly' – meaningless.

Do you have children, if so would you mind telling me how you keep their hopes alive that the nuclear arms race will stop when there is no progress?

Who would have ever thought that the Stars would one day belong to the Superpowers? They'll have to rewrite the nursery rhymes . . . no longer the cat and the fiddle jumped over the Moon. . . .

The ultimate frustration is knowing that my children's future is being shaped by such rigid, inept, unimaginative people. How I wish that other Mothers who feel like me could get together and do something to influence this lot. For starters a good kick up the arse.
Yours sincerely,
Deirdre Rhys-Thomas

The International Institute for Strategic Studies
London WC2

Dear Mrs Rhys-Thomas,
Thank you for your letter of 5 May. I enjoyed the freshness of your expression as well as sympathised with your feelings of frustration.

I have two teenage daughters, the elder of whom takes a keen interest in international affairs. Their faith in the future is sustained essentially by what they achieve in their own personal

234

lives and studies at school, all of which keeps them very busy. When we discuss questions of the military competition and arms control I place my pessimism about the future of the Geneva negotiations alongside the reality that for the present, and for at least the coming generation, any act of nuclear warfare by one or the other of the superpowers would be virtually an act of suicide. Despite their rhetoric I think they know this to be a real situation and although problems continue to pile up, I believe that peace, in terms of absence of direct conflict between the superpowers, is likely to be preserved for a long time to come.

That having been said, I share your view that there is a strong need for change in the policies of each side and we must continue to work for it.

Perhaps the best thing that we as parents can do for our children is to educate them to take a keen and responsible interest in the political debate so that more voices of sanity and expertise are raised against those who advocate crude and simplistic solutions to our difficulties from both sides of politics.
Yours sincerely,
Robert O'Neill
Director

29 April 1985

To: Mr Robin Grove-White,
Director,
Council for Protection of Rural England,
London SW1

Dear Mr Grove-White,
On this Saturday's 'Week ending' programme the British Nuclear Police and Hilda Murrell[70] were mentioned in the same sketch satirizing the use of euphemisms.

This triggered the thought that I don't know what the British Nuclear Police do? I suppose just guard nuclear power stations.[71]

I've been told your book *Nuclear Power* describes their role, the numbers and the powers of Britain's Nuclear Police, would you be kind enough to tell me what they are?

Thank you.
Yours sincerely,
Deirdre Rhys-Thomas

Note 70: Hilda Murrell was found murdered on 24 March 1984. She was 78, and a renowned professional rose-grower. Miss Murrell was a highly educated woman who was sufficiently concerned over the management of radioactive wastes from the nuclear industry to set herself the task of researching the subject in order to present a paper to the Sizewell Inquiry opposing the CEGB application to build a PWR station.

Whoever killed her has not been found, and there has been some speculation that she was under surveillance by a private detective employed by Special Branch. She died of hypothermia (in other words she froze to death) but she had a bruise under her eye, and her body had a number of stab wounds. The paper on nuclear waste management that she intended to read to the Inquiry, which was highly critical of Sellafield's record and of plans for future disposal, was missing.

Her nephew took voluntary redundancy from the Navy after being a high-ranking naval intelligence officer with an important role in the Falklands War. It has been suggested that there might have been a suspicion that his aunt's evidence to Sizewell might have some connection with his work, but he thinks her death was somehow connected with her opposition to nuclear power. He read her paper at the Sizewell Inquiry after her death.

See Cook, Judith, *Who Killed Hilda Murrell?*, Penguin, London, 1985.

Note 71: Because plutonium can be made into extremely dangerous bombs, there is a fear that it might become an attractive target for terrorist theft or sabotage. If it is to be guarded with maximum efficiency, security measures must be secret. This poses a difficult situation in a democracy, where we are used to being aware of security measures taken by the police, who must account for their action before Parliament.

The Atomic Energy Authority (Special Constables) Act of 1976 gave the AEA a permanently armed Constabulary, originally a force of 400 men, now 600 plus, although the number and location of nuclear installations is unchanged. They are required mostly to guard AEA/BNFL installations handling special nuclear materials, that is Harwell, Winfrith, Dounreay and Sellafield, and their associated transports. They are empowered to carry arms, to engage in hot pursuit of actual or attempted thieves of special nuclear materials and to arrest on suspicion. They are directly employed by the AEA, who are formally responsible to the Secretary of State for Energy; he is not answerable to parliament for their day-to-day activities.

The handling of plutonium in a place of work imposes stringent security measures on the workers whether or not they themselves handle the fissile material. All professional staff and many of the industrial staff employed by the AEA and BNFL are 'positively vetted' and the installations are 'prohibited places' under the Official Secrets Acts (1911 and 1920). This has a bearing not only on the private lives of employees, but on their health if they are dismissed, since their accumulated exposure dose to radiation is prohibited material, and is not made available to their GP.

Groups and individuals who oppose the production of plutonium, or any aspect of the nuclear industry, are regarded with suspicion by the authorities, who are concerned over possible infiltration by potential terrorists. The climate of mutual suspicion and mistrust in every society is raised, and civil liberties eroded.

Council for the Protection of Rural England
London
8 May 1985

Dear Deirdre

My apologies for the failure to respond to your letter of 29 April as promptly as I would have wished.

I enclose a copy of my 1976 booklet *Nuclear Prospects*. Pages 19-23 deal with the UK Atomic Energy Authority Special Constabulary. It has grown in numbers of personnel, from 400 in 1976 to 653 in 1983, an increase of 60 per cent over a period when there has been no significant corresponding increase in civil nuclear power installations. Bear in mind that the Constabulary is not deployed at ordinary nuclear power stations – just fuel fabrication, reprocessing and experimental facilities. I enclose a copy of an article I wrote for *Nature* in December 1979, which summarises some of the background.

I hope this is helpful.

With good wishes.

Yours sincerely,
Robin Grove-White
Director

24 July 1983

To: Mr Enoch Powell, M.P.,
The House of Commons,
London SW1

Dear Mr Powell,

Can you tell me why in a Democracy those people who democratically voice their concern about the nuclear arms race and indeed 'all things nuclear' from pollution in the Irish Sea to storage of intermediate nuclear waste underground, may be classified subversive, suffer harassment, and be put under surveillance?

And why in the build-up to a nuclear war should the

Government contingency plans recommend the removal of such people from their homes to labour camps, or worse?

In conclusion, do you think it is democratic that the hierarchy have allotted places in nuclear shelters paid for out of public funds?

Yours sincerely,
Deirdre Rhys-Thomas

House of Commons
London SW1

28th July 1983

Dear Mrs Thomas,
In reply to your letter of 24th July, I had not seen references to the facts which you mention, and would be grateful if you could refer me to the authority for them.

Yours sincerely,
The Rt. Hon. J. Enoch Powell, MBE, MP

14 September 1983

To: The Rt Hon. J. Enoch Powell, MBE, MP,
House of Commons,
London SW1

Dear Mr Powell,
Thank you for your letter of 28 July. As is being shown by the BBC 1 series *Secrets*, it is very difficult for an ordinary person to find out the facts and that is why I used 'may be' in my letter to you.

May I refer you to – *Beneath the City Streets* by Peter Laurie revised 1983: *The Political Police in Britain* by Tony Bunyan: *Low Intensity Operations* by Frank Kitson: and the *Daily Telegraph* 6 August – 'Anti-CND Unit to Close. The M.O.D. Secretariat 19 which combats the Peace Movement and the Campaign for Nuclear Disarmament is being disbanded on Sept. 1. Its role of explaining Government nuclear policy will be handed to Secretariat 17 which deals with nuclear policy as a whole. . . .' I would like to know what was the precise function of Secretariat 19, and what is the precise function of Secretariat 17?

Ref. my para 2. 24/07 – may I refer you to *Civil Defence: The Cruellest Confidence Trick* by Phil Bolsover, pages 35, 38, 48, 49, 50.

Ref. my para 2. 24/07 – may I refer you to *Civil Defence:* hierarchy personally paying for their allotted places in nuclear shelters. As an example I give the nuclear bunker being built at Leominster at a cost of £70,000 for the Chief Executive and Senior Officers of Leominster District Council.

I trust you appreciate how difficult it is for an ordinary person to get the facts, and I look to you for help.

Yours sincerely,

Deirdre Rhys-Thomas

House of Commons
London SW1
26th September 1983

Dear Mrs Thomas,

Mr Powell has asked me to acknowledge your reply of 14th September, posted the 19th, and thank you for the references to your information which you have given him.

Yours sincerely,

Monica Wilson

Private Secretary

16 September 1985

To: Dr Richard Garwin,
IBM Fellow,
IBM,
Thomas J. Watson Research Center,
Yorktown Heights,
New York
U.S.A.

Dear Dr Garvin,

I was amazed to read in my Sunday paper that you and leading American scientists have asked Reagan to stop his Star Wars[72] because it would 'significantly increase the likelihood of nuclear war.' As you're a Pentagon consultant I can only hope the hawks will listen to you.

239

Because of our so-called 'special relationship' and Maggie's support of Ronnie's Star Wars it seems to me that a lot of British people seem to still be relating Star Wars to fighting the Jedi, and not to the complexities of computers, 'space mines', etc. Could you, Dr Garvin, or one of your scientist friends come over here to Britain and tell us about the difficulties of making SDI 100% successful?

Who would have thought we would have to re-write our nursery rhymes – no longer the cat and the fiddle jumped over the Moon . . .

Thank you for having the guts to speak out.

Yours sincerely,
Deirdre Rhys-Thomas

P.S. I just hope IBM London have given me your correct address.

P.P.S. How much opposition is there to Star Wars in America?

Note 72: Star Wars, or to give it a military sounding name rather than a film title, Strategic Defence Initiative, seems to have been President Reagan's own idea, not a proposal he was asked to put forward by his military advisers in the Pentagon.

In 1982 the United Nations Second Special Session on Disarmament was held in New York. The Freeze movement – based on the determination to call a halt to the development of nuclear weapons as a first step in multilateral disarmament – gained ground so rapidly in America that by November 1982 eleven states had voted in favour of the Freeze. In that month a strong statement of support came from the conference of Roman Catholic bishops, who said: '. . . the danger of escalation is so great that it is an unacceptable moral risk to initiate nuclear war in any form.'

President Reagan responded to this movement by the speech he made on the 23 March 1983, when he painted a beautiful picture of the USA and its allies protected for all time against the nuclear weapons of the USSR by a protective umbrella of high technology equipment, poised in space ready to destroy any incoming missiles. He asked: 'Wouldn't it be better to save lives than to avenge them?' Well, you can't argue with that. Except that as it turns out, the SDI is disturbing the balance of power between the USA and USSR, it is distorting the work of thousands of scientists, it is diverting billions of dollars into a futile exercise at the expense of America's own poor, and it gives the USA an excuse to control the trade in technology of just about every firm engaged in making electronic equipment. It also exposes greedy and unethical trends in the scientific establishment in many European countries, since they are unable to resist the lure of the dollar, and undertake work that they know is concerned with increasing nuclear capabilities and not with putting up a

240

magic umbrella of protection. It will not even work. But it brought the growth of the peace movement in the USA to a standstill.

See Thompson, E.P. (ed), *Star Wars*, Penguin, London, 1985.

IBM Thomas J. Watson Research Center
Yorktown Heights, NY
September 24, 1985

Dear Ms Rhys-Thomas,

Your letter of 09/16/85 reached me 09/20/85 so you need have no concern that IBM London had done you wrong.

Indeed, the large majority of scientists in the United States not working for the SDI program oppose the SDI. This includes many consultants to the program. You may be interested in the enclosed UCS material, including the text of a letter signed by the majority of the U.S. Nobel Prize winners in science and also the majority of the members of the National Academy of Sciences.

I have indeed talked at the Royal United Services Institute on Star Wars as well as the International Institute of Strategic Studies. Enclosed are some of my recent more popular publications on Star Wars, as well as some very good items by Lawrence Freedman and R.V. Jones. Please give these remarks as wide a distribution as you can. I am sending a copy of your letter and my response to Howard B. Ris, Executive Director of the Union of Concerned Scientists, who might in fact have more opportunity to see that people speak publicly in Britain about Star Wars.

Thank you for writing to me.

Sincerely yours,
Richard L. Garwin
Also Adjunct Professor of Physics at Columbia University
(Views not necessarily those of IBM or Columbia)

If we hadn't been having supper with Mummy I would have missed the Channel 4 programme on Cannonsburg: Knighton must be one of the only places which hasn't got Channel 4.

In December 1985 the *Sunday Times* colour magazine carried an article written by Sylvia Collier about the town of Cannonsburg in Pennsylvania. From the 1930s there had been a factory on the outskirts of the town using radium in the manufacture of a range of goods, from watches to medical instruments. After the war business ran down and the factory closed at the end of the 1950s, leaving a considerable amount of radioactive waste, which was buried in a large field. This field was used by the children of the town as a playing field; baseball teams practised and played there, and the children tobogganed down its gentle surrounding slopes in the winter snow.

Gradually many people in the town fell ill, and the number of young men and women who developed cancer became worrying. It was not until Janis Dunn went out with a notebook and pen to ask her neighbours if they had noticed anything strange about their family's health that it came to light that in some streets near the field every family had a cancer sufferer, and some several. One man whose house faced the secret waste dump had lost fourteen members of his family, some of them in childhood.

Thanks to the refusal of Janis Dunn and her friends to be silenced or intimidated, steps are being taken to deal with the waste, and compensation for the victims is being sought.

If only there were more women like Janis Dunn.

19 December 1985

Mrs Janis Dunn,
Box 85 RD1,
Thomas Road,
Cannonsburg,
85 PA 15330,
U.S.A.

Dear Janis Dunn,
I can't forget you. I saw you this summer on TV talking about

242

how you're trying to get together information on the nuclear waste buried under your town and the people who have died of cancer and leukaemia in Cannonsburg.

Yesterday I phoned the TV producer here for your address. He tells me you're still battling with the U.S. authorities.

The fear of cancer must be difficult to live with.

It's marvellous, for all their assurances the nuclear authorities are still unable to agree on the lowest dose of radiation which might lead to the development of cancer.

I don't know if you know, but the Irish Sea is now the most radioactive sea in the world — more radioactive muck has been pumped into it than any other sea — and years and years of nuclear reassurances and 'safe' radiation levels have resulted in about a $\frac{1}{4}$ ton of plutonium in it.

So nuclear reassurances are worthless. That's only too obvious when you read scientific/medical reports. and cross-check bureaucratic statements. There are still great areas where research has yet to be done.

It suits the nuclear authorities to keep us ordinary folk ignorant: they play on the fact that 'all things nuclear' are so complex and intimidate us with this so that we feel under-confident to ask questions.

It's only too obvious, Janis, from your experience in Cannonsburg, and what's happening in the Irish Sea, that we have got to have a central pooling system where any member of the public can get information — for specific queries or just to read so that they don't feel so ignorant. We've also got to stop being so selfish: the 'if it's not on my doorstep, or in my back garden it doesn't concern me' has got to go. It does — the world's too small. If there is anything I can do, please let me know, and if you would like copies of letters I have had about low level radiation, please let me know.

We all watched you on TV — Peter, my husband, Theo and Toby our sons, and we would like to send you and your family our kindest regards.

Yours

Deirdre Rhys-Thomas

Deirdre Rhys-Thomas
Wales

Dear Deirdre,

Please forgive me if I have interpreted your name
incorrectly. I have received many letters from England also, and
have had a little trouble making out some of the letters. Seems
we write our letters a little differently.

Thank you so much for your caring letter and the time you
took to get my address, etc.

Our story was told for the first time nationally in the U.S.
Sunday, January 12, 1986. We tried so hard to get national
attention on our problem for 6 years and finally it has
happened. I have been receiving many letters and phone calls
from all over the country and am trying to answer all.

It has been a real struggle here. We have so much evidence
of cancer and other health problems near the radioactive waste
site and yet we receive nothing but opposition for our attempts
to get a comprehensive study done of the situation. Believe it or
not the local residents, even those with cancers, etc., tell us to
shut up because we are devaluating their property.[73]

The Mayor and town council are concerned that the bad
publicity will damage the town business and keep people from
moving into the area. They said that millions of dollars have
been spent to make Cannonsburg an ideal place in which to live
and we are hurting the image of the town. Of course the federal
government loves all of this bickering and in-fighting – it takes
the heat off them.

We found documents that tell us that our town council
knew of the problem as far back as 1962 and pledged their
cooperation with the federal government in trying to cover the
story so that the town would not get a bad image. Can you
imagine it!! No concern for the health of the people at all.

I am working on a book with Pittsburgh Press reporter,
David Templeton in which we hope to reveal more than has
been told previously by press or television. Together we have
uncovered much that officials – local and federal – had hoped
the people would never know. Even with evidence they twist
everything around with half-truths and twisted truths. I have
had them tell me one thing to my face and another publicly. It's
a crime.

244

We also know that much of the eastern coast of the U.S. is contaminated from radioactive material that was dumped in the Atlantic Ocean in the mid and late 40's – leftovers from the Manhattan Project which built the Atomic Bomb. The wastes were put in barrels and dumped in the Ocean and now the barrels are deteriorating and the radioactivity washing to shore.

I have worked with Italian T.V. to produce a documentary which was shown nationally in their country. Also the Japanese have written a book called, *Hibakusha, USA*. Hibakusha is the Japanese word for Atomic Bomb victim. They sent me a copy which I cannot read, of course, but promised that it would be translated in other languages, including English.

And so, this is my way of fighting back. It is a problem which started out as a personal one – in my backyard and now has spread all over the world. It is good to know that others are being alerted to the problem and are joining in the battle . . .

We must keep complaining, fighting back, writing letters of protest to authorities and getting others involved. Together we can make a difference.

Best wishes to you, Peter, Theo and Toby. God Bless!
Sincerely yours,
Janis Dunn

Note 73: Radiation Roundtables have been set up in several countries, to collate information on those who may be victims of radiation exposure. An International Radiation Exposure Forum will be held in Japan in 1987 with seven aims:

1 To bring forth the plight of radiation victims worldwide.
2 To demonstrate that low-level radiation is more harmful than current exposure standards assume.
3 To illustrate that we already have victims of World War III – those injured by the production, deployment and testing of nuclear weapons.
4 To secure the maximum possible media coverage of the event and the issues.
5 To forge international ties among radiation victims/survivors, groups, and support groups and to further ongoing communications.
6 To share the personal stories of radiation victims with other victims and with the media.
7 To provide an opportunity to develop resolutions, organising strategies, and mutual actions on relevant issues.

Further information can be obtained from the Radiation and Health Information Service, PO Box 805, London SE15 4LP.

12 December 1985

To: Mr David Puttnam
Enigma Productions,
London SW7

Dear David Puttnam,
The Fireside Chat hasn't gone down well with my son Theo,
nor I gather most of his friends – all 16, just started their 'A'
levels. It was the ultimate in hype: wouldn't have looked out of
place in *Dynasty*. Both Super-Leaders wanting to look good just
for the world ratings.

So we've been conned by the cosy fireside flicker. It's given
the military and nuclear hawks the extra time they wanted.

Only in music – Lennon's 'Imagine', 'Nineteen', Billy
Bragg, Lennon's 'Happy Christmas (War is Over)', does Theo
find consolation.

Surely, there has to be the blackest comedy film waiting to
be made about where we are today in the nuclear saga – have
you ever stopped and actually listened to Weinberger
expounding on world relations?
Yours sincerely,
Deirdre Rhys-Thomas

17 March 1986

Dear Mrs. Rhys-Thomas,
I am sorry to have taken so long to reply to your letter of the
12th December, but I thought you would be pleased to know
that the next *major* film I plan to make for Warner Bros. will be
the story of the (malign) creation of the atomic bomb.

I don't know if you will find it satisfying in terms of a black
comedy, but I promise you, if we do our job properly, it will at
least get people sitting up and talking.

By the time the film is released Theo will have finished his
'A' levels and hopefully set about changing the world from
University.

Thanks for writing.
Warmest regards,
David Puttnam

246

Epilogue

Tuesday 15 April 1986

I was late leaving home. I had arranged to meet Geraldine at the Little Chef in Newtown, call in at the accountant's and go on to the printers in Welshpool to check the new brochures for our new food products. Frustrating drive over as lambs kept on popping out of the hedge onto the road.

Turned on the radio: Americans have bombed Libya. US Bases in Britain used. Mrs Thatcher gave permission. Military targets hit, civilians killed and injured.

I couldn't believe it. How could anyone in their right mind think this bombing will make the world a safer place? Hasn't Reagan read a history book? There'll be terrorist bombings, hostages killed, fanatics eager to be martyrs. I just wanted to go home, to be with Toby and Theo and Peter, and I felt so sickened by it, and this feeling hasn't left me.

Nothing has brought home to me more clearly how stupid we are having American nuclear Cruise missiles in Britain 'protecting us' than the American bombing of Libya. The *Sunday Times* (20 April) says 'The American raid on Libya last Monday was much bigger and struck at more targets than had been agreed with Mrs Thatcher in return for the use of British bases.' Apparently 44 F-111s were used, not the 29 as the Pentagon officially admits. Mrs Thatcher didn't even have any say in what weapons could be used – 'It is for the Americans to choose the weapons to secure the defeat of those targets within the target permission we gave,' she said. And we are expected to believe that the agreement between America and Britain will work 100 per cent in a nuclear crisis.

And what on earth was the Ministry of Defence thinking of, allowing Cruise missile launchers, the largest number at any one time, under heavily armed American servicemen, to leave Greenham Common at such a time? Or perhaps they don't have any authority to stop the Americans?

68% of our population objected to US Bases in Britain being used, and to the bombing of Libya.[74] We have been warned. We can't just slip back into apathy, we have got to make them hear us. Otherwise we may never have another warning.

Tuesday 29 April 1986

The worst accident in the short history of nuclear power has taken place – probably last Saturday – at the Chernobyl Nuclear Plant near Kiev.[75]

Oslo has recorded radiation 50 per cent higher than normal background radiation. Because of the overnight rain there has been ground contamination. There are no iodine tablets to be bought in Copenhagen and Oslo, people have been queueing all day for them.

It looks as if the reactor core is still on fire as the Russians are seeking West German and Swedish advice on how to deal with it. They have no practical experience, and yet they go on building them. Look at Windscale, look at Three Mile Island (that was just very lucky), now Chernobyl. They may say they dealt with the incidents, but how do we know in the long term they did? Cancers take 10 to 30 years to appear. It is all too experimental. There are alternative fuel sources. The risks are too great.

Thursday 1 May 1986

Part of the radioactive cloud is now drifting across Austria and heading for Switzerland, and by Saturday will be going towards Italy. 10,000 may die from cancers over the next 20 years from this accident. A conservative estimate; all this from just one nuclear plant. How many are there in the world?

This accident has shown how unpredictable the fallout pattern is.

Only this March, the Energy Secretary Peter Walker said, 'Nuclear power is the safest form of energy yet known to man.' Now the Swedish are concerned about the high levels of radioactive caesium recorded there: 'There is far more caesium than we previously suspected. We are uncertain what this means and have to look into the possible effects. Caesium has a very long-lived half-life. Furthermore while we are a long way from lethal radiation levels in Sweden, there is a risk of damage in the long term' – Director of the National Institute for Radiological Protection. So much for the bland reassurances about the safety of low-level radiation.

Sweden is about 800 miles from Chernobyl – how many nuclear

stations have we got? I haven't been the slightest reassured by Lord Marshall's TV appearances telling us British nuclear plants are so safe. His complacency appals me. He forgot to tell us that none of Britain's nuclear reactors have secondary containment.

Saturday 10 May 1986

The radiation cloud didn't go over Italy last Saturday. Instead it came over Britain, on Friday. It has now passed over us twice. Look what we've done to our world. It rains. Mothers in Europe and here wonder if they should let their children out to play. It's sunny. Better stay inside again today? I can understand why Janet won't let her two toddlers play in their sandpit. The scientists, the experts, the National Radiological Protection Board talk of 'hot spots', of finding particles on the ground. Don't drink rainwater. Levels found in milk. We can't taste it, smell it, see it.

'None presents a risk to health in the United Kingdom,' says Kenneth Baker, Environment Minister, in the House; and Dr Dunster, Director of the NRPB, says about 500 people in Britain will die from the Chernobyl disaster.

This cleverer-than-thou attitude of the pro-nuclear lot terrifies me. Mrs Thatcher says we must have 'the highest possible standards in the nuclear industry'. That isn't good enough. It has to be 100 per cent safe because look what happens if it isn't. But we all know only too well that life isn't like that. Think of the domestic appliances that go wrong, new cars – because of bad design, engineering, maintenance. American shuttle and Titan failure, the unreliability of Cruise, human error – it's totally unrealistic to think that the nuclear industry is uniquely free from potentially catastrophic failures.

There are 306 nuclear plants operating in the world today (or is it 305 after Chernobyl?) and 224 are under construction or on order. And still the nuclear industry tells us that nuclear power is 'the great white hope', peevishly telling us on TV that France has gone nuclear, how competitive and economic French nuclear energy is. Oh yes? Well why does Electricité de France owe 200 billion Francs, making them the 6th or 7th biggest debtor in the world?

We've got 300 years of coal, there's wave energy conversion, solar power, the Severn barrage, and I've read of the commercial excitement of large-scale fuel cells which Japan and America are

investing in. Wouldn't you know it, it was a British invention –
but I suppose because of our obsession with nuclear power, we
didn't develop it.

And the radiation cloud may come back again, weaker but for
how long? and what will be the long-term effects? Insignificant
low levels say the Energy Minister, the Environment Minister, the
NRPB, the CEGB, but THERE IS NO SAFE LOW LEVEL OF
RADIATION and Chernobyl's radiation level has to be added to,
not compared, to natural radiation and added to background
radiation. And what do several 'safe levels' added together add up
to?

Tuesday 13 May 1986

I've just been sitting in the garden with Puzzle, today is the first
really warm sunny day. A near miracle after this seemingly never-
ending winter. But those people near Chernobyl can't share this
sunny day with me; mothers must be so worried about their
children, not knowing what the future holds for them. Everyone
who has been subjected to this radiation fallout must in their heart
wonder.

However one looks at nuclear power it is fraught with danger,
with risk. Malfunctions, waste disposal, possible terrorist action.
The risks are too great, we cannot continue to build them.

Yesterday the British Government announced tighter controls
on radioactive discharges into the Irish Sea from Sellafield.

Sunday 20 July 1986

What a surprise, another invitation to Sellafield stuck in today's
Observer. It's only too obvious that this slick public relations
advertising campaign is to stop us natives getting restless about
nuclear power and reprocessing after Chernobyl. I just find it so
tragic it had to take Chernobyl to bring it home to most people
exactly what nuclear power means.

I can remember so clearly talking to somebody at the
Trawsfynydd nuclear station who was doing the monitoring of
radioactive levels and him telling me that it was just a matter of
procedure, absolutely no cause for alarm and no way would any
livestock be affected: on 20 June a ban was placed on sheep

movement in North Wales and Cumbria, and later part of Scotland, because of radioactive levels in lambs.

And still the Energy Minister, Environment, all their sidekicks, and Walt at the CEGB tell us it's all OK, but of all the people who will die in Britain as a direct result of Chernobyl, which of us will draw the short straws?

I have read that a substantial proportion of the fallout is in a form whose effects cannot be inferred simply by average measurements of radioactivity. This 'hot particle' problem, in which a significant proportion of the radioactivity is concentrated in or on small dust particles which, as an aerosol, can be carried hundreds or even thousands of miles, is very similar to the problem already identified around reprocessing centres such as Sellafield. Apparently this means that farmers who store grass, hay and make silage contaminated by Chernobyl will be feeding their livestock radioactive feed this winter. So caesium will get back into the food chain in milk and meat next year, 1987. German physicists have found that caesium and 'hot particles' – beta-emitting – will accumulate in barns and silos endangering farmers and their children. 'They can be expected to be trapped permanently in the lungs of individuals exposed to contaminated hay' the physicists warn (gives a new meaning to farmers' lung). And what does the National Radiological Protection Board spokesman say? 'Nonsense; the concentrations are too low.' Mind you, the same spokesman recognises that caesium will be in milk and meat next year and says, 'I would not like to predict the effect on people.'

The Ministry of Agriculture and the Farmers Unions are hoping it will rain enough before harvesting to wash the caesium away; but it's mid-July, we've not had much rain since Chernobyl and harvesting is in full swing.

Is it any wonder people are frightened? I was down Llandovery last week and people were telling me a man from the Ministry had been round going over their tractors with a geiger-counter.

The weather's been so good there are Pick-Your-Own-Fruit signs up all over the place and yet people seem to be reluctant to pick this year's fruit and veg.

I sometimes find it difficult to believe it's five years since I wrote my first letter and in that time some of my worst fears have been realized. We've even managed to destroy the comforting reassuring childhood image of Father Christmas and his reindeer: as many of the Lapland reindeer are contaminated from the

Chernobyl fallout and they will have to be killed.

And while many, many people in Britain don't give Cruise a second thought — 'it's been here several years now, nothing's happened just those stupid women going on and on about it, the same old thing' — what they don't realise is that Cruise has changed everything. With the new modernised tactical nuclear weapons the military are now thinking 'the unthinkable', that it will be possible to fight a limited nuclear war, even thinking they could win a nuclear war. The USA is changing its nuclear policy from MAD (Mutually Assured Destruction) to NUTS (Nuclear Utilisation Targeting Strategy) policy. That's exactly what all we women who went to Greenham Common feared.

I can't understand how parents who love their children allow themselves to be deceived by this nuclear confidence trick.

Note 74: At a meeting in Bristol Postgraduate Medical Centre on 28 June 1986, Dorothy Rowe spoke about her recent visit to the States to publicise her book, *Living with the Bomb* (Routledge & Kegan Paul, 1985). The US attack on Libya took place while she was there, and she was questioned closely about the British and European responses to the bombing. She found that many of the interviewers did not know that the total population of Libya is around 3 million, half of whom are under 15 years old.

Note 75: The core of a nuclear reactor — that is the part where the fission takes place in the fuel rods, and gas or water circulates in pipes to extract the heat — has a building around it that is carefully constructed to withstand a build-up of pressure. This is called the containment vessel. This is inside a huge tall building. with a lot of machinery and equipment. The building is made of thick concrete. Some reactors, especially the PWR where the water collecting the heat is kept under pressure so that it doesn't boil into steam, are inside a pressure vessel, and this itself is inside another strong building, called a secondary containment. The early Magnox reactors in Britain do not have a secondary containment. Chernobyl was built with a very strong shell, but the force of the explosion blew the roof off.